SOUTH KOREA

The Price of Efficiency and Success

SECOND EDITION

Dr. John Gonzalez and Young Lee

SOUTH KOREA: The Price of Efficiency and Success, Second Edition

Independently published.
Printed in the United States of America
Cover by Enrique Arredondo at ArsDesigns
Typesetting by S4Carlisle Publishing Services, Chennai, India
Publisher: John Gonzalez
Email: skoreaefficiency@gmail.com

First edition, 2019; Second edition, 2024

ISBN: 978-1-7376513-2-1

For the victims of the *Sewol* ferry tragedy.

Contents

My Journey to Korea

On April 16, 2014, I came home to find out that a boat accident had claimed the lives of over 300 people. Most were high school students on a field trip to Jeju Island. My first thought was, "My students and I could have been among the victims!" I also thought about how devastating the accident would be for the victims' families, the school, and the whole country. Some people were shocked; others appeared traumatized. I knew then that I would write a book about Korea. Such was my initial reaction to the *Sewol* ferry accident, one of Korea's worst tragedies in the recent past.

Before stepping foot on Korean soil in the 1990s, I had made a few Korean friends who told me how beautiful their country was, so I wanted to see it for myself. Some of my initial trips included meditation tours that enabled me to visit Buddhist temples in rural areas. At the end of the tours, I would take the time to see large cities, like Seoul and Busan, to get a different perspective.

As I visited Korea for the first time, the country's technological advancements impressed me to no end. It was convenient, even back then, to rent a cellular phone at the airport to be in touch with friends and family in the country and back home. It was impressive to walk around Seoul, where I saw many people using cell phones in the late 1990s. Back in the States, a smaller percentage of people seemed to own one. After thinking about it, I realized it made total financial sense for a country like Korea, which was undergoing a technological transformation, to skip expanding landlines and embrace broadband and wireless technology instead. After all, it is more efficient.

The efficient use of technology continued to impress me even at restaurants, where I noticed inconspicuous buttons at the end of each table that customers used to summon a server. While researching this book, I found that these devices are known in the industry as "push-for-service systems." When customers pressed the button on their table, a buzzer sounded, and a server immediately said something aloud to acknowledge the call. The server signaled to the client who had pressed the button that someone would arrive any second to find out how they could be of service. Based on my observations, the use of this system appears to have expanded since I started visiting Korea.

This technology aims to enhance customer service, but using the button was, first and foremost, efficiency-driven. The customer quickly gets a server's attention; the servers immediately know which table needs assistance; the customers' needs are promptly met, and they can enjoy a more pleasant visit. What a difference between this experience and one in the States, where flagging a server in a busy restaurant may take significant effort! In most American restaurants, a server is assigned to specific tables, meaning other servers may or may not be able to help you.

Another instrument widely used in Korean coffee shops for quite some time is the guest pager. This device notifies customers that their order is ready. In the U.S., even today, baristas are still calling out customers' names.

As I continued to visit the country for short intervals, I admired the glittering shopping centers, the tall skyscrapers, the efficient subway system in Seoul and Busan, the expansive national highways with long tunnels that significantly shorten travel time in a mountainous country, and of course, the high-speed train system. The latter is better known as KTX (Korea Train eXpress). In short, Korea possessed every infrastructural and technological attribute that one would expect in a developed country.

I took early retirement and struggled for a year to adjust to my new lifestyle after being extremely active and involved in education from the classroom to counseling and finally to administration. Since I had so much free time, I decided it was time for me to experience an unfamiliar environment.

The attachment I had to Korea made it an ideal place for me to explore. So, I decided to rent an apartment near Seoul for one year. Having lived in large cities most of my life, I sought a less hectic environment. I settled in Jukjeon, a small town south of Seoul. It was close to the big city and convenient for travel purposes. Since I did not have Korean residency then, I could only live in the country for 90-day intervals as a visiting tourist. I spent much time traveling to nearby towns, trying Korean dishes, attending yoga classes, and visiting cafés.

The most valuable part of this experience was my contact with Koreans through my yoga classes. I learned much about Korean culture from my observations and conversations with them. I did not own a car then; therefore, I used public transportation, which limited my explorations of the country. I was particularly fond of visiting and walking around Jukjeon café street (to Koreans, this street is known as Bojeong-Dong Café Street or 보정동카페거리). Even though the difficulty of relying solely on public transportation was somewhat limiting, it gave me the confidence that I could survive in a foreign country. It propelled me to a much more enriching experience in the ensuing four years.

After my one-year sojourn in Korea, I returned to the U.S. Since my adjustment to retirement was still a challenge, I decided to turn it into an opportunity. During my American teaching and administration career, I knew a few teachers who taught in foreign countries during their sabbaticals. Their sense of adventure fascinated me. I was confident that one day, I would have the courage to go to a foreign country to practice the profession for which I have an enormous passion.

This was the perfect time to achieve the dream of practicing my cherished profession outside the U.S. I applied for a few teaching positions in the late spring of 2012. My fascination with the country, the advanced technology level, and my interests in philosophy, religion, and teaching motivated me to consider a teaching assignment in Korea. I was invited to interview via Skype for a job at an accredited American high school that operated under the auspices of a university.

The prospective job was a teaching and guidance counseling position, which would afford me the additional opportunity to teach an English class for the university. This job was tailor-made for me, given my professional background. I was offered the position, and I accepted it. My dream had become a reality faster than I had imagined. Suddenly, I was in Korea, ready to begin my new assignment in early August 2012. This once-in-a-lifetime opportunity was feasible because I was single and had no children. Had this not been the case, the feasibility would have been challenging, perhaps even impossible.

As I started my assignment, I had no idea of the profound impact my experience would have on my consciousness. I was about to learn what many expats grow to realize: Living in a foreign country is very different from visiting one as a tourist. As a resident, I was about to delve into the fabric of society and learn the nuances of Korean behavior, both subtle and otherwise. I was about to have the privilege of looking at the country's underbelly from within it. Also, I was about to undergo a reality check about my view of Korean society. This experience would enable me to compare the Korea I remembered as a tourist to present-day Korea as a "resident."

In retrospect, I am grateful for the opportunity to live and work in Korea. I am thankful to the Korean people, those who embraced me with open arms, put aside their shyness, and tried to speak English to me, and those who chose to keep their distance. I could immerse myself in their culture through their approach to social interaction with someone who looks, talks, and acts differently from them. Thank you!

On a more practical level, thanks to this opportunity, I could witness and confirm the country's beauty that my friends had relayed. I traveled throughout the country in the five years I lived there. On weekends in spring and fall, I particularly enjoyed visiting unfamiliar places. My travels enabled me to witness the fantastic palette of Korea's natural colors and the inherent beauty of the country.

Both spring and fall are equally beautiful in their unique way. Still, if I had to choose, my favorite would be autumn because it is exhilarating to the senses, particularly sight and taste, and it touches me at a more profound level. It is a live visual tapestry that evokes the cycle of life in the body and mind. Persimmon trees adorn the landscape with their turning leaves and bright orange fruit, particularly in rural villages throughout the autumn months. The fruit is harvested from October to early December. I enjoyed eating persimmons and the earthy, ever-present roasted chestnuts. The latter are in season from October to March and can be enjoyed anywhere in the country, from big cities to small mountain towns and from the most crowded Seoul neighborhoods to rest stops along the highways.

The kaleidoscope of colors starts every year with the ubiquitous cherry blossom trees that bloom during a very short period from late March to early April. This event marks the end of the winter season and the beginning of spring. One of the most impressive and stunning images that will remain forever engraved in my memory is the variety of flowers that form a colorful landscape in cities, highways, and mountains throughout spring, summer, and fall. The color of the landscape changes every two or three weeks, depending on the blooming flower. Autumn concludes with a spectacular shower of ginkgo biloba tree leaves and others that turn from green to bright yellow, red, and brown. The changing leaves in autumn are a sight to behold, especially in the mountains and around Buddhist temples.

Located primarily in the mountains, Buddhist temples with streams or rivers running nearby attract Koreans and tourists alike. They provide a place to rest, meditate, or pray before or after an invigorating mountain hike. Streams and waterfalls are delightful and refreshing any time of the year, particularly in the summer. Both adults and children relish playing and getting wet in a stream. Entire families enjoy a picnic by a river in the spring, summer, or early fall. The sounds of children playing echo up and down streams and make the mountains even more vibrant.

On the way to and from the mountains, hikers—millennials and baby boomers—and Buddhist temple visitors can satisfy their hunger with *bibimbap*. It is served at any number of restaurants leading into or out of the town.

The iconic blend of rice, mountain-grown vegetables, such as beansprouts, carrots, radish, cucumber, your choice of meat or no meat, a fried egg, and red pepper paste is served in a dish of your choice, either in a hot stone pot or a bowl at room temperature. *Bibimbap* is garnished with numerous side dishes of nutritious and wholesome mountain-grown vegetables. Some side dishes may include fermented sesame seed leaves, radish, seaweed, and the ubiquitous *kimchi* or fermented cabbage, which most Koreans eat with breakfast, lunch, and dinner.

A meal in a mountain town is not complete unless it includes the traditional *soju*. For those unfamiliar with *soju*, the national drink of Korea, it is a neutral-tasting, clear spirit. *Soju* was traditionally made from rice, but nowadays, it is made from a blend of grains and starches such as wheat and sweet potatoes.[1] It is somewhat like vodka but has half the alcohol. The alcohol content in *soju* is around 20 ABV (Alcohol by Volume), whereas vodka is 40.[2] *Soju* is customarily consumed straight in small shot glasses and used in cocktails.

One interesting cultural detail about drinking *soju* among Koreans is that consumers do not serve themselves. They serve each other. For instance, if I am having dinner with a Korean friend and we are both drinking *soju*, when our glasses are empty, my friend fills my glass, and I refill his. We toast, we down the *soju*, and we start over.

About this Book

I decided to author this book to show my appreciation for Korea and the Korean people. It is my way of giving back to the country that opened its doors and enabled me to relish its long history and natural beauty. My co-author, Young Lee, and I examine social behaviors and attempt to identify patterns that tend to repeat from one area of society to another, thus indicating that they are firmly ingrained in the fabric of the culture. We question the source of behavioral patterns and attempt to determine whether efficiency is the driving force, thus the book's title. Recognizing that Korea has arrived on the world stage to join other economic powers in record time, we ask these questions: What has been neglected in this evolution? What have been the individual and collective sacrifices and the human toll associated with the national progress?

We present the set of observations for individuals, Korean or otherwise, who are open-minded and realistic enough to accept that, as in all societies, including those in the West, there is work to be done to achieve real, lasting, and sustainable progress, and for society to be more equitable and compassionate. Compassionate societies recognize that values must be revisited and questioned to ensure their relevance. They also acknowledge that attempting to get around a rule or regulation may give one person or a select group of entities an advantage. However, it places others at a distinct disadvantage and may endanger the safety of many.

This book is meant not as a criticism but as an observation from an outsider's perspective about culture and its role in the evolution of economic progress. The commentary is intended to show how a country's policies and procedures and resulting attitudes must be revisited to ensure congruence with the pace of financial and technological advancement. It is meant to place a mirror in front of the Korean people so they can judge whether they can use their current situation as a springboard toward the country's overall evolution. Or do they need a thorough and systematic review of policies and procedures at various government, business, and industry levels? Do these entities need to ensure appropriate safety regulations are in place, consistently followed, and rigorously enforced? Also, do they need to recognize that taking shortcuts with selfish motives is usually done at someone else's expense and may be accompanied by unintended consequences? These repercussions may include casualties of innocent bystanders. Finally, we pose the question, is the country adequately prepared to overcome the nation's challenges? Given the demographic projections, economic conditions, and behavioral patterns discussed in this book, are Koreans ready to commit to the long-term solutions needed to prevail over the apparent perfect storm gathering on the horizon? Meaningful, fundamental, and profound change is up to the Korean people.

Since this book focuses on Korea, I made a concerted effort to avoid passing judgment and making value-loaded comparisons to other cultures, societies, and economies. However, it is difficult, if not impossible, to be objective when the observer, in this case, me, is born and raised in a radically different culture. Consequently, the observer's perception of reality is affected by their culture, socioeconomic background, level of education, religious framework, and upbringing, to name a few factors. In those instances where I make comparisons, it is to point out where Korea is in relation to other countries, not to judge Korea, for the only fair judgment is to compare today's Korea to the Korea of 10, 20, or 70 years ago.

This book provides a historical perspective only when needed to understand how a specific current situation developed. A substantial number of books about Korea delve thoroughly into the historical perspective. Instead, the present work focuses on describing the current condition based on extensive research, the power of observation, and systematic analyses of behavioral and cultural patterns.

Many sources cited are from credible Korean newspapers or news outlets that offer an English version of their website. A handful of the citations are from news sources published or broadcast in Korean. Young Lee, the co-author, translated articles or news reports in these cases. These instances are noted in the endnotes at the end of the book. The remaining articles and reports are from English-speaking countries. We purposefully consulted various sources to validate the information and balance the references.

For the present edition, we have updated the most critical data. The COVID-19 pandemic has profoundly influenced human behavior worldwide. As a result, some statistics have been affected, such as those related to trade. In some cases, we have decided to retain the data generated before the pandemic to project an image as close to "normal" as possible and avoid contaminating them with affected statistics. Lastly, whenever we quote amounts in "dollars," they represent U.S. dollars.

Finally, it is humbling and reassuring to recognize that societies often be-have in ways that reflect nature, particularly concerning the large spectrum of human progress. Economic and technological advancement go hand-in-hand. However, consciousness-level development appears to happen independently of the first two, like autumn leaves change colors at their own pace rather than in unison. This natural process gives us hope that Korea's consciousness level will not only equal but surpass its economic and technological progress soon.

John Gonzalez and Young Lee

- What impressed me most about South Korea?
- Why does a resident's impression of a country differ from that of a tourist?
- What is the purpose of this work?

What Factors and Cultural Values Contributed to the Transformation of the Korean Economy?

Economic Transformation

A discussion about South Korea would be incomplete without touching on the economic transformation that the country has undergone since the end of the Korean War (1950-1953). The information in this chapter will serve as the backdrop to put the rest of this work into perspective. South Korea ("Korea," hereafter) rose from the rubble after the war. Observers and historians often refer to the nation's remarkable economic transformation as the "Miracle on the Han River."[1]

Since the 1950s, the country has shifted from being among the poorest in Africa and Asia to one of the top 20 economies in the world. The country's Gross Domestic Product (GDP) expansion since the 1960s has been spectacular. According to World Bank data, Korea's GDP grew from $2.418 billion in 1961 to $1.053 trillion in 2006, surpassing the one trillion-dollar mark for the first time.[2] According to the World Bank, Korea's economy is the fifth largest in Asia and 13th in the world, based on its 2022 GDP of $1.67 trillion.[3] The chart below shows the country's GDP growth trajectory from 1962 to 2022 in current U.S. dollars. See Figure 1.

Another indicator of this fantastic transformation is Gross National Income (GNI) per capita, formerly referenced as GDP per capita. Korea's GNI per capita experienced an astounding increase from 1962 to 2022. According to the World Bank, GNI per capita grew from $120 to $35,990 in that same period. See Figure 2.

The Korean Economy

Today, Korea's economy is export-based. As such, the historical trajectory of exports follows the patterns established by GDP and GNI growth.

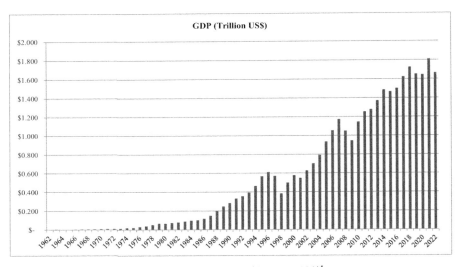

Figure 1: Korea's GDP (Current US$)[4]

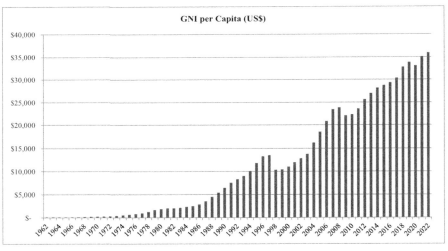

Figure 2: Korea's GNI per Capita, Atlas Method (Current US$)[5]

"South Korea's exports, which amounted to only USD 32.82 million in 1960, surpassed the USD 10 billion mark in 1977 and reached USD 542.2 billion in 2019."[6] The country's five top export items are as follows: 1) semiconductors, 2) automobiles, 3) petroleum products, 4) auto parts, and 5) flat panel displays and sensors.[7]

Korea's economy is considered mixed. According to the *Business Dictionary*, a mixed economy is "An economic system in which both the private enterprise and a degree of state monopoly (usually in public services, defense, infrastructure, and basic industries) coexist. All modern economies are mixed, where the means of production are shared between the private and public sectors. Also called dual economy."[8]

It is widely known that the economy is dominated by family-owned conglomerates called *chaebols* that produce everything from cars to television monitors, laptops, cell phones, and more. They also own major supermarket chains, hotels, apartment buildings, department stores such as Lotte Mart and Lotte Department Stores, and bakeries like Paris Baguette. As a result of the overwhelming influence that these *chaebols* have on the economy, the country and the people depend heavily on the success of these corporations. Not surprisingly, from a very early age, Koreans aspire to join one of these conglomerates as full-time employees after college graduation for economic security and to assure themselves of a successful life-long career.

The Efficiency Factor

Korea produces some of the most advanced technology capable of competing with similar products assembled by major companies worldwide. Koreans have accomplished this impressive achievement through efficiency, a pillar of capitalist economies, in a highly competitive environment that permeates the culture. These two themes—competitiveness and efficiency—will resonate in our observations of Korean society.

The Competitiveness of Korean Companies

Companies like Hyundai/Kia Motors, LG, Samsung Electronics, and others successfully compete on the world stage against renowned corporations like Apple, Ford, GE, GM, Google, Honda, Intel, Kenmore, Toyota, and Whirlpool. However, even among Koreans, there is a sense that for conglomerates to maintain their competitive edge, they must continue to promote growth, creativity, and innovation—but especially growth.

Technology, business, and industry have set the pace for the unprecedented trajectory in the above charts. For example, in 2020, Korea ranked fifth among electronic circuit component exporting countries, behind only Hong Kong, Taiwan, China, and Singapore.[9] According to *IC Insights*, as of December 20, 2021, Samsung Electronics was the largest semiconductor company in the world, with sales of $83.09 billion. The number two semiconductor company was Intel, selling $75.55 billion.[10]

A characteristic that will become evident in this book is that Koreans are early adopters and trendsetters, especially regarding the efficient use of technology for convenience. Today, the extensive use of technology is even more pronounced than in the 1990s when I first started visiting the country. A prime example of this increased use of technology is the ubiquitous access to the Internet. Broadband is accessible from practically anywhere in the country. Moreover, it is fast. It is faster than the bandwidth available in many parts of the United States. According to *Fastmetrics*, in the first quarter of 2017, Korea enjoyed the number one spot among the top 10 countries in the world with the fastest Internet. It had a 28.6 average Mbps (megabits per second) at the time. The global average Internet speed was 7.2 Mbps. In the same quarter, the United States finally cracked the top 10 countries at number 10 with an average Mbps of 18.7, or 10 Mbps slower than Korea. By comparison, Korea has held the number one spot continuously since *Fastmetrics* first began documenting data in the fourth quarter of 2015.[11]

From the end of 2018 to April 2019, companies from Korea (KT) and the United States (AT&T and Verizon) raced neck-and-neck to the finish line to be the first company in the world to launch a 5-G network or fifth-generation cellular technology. In the end, companies from both countries claimed to be first. Regardless, the point is that Korea has developed cutting-edge technology capable of competing with the most technologically advanced countries.[12] This reality is a testimony to the remarkable technological transformation achieved since the end of the Korean War.

Effective Use of Technology

Another example of the effective use of technology is the universal use of dashcam recorders, which are inconspicuously located on the windshield next to the rearview mirror of a vehicle. Koreans refer to this type of camera as a "black box." These instruments record everything that happens in front of the car. Nowadays, some cameras can record video and sound in front of and inside the vehicle. Consequently, if an accident occurs, there is no need to argue about whose fault it is. It is all recorded.

Although these cameras are readily available in the U.S. at stores such as Best Buy and Amazon and are reasonably priced below $200, some at less than $100, their use is still limited. Regarding technology, Koreans tend to be much more early adopters than Americans. One reason is that Koreans generally appreciate efficiency, particularly the efficacy that technology generates. It is worth noting that this attitude has recently changed in other developed countries due to the COVID-19 pandemic. In this instance, however, adopting the automation concept is not necessarily a result of an early adopter propensity or motivated by a desire for efficiency but by necessity.

Another convenient and clever innovation that impressed me recently was the proliferation of power-folding-side-view mirrors (or wing mirrors) on cars. Undoubtedly, one of the reasons for the extensive use of this device is that some of the streets in Korea are narrow, particularly in the older sections of cities, as in other countries with a long historical trajectory. The capability of folding the side mirrors gives drivers more room to navigate. Nowadays, this convenience is available in luxury cars in the United States.

In a more recent development in the utilization of advanced technology, on December 3, 2023, the Seoul Metropolitan Government announced the implementation of a pilot program using two autonomous overnight buses across 40 stops beginning on December 4 between 11:30 p.m. and 5:10 a.m. The buses are scheduled to travel 9.8 kilometers (6.1 miles).[13] The bus operator is taking precautions to ensure passenger safety during the trial run. Specifically, "two safety staff will be on board each bus."[14] Also, the number of passengers will be limited to 23, as the pilot trial will not allow standing passengers. A fifth-generation communication infrastructure is supporting the autonomous technology in this pilot program.[15] Once again, Korea is leading the way in using cutting-edge technology that supports efficiency.

An Image Renewal through International Events Exposure

Korean people have many reasons to be proud of their country's achievements. Some of the nation's advancements have been showcased during international sporting events, commencing with the 1988 Seoul Summer Olympics. Korea also co-hosted the 2002 World Cup bi-nationally with Japan. More recently, they hosted the 2018 PyeongChang Winter Olympics. The 1988 Seoul Summer Olympics, however, had a special significance. Lee Charm, former head of the Korea National Tourism Agency, referred to it as the country's "coming-out party."[16] In today's parlance, it may be called Korea's debut on the world stage.

Before this event, people around the world associated Korea almost exclusively with the Korean War. However, by the time the torch was extinguished, the country's image had become that of a nation where rich traditions coexist with a vibrant, modern, youthful, economically strong, highly industrialized, and technologically advanced society. The infrastructure built for these events has enhanced mobility, communication, and entertainment. This effort continues today with the constant expansion of highways, tunnels, railways, high-speed trains, and broadband accessibility. The infrastructure buildup and worldwide exposure through international events contributed to the Korean economy by facilitating the movement of goods and services, expanding international tourism, and cementing the country's image as a potential business partner.

Korea Exports Its Pop Culture

Today, Korea exports much more than cars and technology. The country exports its pop culture to the world through K-pop and soap operas, better known as K-dramas, since these two forms of entertainment are in high demand worldwide. According to the Korea Creative Content Agency, in 2016, global sales related to K-pop, including revenue from CDs, concert tickets, streaming music, and related merchandise and services, reached 5.3 trillion Korean won (KRW) (~$4.7 billion).[17]

Those who had been living under a rock, so to speak, and were not familiar with K-pop, experienced a taste of the infectious music during the closing ceremony of the 2018 PyeongChang Winter Olympics with the performance of the popular group EXO. Furthermore, as of this writing, BTS, the most successful K-pop group in history, has reached the number one spot on Billboard Hot 100 six times.[18]

Similarly, K-beauty cosmetics have become a worldwide phenomenon. The country also exports in-vogue trends. Two such fads are the extensive use of Botox and plastic surgery. Even though Koreans did not invent either of them, through K-drama exports, they have been successful at attracting people from other Asian countries to receive these types of treatments in Korea. Globalization has facilitated the spread of these trends, especially when these phenomena are congruent with a receptive culture.

Lastly, Korean food has become popular around the world. Thanks to the entrepreneurial nature of Koreans, people around the globe can enjoy Korean cuisine from Abu Dhabi to Beijing, London, Los Angeles, New York, Paris, and Siem Reap.

Values Contributing to the Economic Transformation

The nation's accomplishments discussed in the above section did not happen accidentally. Koreans have demonstrated that they are goal-oriented, tenacious, efficient, hardworking, and entrepreneurial, as evidenced by the high percentage of self-employed. They have also shown robust support for the national agenda. This tendency is reflected in the universal willingness to make the necessary individual and collective sacrifices for the good of the nation. These qualities have contributed enormously to the nation's evolution from an underdeveloped state following the war to one of the most technologically advanced countries in the world.

Koreans also espouse fundamental values that account for the nation's high standard of living, including a strong work ethic, a solid healthcare system, and an emphasis on education. In our analysis, we will examine these and other characteristics. We will also demonstrate how efficiency permeates society. It is the driving force behind the country's astonishing rise from the ashes since the end of the Korean War. Unfortunately, the emphasis on efficiency has taken its toll on some segments of society and the nation's psyche, hence the title of this book.

- The Korean economy is export-based.
- The country has experienced an extraordinary increase in productivity since the end of the Korean War.
- How did Korea change the world's image of the country?
- In addition to advanced technology and cars, Korea exports its culture through K-pop, K-drama, K-beauty, and emerging trends.

CHAPTER TWO

Cultural Values and Behavioral Patterns

Background

Korean societal values have followed Confucian and Daoist traditions for thousands of years. As such, family values were cherished, and respect for elders was upheld above all else. Confucian values emphasize respect for authority, filial piety, and social harmony. This philosophy shaped Korea's traditional family structure, governance, and interpersonal relationships, fostering a hierarchical system where individuals are expected to adhere to their assigned roles and show deference to those in higher positions. While modern Korea has evolved, remnants of these Confucian-influenced hierarchical values persist in certain aspects of society. For example, in the past, Korea promoted itself as *dongbangyeuijiguk* (동방예의지국), which translates as "the country of courteous people in the East." Nowadays, it is still customary for individuals to bow their heads when greeting each other and to use more formal or polite speech when speaking with strangers or older adults.

Modern Korea

Modern Korea is a land of contrasts. It is a blend of traditional cultural norms, cutting-edge technology, democracy, and capitalism. Given the extensive divide between conventional norms and modern values that emphasize efficiency, competition, and materialism in the form of wealth, glamour, beauty, and youth, the contradictions often result in a clash, creating disharmony and imbalance.

Korea's modern history began at the end of the Korean War. The peninsula's split after the war meant South Koreans had to adopt an ideology different from what they had as a reference. They were pressed to begin the country's reconstruction and modernization, given the massive destruction of infrastructure, industry, agriculture, and human lives caused by the war. An estimated ten percent of the population, or approximately three million people, were killed, wounded, or missing. The war also created social problems, such as poverty, inequality, unemployment, and displacement. Many people lost their homes, families, and livelihoods. Refugees from North Korea and orphaned children from the war increased the population pressure and social welfare needs. As expected, after an all-out war, people experienced hunger, disease, and trauma.

After the war, South Korea's financial and physical conditions were challenging and dismal. However, when we put things in perspective, overcoming these bleak conditions and rebuilding the country took Koreans a relatively short time. To assert their sovereignty, prevent a possible communist takeover, and avoid a case of history repeating itself, e.g., the Japanese occupation (1910-1945), South Koreans had to adopt an imported ideology that combines democracy and capitalism. The modernization process required Korea to

[urbanize] the people and the land, taking a largely agricultural and rural population and turning them into urban apartment dwellers in but a few decades with towering vertical concrete structures replacing the more spacious horizontal dwellings of the farms and hanoks [traditional Korean houses that were first designed and built during the Joseon dynasty (1392-1897)].[1]

As a result of the rapid, radical transformation, the most salient Korean values and behavioral patterns represent a blend of the nation's past and present realities. Since efficiency is a pillar of capitalism and Korea has a capitalist economy, it is not surprising that the culture is imbued with a competitive environment within an efficiency paradigm. However, Korea's competitive milieu seems more expansive and relentless than other capitalist economies.

Other cultural and behavioral patterns have contributed to the country's economic success as measured by GDP. In turn, consistent GDP growth has a positive impact on individuals as well as the nation's education level. Eventually, this generates financial success for the people in terms of GNI (Gross National Income) per capita and for corporations as determined by profits. The cultural values and behavioral patterns that have contributed to the nation's financial success include an emphasis on education, unity, harmony, consensus building, individual and collective sacrifice, the *pali pali* (빨리빨리) or hurry, hurry culture, and *gap* (갑) and *eul* (을). The latter refers to a relationship between two parties, one with power and another without. Overlaying these cultural and behavioral patterns is the pervasive efficiency construct. In the remainder of this chapter, we discuss some of these cultural values, behavioral patterns, and their role in a competitive environment within this efficiency paradigm. Due to the complexity of the emphasis on education, we purposely decided to dedicate an entire chapter to this topic.

The Concept of Unity

One of the fundamental differences between Korean and Western societies is the emphasis on unity or group conventionality in the former and individuality in the latter. At least as far as Korea is concerned, it seems that the prominence of unity has geographic and historical roots. A strategically located peninsula surrounded by historically powerful nations like China, Russia, and Japan, Korea has been susceptible to foreign aggression and, in some instances, invasion and eventual occupation. Consequently, Koreans have recognized the advantages of being a united people.

United, they have repelled aggressors and freed themselves from the shackles of oppression by foreign countries, including Japan. Also, united, they recovered from the devastation of the Korean War to transform the country into the 13th largest economy in the world. Therefore, the concept of unity runs deep in the fabric of society. This widespread commitment to solidarity is expressed in the slogan 뭉치면 살고 흩어지면 죽는다, which translates as "united we stand, divided we fall." However, the Korean expression carries a much stronger connotation. It means, "If united, we live; if not, we die." Some administrations have used this slogan to rally the people behind initiatives considered beneficial to the nation. It is also emphasized in the armed services, the workplace, schools, and families.

The national unity fervor was evident before and during the 1988 Seoul Summer Olympics and the 2002 World Cup when Korea and Japan co-hosted the FIFA (International Federation of Association Football) event. The spirit of solidarity was also evident in the heartwarming show of unity between the two Koreas during the opening ceremony of the 2018 PyeongChang Winter Olympics. The two delegations made their appearance under a single flag. The same spirit showed unconditional support for athletes representing South Korea during specific events.

The 1988 Seoul Summer Olympics, including infrastructure build-up, cost Korea $8.2 billion in today's U.S. dollars.[2] In addition to showcasing the country and transforming the nation's image, the event provided a morale booster for the people. In retrospect, the money spent to organize the games and introduce modern Korea to the world was well spent.

According to the *Washington Post*, Korea spent $2 billion on stadiums, roads, and related infrastructure in preparation for the 2002 World Cup.[3] Government and business leaders valued the intangible benefits of co-hosting the event. Kim Joo Hyun, vice president of Hyundai Research Institute in Seoul, is quoted as saying: "This is a total makeover of Korea's image to the world."[4]

The unprecedented infrastructure build-up in preparation for the 1988 Seoul Summer Olympics and the 2002 World Cup made Korea an ideal host for subsequent international sports events. Aside from the 1988 Seoul Summer Olympics, the 2002 World Cup, and the 2018 PyeongChang Winter Olympics, the country has hosted other major international sports events, such as the Asian Games in 2002 and 2014. These athletic competitions had a lesser unifying impact, most likely because Koreans recognize the unparalleled intangible benefits of hosting events on the scale of the World Cup and an Olympiad versus the regional games.

Koreans were justifiably proud of co-hosting the 2002 World Cup and showcasing their country to the rest of the world. The entire nation rallied behind their team. People in Seoul, Busan, and other cities in Korea, and even expatriates in Los Angeles, took to the streets by the thousands, wearing the traditional red T-shirts and matching bandanas to watch and root for the Korean national team on giant TV screens. This enthusiasm and energy undoubtedly contributed to the country's best showing in a World Cup event: Korea took fourth place.

History will judge the performance of Korea as the host country of the 2018 PyeongChang Winter Olympics. However, based on first impressions, the highly polished image transmitted was that of a much more mature, confident, and technologically advanced nation than in prior worldwide events. The 2018 PyeongChang Winter Olympics was no longer the country's debut on the world stage but more akin to an encore or a return engagement. The world was much more familiar with Korea as an economic power and a nation that exports quality products. The 2018 event reaffirmed that Korea has a respectable place on the world stage despite the tensions with its neighbor in the north.

Unity and Harmony

Racially, ethnically, culturally, and linguistically, Korea is still a largely homogeneous country where unity and harmony are universal values. These concepts are evidenced by national symbols and practices, including the *Taegukgi* (also *Taegukki*) or the national flag. The white background represents the purity of the Korean people and their quest for peace. The inner circle, or *taeguk*, is divided equally and represents the harmony and balance between *yin* and *yang*, the two cosmic forces which oppose each other but achieve perfect balance. The bottom blue section in the inner circle represents *yin*, and the red upper area signifies *yang*. Examples of *yin* and *yang* include the following:

Table 1: Examples of Yin and Yang

Yin	Yang
dark	bright
cold	hot
the moon	the sun
night	day
winter	summer
woman	man

The four black trigrams called *Kwae* surrounding the *taeguk* circle are composed of broken and unbroken bars. Individually, they represent the elements of heaven, earth, water, and fire. Together, they stand for the principle of movement and harmony of *yin* and *yang*.

Figure 1: Flag of South Korea[5]

Conformity and Differentiation

Despite the society's highly competitive nature, Koreans tend to conform to social norms. This conformity is congruent with the cultural concepts of unity and harmony. Socially, Koreans avoid standing out and being perceived as different, which theoretically seems like a harmonious social pattern. However, the competitive nature of the culture compels them to differentiate from one another in several contexts. One such distinction involves socioeconomic differentiation. On the surface, they easily navigate this dichotomy of conformity and differentiation. However, as we will see in later chapters, the existing sociocultural contradictions can harm the human psyche.

Associated with this socioeconomic status-conscious tendency is the question related to the university from which an individual graduates, whether domestic or international. Prospective employers give special consideration to candidates possessing a degree from a reputable university abroad, particularly from the United States, because of their anticipated linguistic and cultural contributions to the company. Therefore, Koreans with degrees from a reputable university abroad are highly regarded.

As far as graduates from domestic universities are concerned, the media and Koreans, in general, consider someone with a degree from one of the top universities as having their career and high socioeconomic status set for life. Traditionally, the most prestigious are Seoul National University, Korea University, and Yonsei University. The acronym SKY refers to these three. Many prominent politicians, doctors, lawyers, engineers, professors, and journalists are SKY-university graduates, thus supporting this tradition. More precisely, regarding the influence held by Seoul National University graduates:

> Half of the lawmakers in [the] current National Assembly of Korea are SNU [Seoul National University] alumni. Judges in the high court and the Supreme [Court] are mostly from SNU, which is 88% of all. More than half of [the] cabinet members in the present ministry are also SNU alumni. [Fifty-five percent] of CEOs of [the] top 500 companies in Korea are SNU graduates.[6]

However, with the proliferation of university rankings, the use of different criteria in their development, and Korea's emphasis on technology, the panorama is more fluid. In reviewing the various university rankings available, the musical chairs-esque movement becomes apparent. Therefore, the concept of the three top universities that compose SKY has become purely symbolic. They remain highly ranked, but not necessarily as number one, two, and three. For instance, for 2021-2022, *U.S. News & World Report* ranks the top five global universities in Korea as follows:

1. Seoul National University
2. Sungkyunkwan University
3. Korea University
4. Korea Advanced Institute of Science and Technology (KAIST)
5. Yonsei University[7]

In addition to the university where a person graduates, Koreans consider other factors within socioeconomic differentiation. These include the type of car people drive, their job, their father's occupation, whether they wear designer clothes, carry designer-label accessories, or own their own home.

I realize that people in the West also use similar factors to judge a person's socioeconomic status. However, Koreans tend to be inquisitive once they feel comfortable with someone they just met. To get to know the person better, they ask very direct, personal questions that would be considered inappropriate in the West. The questions may include the person's marital status, their father's occupation, the type of car they drive, the number of children they have, and the universities they attend. The question about the father's occupation generates the most information regarding a person's socioeconomic background. The answer is considered an indicator of such variables as how much support they received in terms of supplemental education while growing up, whether they live in an upscale neighborhood with the best *hagwons*, after-school academies, or "cram schools," and how much wealth they may inherit from their father. The questions also reflect the values of present-day Korean culture. Even in this seemingly trivial social aspect, Koreans are very efficient. They learn as much information about another person in as little time as possible.

Another area where the differentiation is palpable, certainly much more pronounced than in the West, is age. Koreans are highly conscious of age. They tend to associate with, date, and marry people their own or very close to their age. Age-mismatch associations are rare. When someone associates with someone outside their age group, it is considered more than a faux pas; people wonder what is wrong with that person.

Unity and Conformity

Children learn the concepts of unity and conformity at a very early age. They are teased by other children and even bullied if they stray from established norms. As a concrete example, because historically Korea has been racially homogeneous, Koreans can intuitively tell when someone is from a mixed marriage, even if to a non-Korean, the person looks and talks like a full-fledged Korean. Consequently, it is not uncommon for children of diverse racial backgrounds to be bullied.

Traditionally, children are expected to follow the conventional path, including being studious, earning good grades, and obtaining commensurate test scores. These achievements will enable them to gain admission to a top-tier university, eventually making them candidates for the "ideal job" at one of the nation's conglomerates. Men must perform their military service unless granted an exemption for medical reasons. Eventually, men and women are expected to secure a "dream" white-collar job at a multinational corporation, get married, raise children, and sacrifice themselves for their children's education, as their parents sacrificed for theirs. Thus, their children can follow the time-tested path to economic stability and success. White-collar jobs exist in smaller companies; however, the initial goal is to obtain the "dream" white-collar job in one of the *chaebols*. The reasons are the higher compensation, better benefits, security, and prestige associated with those jobs compared to similar positions at a smaller company.

The differentiation between university- and non-university-bound students begins before they enter high school. Pupils with solid academic potential attend regular high schools unless their parents can afford private or international school tuition. Conversely, students whose grades and test scores show a lesser academic potential in elementary and middle school can attend an occupational or technical high school. Regular high school students who do not earn good enough grades with matching test scores to enter university are relegated to blue-collar jobs. They can enroll in a university specializing in career and technical education, or if they are fortunate enough to have parents who own a business, they may be incorporated into it. Suppose they are entrepreneurial, and their parents have enough money to support a business venture. In that case, they may start a business of their own. Another option is for them to complete any number of certificates to obtain the necessary skills for an entry-level position at a small company.

The Tendency to Follow Collective Norms

The emphasis on wearing school uniforms in public and private schools exemplifies the tendency to follow group norms. This is not to say that all schools require uniforms; however, many schools espouse a uniform policy.

A more widely observed example of this tendency to conform to group norms is a behavior that appears to apply almost exclusively to Koreans. As I traveled extensively throughout the country, on weekends or holidays, particularly in areas Koreans frequented from various parts of the nation, I noticed a very peculiar behavior. In today's experiential age, when smartphones with cameras are ubiquitous, young Koreans extensively use their cell phone camera and selfie sticks to take selfies and post them on social media. It is true that millennials particularly have universally embraced social media. However, in typical fashion, Koreans have taken it to the next level when adopting new trends. They seem to have a love affair with social media, especially when taking pictures of food or selfies in restaurants they visit for the first time and sharing them online with their friends. In short, the difference is the degree of intensity.

Despite the general tendency to adhere to group norms, frustrated and disheartened young people choose not to follow the traditional path. They refer to Korea as *Hell Joseon*, alluding to the Joseon dynasty (1392-1897), to express their struggle, especially the poor, to live up to society's expectations. We discuss this trend in more detail in Chapter Ten.

Consensus Building

In addition to the pressure to conform to social norms, Koreans have an innate desire to reach consensus, the underlying belief that the best decision is the one most endorsed. In other words, other people's opinions are valued highly in decision-making. For example, when selecting a *hagwon* for their children, mothers of elementary, middle, and senior high school students consider the opinion of other mothers in their network whose children have gained admission to prestigious universities. Mothers utilize the consultation process when choosing a private tutor or an international school for their children.

Consultation and consensus building are especially applicable to potentially life-changing events, such as when Korean students face personal decisions, including submitting an essay for the U.S. university admission process or choosing a country for a job internship. Three fundamental motives in consensus building for Koreans are the desire to fulfill societal norms, to gain an advantage in a competitive environment, and to develop maximum efficiency. The latter signifies taking the road well-traveled as determined by the consultation process, thus minimizing mistakes and increasing the probability of success.

The intensified pressure to ensure their own and their family's future financial well-being forces students to behave obsessively. For example, most of the students I counseled asked two or three teachers, and sometimes university professors, to review their autobiographical essays before submitting them with their college admission applications. By taking this action, students demonstrate that they recognize the essay's crucial role in university admission. Furthermore, they believe that procuring the opinion of several people on the essay structure and content gives them the best chance to put their best foot forward.

For students who apply for college admission abroad, selecting an institution from among several admission offers presents yet another example of the role that consensus building plays in Korean society. Being aware of the competitive nature of their culture, high school students recognize that the university selection process is of utmost importance to their future financial security.

Aside from the culture-driven behavioral patterns, ethical issues are at stake when these actions are viewed through the lens of a Westerner. Directions for essay writing on admission applications are explicit and specific enough for applicants to follow. These instructions are there to ensure a leveled playing field. Suppose admission committees utilize essays to determine the applicant's potential to succeed in a rigorous academic environment. Are essays providing a false measure? The substantial input provided "by committee," through consensus, or by someone other than the applicant can significantly alter the quality and meaning of the essay.

Without exception, the students I assisted with the Western university application process engaged in lengthy consultations with relatives, friends, family friends, and respected community members, including teachers, pastors, and university professors, before finally arriving at a decision. Although the students were well-guided by an area expert, they were still compelled to go through this informal consultation process to reassure themselves of success and efficiency in decision-making.

It may take a while for a Western counselor who is used to dealing directly with the students and their parents regarding these crucial decisions to realize that when counseling Korean students, additional players with considerable influence on the decision-making are not sitting at the table. Instead, they are standing in the background and are only accessible to the students and their parents.

A prime example is a senior, whom I assisted with the college application process, who received acceptance letters from about ten institutions in the United States and a $25,000 scholarship. He consulted with his parents, relatives, university professors, and family friends before making his final choice. These situations present students with decisions that may have profound personal and professional repercussions. Concerns arise when they ask non-experts for advice before making such choices. They may receive incomplete information, disinformation, or biased opinions that may not be in the student's best interest.

A similar example, but at a different level, is one of a university student I met. He consulted extensively with relatives and friends, professors, and former supervisors before finally choosing Singapore over Australia for a job internship in hotel management. After he returned to Korea from his training in Singapore, I had the opportunity to ask him about the usefulness of the consultation or consensus-building process concerning his choice between Singapore and Australia. Below is his answer in his own words:

> I consulted professors, friends, and parents about my problems. In fact, at that time, I wanted to go to Australia rather than Singapore. However, I went to Singapore because I had to consider various factors such as [my financial] conditions and career. People around me said Singapore would help me more in terms of my introverted personality, career, and [financial condition]. People around me [...] [helped] me from a more objective point of view. Among them, the [financial] question [was] the biggest [factor] in determining which country to go to.
>
> The language training [in] Australia was very expensive, but in Singapore I was able to earn money and be self-sufficient. So, I chose Singapore.
>
> It's hard to say that I didn't regret my choice after going to Singapore. When I heard about my friends who planned to go to Australia together, I thought I would like to live in Australia. But [in the end], I don't regret the year I spent in Singapore. If I [had gone] to Australia [instead], I could have made another memory, but life in Singapore helped me a lot and made many unforgettable memories.[8]

Even though this case study is anecdotal, it provides a glimpse into why Koreans engage in similar consultation or consensus-building processes. They resort to this method when faced with a critical decision and perceive the benefits of the engagement.

This consultation process appears to be the rule rather than the exception. Such observed behavioral patterns reflect the value Koreans place on consensus building and opting for well-traveled roads. They choose it because it is the one that has produced positive results for others. By taking the established path, they enhance the probability of experiencing success. The rationale is that there is no need to "reinvent the wheel" and take unnecessary risks by making an independent decision. The concept of efficiency also comes into play in these decision-making situations. Individuals avoid wasted effort and disappointments by consulting with those who know them and their circumstances well and have had successful experiences in similar events.

Consensus Building in Other Areas

Consensus-building patterns of behavior are evident outside of education as well. An example of the consultation process that leads to consensus building is palpable in the real estate industry. When purchasing property, Koreans usually consider the opinions of family members, relatives, and friends, especially if these individuals have had successful experiences in real estate. This consultation process and consensus building is a way of conducting an informal survey of the people within their sphere of influence whose opinions they trust. The results of such an inquiry make Koreans feel confident that they are making a decision that will benefit them eventually. It is an efficient way to ensure success. They apply it in many areas, aside from those already mentioned, including doctor and hospital choices for medical treatment, stock selection for investment purposes, fashion trends, restaurant options, and acquisition of goods and services.

The Concept of Sacrifice

The concept of sacrifice runs deep in the collective psyche of the Korean people. Specifically, individual sacrifice for the benefit of the group or the larger society holds particular significance. This idea is evident throughout society. Individuals not only voluntarily sacrifice but are expected to do so. For example, family members sacrifice their interests for those of the family; individual employees sacrifice for the benefit of the unit or the entire corporation; students sacrifice for the good of the whole class; soldiers sacrifice for the good of the platoon. The concept is so ingrained in the culture that it is prominent in the Korean lexicon. It is common to hear in everyday conversation the motto 대를 위한 소의 희생, which means: "For the large, sacrifice the small." In other words, "individuals should act or sacrifice for the benefit of the group." This saying should not be confused with "all for one and one for all" since the latter implies a reciprocal benefit to both the individual and the group. The Korean slogan reflects the culture since it incorporates the concepts of unity, conformity, and harmony. More importantly, it accentuates the devaluation of the individual vis-à-vis the group, which is observed in various contexts, including the classroom, the armed services, and social gatherings.

Unless exempted for medical reasons, all males must complete their military service and sacrifice approximately two years of their lives for the nation's good. The service length depends on the military branch; hence, there is variability in the time served. Their sacrifice is viewed as contributing to repelling a possible invasion from their neighbor to the north.

In most Korean companies, entry-level employees are required to participate in company drills. This training often includes trust-building exercises and physical activity. Some drills may consist of army-style exercises with overtones of acculturation to the company values. This practice is meant to impress the importance of individual employee sacrifices for the good of the company.

At a more sublime level is the conviction of the older generation, those who lived through poverty before, during, and after the Korean War. Their firm belief is that individual citizens should sacrifice their happiness, if necessary, for the good of the country. The following are concrete examples of notorious collective sacrifices.

Historically, Korea has frequently been compelled to fight outside invaders, primarily due to its strategic geographic location between China and Japan. In its modern history, the nation overcame the Japanese occupation from 1910 to 1945 and the Korean War from 1950 to 1953. The individuals who made the ultimate sacrifice to help liberate the country from the Japanese have been justifiably immortalized as heroes. Their heroic deeds are still emphatically taught in schools.

A more recent example of a collective sacrifice occurred during the Asian Financial Crisis (ca. 1997–2001) that affected some East Asian countries beginning in July 1997. Korea was one of the countries that was affected the most, alongside Thailand and Indonesia. Other nations were affected to a lesser extent. During the time leading to the crisis, Korea accumulated an increasing trade deficit. Conglomerates borrowed recklessly, jeopardizing the solvency of banks. The country practically depleted its foreign currency reserves, which led to sharp devaluations of its currency, the Korean won. Also, according to *Forbes*: "Foreign investors yanked nearly $18 billion out of the country. Hundreds of thousands lost their jobs."[9] The Asian Financial Crisis is known among Koreans as the IMF (International Monetary Fund) Crisis. In exchange for a $55 billion bailout, the most massive IMF bailout up to that point, Korea reluctantly agreed to implement severe cuts in public spending, open its markets to foreign goods and investors, and reduce the ability of conglomerates to expand.

Realizing the individual and collective impact of the IMF conditions, about one-quarter of all Koreans, almost 3.5 million people, participated in a national campaign to pay back the IMF loan as soon as possible by donating their gold jewelry, coins, trinkets, and medals. They showed a profound sense of unity, collective sacrifice, and nationalism vis-à-vis this problematic situation. They stood in line outside donation centers to offer their gold for a national cause. According to *Forbes*, the campaign yielded 226 metric tons of scrap gold, totaling $2.2 billion. The donations were melted into gold bars and delivered to the IMF as an initial payment on the loan. Even though the gold contributions made only a small dent in the bailout amount, the campaign served as a national call to action and inspiration to pay off the loan before the end of 2001, almost three years ahead of schedule.

Pali Pali Culture

One cultural characteristic that is extremely specific to Korea is the tendency to do everything quickly. This characteristic is called "*pali pali*" or "hurry, hurry." We will examine in detail instances that reflect this tendency. Therefore, this section will serve as an introduction to this peculiarity. Koreans are keenly aware of this cultural concept, which they view as a tool for success. They teach it to children from an early age. Schools, *hagwons,* and private tutors promote the adoption of the "*pali pali*" characteristic by teaching students to solve problems quickly. The reason is that the speed with which they solve problems determines their academic success.

When eating in a restaurant, unless they are enjoying drinks, Koreans like to eat quickly, pay for their meal, and go. Restauranteurs and servers expect no less. Whether eating out or in, Koreans prefer their food delivered fast. Fast food delivery is readily and universally available. They consider it an acceptable alternative since restauranteurs commit to quick delivery.

Koreans also enjoy their fast Internet access. They also build structures fast. We will discuss examples and issues surrounding buildings erected in record time in Chapter Seven. The infatuation with a fast-paced lifestyle is attributed to the rapid economic expansion of the country that took place in record time after the Korean War.[10]

The Concept of Efficiency

Efficiency is embedded into the fabric of the culture, starting at an early age in education and from business to the top levels of the socioeconomic and political strata, including the Blue House (the equivalent of the U.S. White House). The latter is evidenced by the public expectancy of 3% annual growth in GDP. This expectation is based on the country's annual GDP growth for the last few years. Since 2013, Korea's economic growth has hovered consistently between 2.2% and 3.2%, except for 2020 and 2021, the first two full years of the COVID-19 pandemic.[11] This annual metric largely determines the success of a presidency during a single five-year term. Consequently, the emphasis is placed on short-term rather than long-term goals. This expectation exemplifies Korea's obsession with quick results.

Some Koreans I have spoken with feel it is time to revisit the one-term presidential term question and consider adopting a two-term limit. If this change were enacted, it would enable a sitting president to set short- and long-term goals for the nation. The attitudes of other Koreans about this shift run the gamut from hesitant to skeptical. The skeptics are concerned that implementing a two-term limit might open the door to a dictatorship. The thought of dictatorial rule brings back memories of years past, particularly for baby boomers. Furthermore, Koreans seem to have an understandable, instinctual aversion to dictatorships, given the constant threat from the north and their history.

This concern is valid and deserves to be respected. It is clearly up to the Korean people to decide whether they will keep the current format and maintain the focus on short-term goals. Otherwise, they could adopt a two-term limit, providing continuity in national policies and changing the public attention from short to long-term goals with appropriate intermediate measurable objectives. If implemented, this fundamental change at the national level would necessitate a paradigm shift throughout the rest of society. This shift would require less emphasis on quick results and more on solid, long-range goals.

The one-term limit resonates with the concept of efficiency. If, on the one hand, a president implements policies that promote a strong economy and contribute to a "successful" regime, the public will consider the mission accomplished, provided that no mishaps of the magnitude of the *Sewol* ferry or the Itaewon crowd crush occur. If, on the other hand, the public views the president's policies as ineffective in maintaining a robust 3% annual GDP or higher, it will deem the administration as unsuccessful. In such a case, the public endures the pain for only one term. Afterward, a new leader can have the opportunity to change course and guide the country to more prosperous times.

Competition and Efficiency

The preferred method of dealing with the brutal competition pervasive throughout society, from the higher levels to the lower echelons, is through efficiency. To this end, Koreans use quantitative measures represented by numerical values and ranking systems. Efficiency is achievable for educational entities, government agencies, businesses, industry, and the public by implementing a ranking system that assigns numerical values to a set of criteria.

Boiling down simple variables to a numerical value is undoubtedly efficient. The added benefit of using these rankings is the public's perception of fairness. Fairness is highly valued by Koreans primarily because of the extremely competitive environment. They do not shy away from competition if there is a perception of equity in the evaluation process. The reliance on tests for theoretical fairness and efficiency underscores the culture's competitive and cutthroat characteristics. Conglomerates, large corporations, and universities rely almost exclusively upon test results to make life-changing decisions about employment and admission. This overemphasis on testing fuels Korea's costly and universally utilized private education industry.

The challenge, however, is that complex factors, such as personality traits, potential, motivation, and values, are more difficult to quantify. Complex elements such as these can be assigned a numerical value for efficiency. However, even though a qualitative method is more elaborate and time-consuming to design and interpret, it is often more effective at analyzing empirical data generated by complex factors. Finally, the effectiveness and fairness aspects of qualitative measures are enhanced when a carefully designed rubric is used.

Efficiency in the Workplace

Several factors have contributed to Korea's emphasis on efficiency in the workplace. These include globalization, the dependence of the Korean economy on exports that must remain on the cutting edge, and the 1997 Asian Financial Crisis. These three factors directly or indirectly compel corporations to be lean to compete successfully against other global manufacturers on the international market.[12] Korean companies achieve efficiency through the extensive use of contingent workers and outsourcing to minimize labor costs.

EXAMPLES OF EFFICIENCY

Hagwons and Private Tutoring

Cram schools or *hagwons* and private tutoring reflect the priority given to education and exemplify the pervasive emphasis on efficiency permeating Korean culture. They represent an efficient vehicle for making students more competitive. Even though *hagwons* specializing in meeting adults' needs exist, *hagwons'* fundamental role is to provide elementary, middle, and senior high school students with academic support in areas crucial for success in the university admission process. Some *hagwons* specialize in other areas, including the arts. Koreans view *hagwons'* academic support as above and beyond the education delivered by the school system. Consequently, *hagwons* and private tutors have become an industry in and of themselves. These academies emphasize areas such as English education (e.g., conversation), mathematics, science, and performing arts. In addition, they provide support in preparation for the *Suneung*, the Korean university admission test, also known as the College Scholastic Ability Test (CSAT). This exam includes an English section. *Hagwons* also provide training for other tests required for international university admission, including the SAT (Scholastic Aptitude Test), the ACT (American College Testing), the TOEFL (Test of English as a Foreign Language), and the TOEIC (Test of English for International Communication). The TOEFL mainly applies to students planning to attend university abroad, and the TOEIC assesses English proficiency in the workplace. *Hagwons* and private tutoring are discussed in more detail in Chapter Four. However, in this chapter, the discussion will focus exclusively on their function. Also, unless otherwise specified, in this chapter only, the reference to *hagwon* indicates both *hagwons* and private tutoring.

Tools to Level the Playing Field

Parents perceive the test preparation for the *Suneung* available through *hagwons* as a way to level the playing field in a highly competitive university admission process. *Hagwons* provide their children with test-taking strategies, including test practice. Therefore, if a *hagwon* can significantly increase a student's score on the *Suneung* in a brief period through efficient test-taking strategies, the cost of attending will be worth every Korean won spent on it. Because of the highly competitive process for Korean university admission, a student's enrollment in *a hagwon* for test preparation is not an option but a necessity. The challenge for students from families with limited financial resources is that their economic situation may prevent them from accessing the better quality *hagwons* that children from wealthier families can afford, or it may preclude them from participating. Either of these instances places them at a disadvantage.

Student Rankings

Admission to university in Korea is an exceptionally long and competitive process that begins as early as middle school. School officials infuse efficiency into the process by assigning rankings to students. These rankings are called

내신 (pronounced "*naesin*"). Beginning in middle school and continuing through high school, student rankings are derived from locally developed and national tests. Universities consider these rankings when making admission decisions. Therefore, they become integral to the student's life and psyche early on. Students often refer to them when talking among themselves. They know that through these classifications, they are building their case toward university acceptance, the first step toward a dream job, and eventual financial success.

As the guidance counselor, I reviewed transcripts of incoming students from Korean schools and noted the ranking systems. They indicated where the student was in relation to his classmates at the Korean school. However, once the student began earning grades at the American school, the rankings became irrelevant. The grades earned from that point forward were a more realistic indicator of the student's academic ability and potential in a Western-style learning environment.

Two Cultures with Diametrically Opposed Philosophies

The old, well-traveled road to economic success appears less accessible for millennials than it once was for baby boomers. Contributing to this new reality is the prohibitive cost of supplemental private education and test preparation, considered essential and universally used in Korea to provide children with every possible advantage to succeed in a competitive university admission environment. As a result of the exorbitant cost of private education, the gap between the haves and have-nots is widening. It is beginning to show in participation statistics. Consequently, the view that the playing field is skewed toward the more affluent is becoming more pronounced. In theory, this is also true in other capitalist economies; however, it will become evident throughout this book that the difference is the degree of intensity. Competition is more fierce in Korea than in other capitalist countries, including the United States.

Access to higher education is quite different in the United States, where the wealthy may also have a distinct advantage in providing their children with the best preparation possible for university access and eventual career success. However, children from middle-class and economically disadvantaged families in the U.S. can succeed academically. This is true if they demonstrate academic potential, complete a college preparatory curriculum, earn respectable scores on college admission tests, and show through extracurricular activities, community involvement, and leadership that they can succeed in an academically rigorous environment. These students also contribute to the diversity of an academic institution.

The most significant difference is that in Korea, private supplemental education and test preparation, as reflected in the university admission test score, are determining factors in the university admission process. Conversely, in the U.S., private supplemental education is not universally used, primarily because the college admission process is more holistic. Therefore, the competitive aspect is not focused on test performance. Compared to Korean universities, institutions in the United States use multiple criteria much more widely to determine admission. They do so to assemble a diverse first-year class that reflects society as a whole and can potentially contribute to the institution.

A New Paradigm

The trend to make ACT (American College Test) and SAT (Scholastic Aptitude Test) scores optional for university admission is growing in the United States. This movement began in the Winter of 2004-2005 and has gained momentum. As of June 10, 2019, 242 four-year colleges and universities made these test scores optional.[13] Only two years later, on September 9, 2021, *Fair Test* reported that "more than 1,700 colleges and universities will not require admissions exam scores from applicants seeking to enroll in fall 2022."[14]

On June 14, 2018, the University of Chicago announced that it would make the test scores optional. It was the most prestigious educational institution in the United States at the time to join the movement. It was ranked third in the 2018 college rankings published by *U.S. News & World Report* at the time of the announcement, and the acceptance rate for the first-year class of Fall 2018 was seven percent.[15] As to the reason for making the test scores optional, James G. Nondorf, vice president for enrollment, is quoted as saying in an email:

> It is about doing the RIGHT thing… [which] is helping students and families of all backgrounds better understand and navigate this process and about bringing students with intellectual promise (no matter their background) to UChicago (and making sure they succeed here too!)[16]

In short, institutions of higher learning in the United States are leading the way in establishing a new paradigm that, in essence, reverses the practice of utilizing standardized test scores for admission purposes that began in the 20th century:

> [These practices have] the idealistic goals of rewarding academic merit, breaking social class barriers, and giving all students a chance to prove they belong

in college. But studies have found a strong link between scores and economic background. Privileged students, with wider access to books, museums, tutors and other forms of cultural or academic enrichment, tend to get higher marks.[17]

If a correlation between test scores and economic background is statistically valid in the United States, the same conditions are likely true in Korea. If so, that correlation would discredit the Korean belief that utilizing standardized test scores is a fairer way of determining admission. To provide more comprehensive access, some universities in the United States rely less frequently on test scores as predictors of success in an academic environment. This new trend shows that admission officers are beginning to recognize the fallacy of relying on standardized test scores for making admission decisions and the propensity to exclude students with intellectual potential. They have started to assign more weight to qualitative information about the applicant.

Regarding fairness, the *Chronicle of Higher Education* reported that James G. Nondorf had "heard lingering concerns about what some people described as enduring barriers to access: One of those was Chicago's testing requirement." Mr. Nondorf was quoted as saying,

> It was time that we looked at the application process and made sure it was fair for everyone. High-school counselors will tell you about a kid who would be a perfect fit for Chicago, who's not a good tester but who's talented in other ways, but who chose not to apply. You have enough of those interactions, and it tells you that the requirement is holding some students back, that it's scaring them away.[18]

This new paradigm will most likely take time to reach Korea primarily because of the brutally competitive environment and society's trust in objective criteria or quantitative measures for fairness. The irony is that the same test-based process that Koreans perceive as enabling a degree of justice may be doing the opposite by excluding students with intellectual potential and obstructing social mobility.

Other reasons for the under-reliance on supplemental private education in the United States include the accessibility of quality higher education at various levels and the diverse paths students can take. For instance, community colleges in the U.S., with their multiple missions, including transfer preparation, represent an outstanding alternative for high schoolers who may not have sufficiently solid academic preparation or the social maturity to succeed at university. However, after spending some time at community college and completing their lower division requirements, these students generally perform very well at a four-year public or private university. The difference is that after spending time at community college, students are more mature, have a solid academic foundation, and have strong time management and study skills. It is also possible that some high school graduates who are university-admissible may opt to attend a community college first for financial considerations. Their parents may lack the financial means to pay for university costs or wish to save money on tuition while completing their lower-division requirements.

Another key societal difference between Korea and the United States, perceived explicitly by prospective employers, concerns a job applicant's college or university trajectory. In the U.S., it matters little where one begins university studies. What counts is where someone graduates. For example, the fact that a job applicant attended a community college or a state university does not detract from the applicant's accomplishment of graduating from an Ivy League school or a top-level university.

In Korea, however, the institution where one begins higher education studies is paramount. Only the top academic students gain admission into elite universities. The overarching reason is the excruciatingly competitive nature of the admission process. By gaining access to a highly selective university, high school graduates show they are academically and socially prepared to thrive in such an environment. Yet another critical reason is that the transfer phenomenon does not play the essential role it does in the United States. In summary, because of systemic differences, Korean students do not have the variety of options their American counterparts have. Therefore, the pressure to perform well in high school and on the *Suneung* is exceptionally high.

Gap and *Eul*

Another code profoundly ingrained in the fabric of the deeply hierarchic Korean society is the *gap* and *eul* relationship. These terms differentiate between two parties: one with money, influence, authority, or power and another without them. In English, one might use such antonyms as big and little, large and small, strong and weak, or perhaps even top dog and bottom dog. Many relationships are based on these two concepts. The critical difference between these two terms is that the person in the *gap* role has a repressive function, while the one in the *eul* role has a submissive attitude.

An example of the *gap* and *eul* relationship is the "nut rage" incident aboard a Korean Airlines flight. One of the passengers, who happened to be the vice president and daughter of the current company owner and president, was served macadamia nuts in a bag instead of a bowl. She ordered the flight to abort the takeoff and return to the gate so the flight attendant who had served her the nuts could be escorted off the plane. Authorities later charged her with, among other things, violating aviation security as well as employing violence against a flight crew member. In this example, the company vice president felt she had power, but the flight attendant did not. Therefore, in the vice president's judgment, she felt her action was justified.

The *Gap* and *Eul* Concept in the Relationship between Consumers, Food Vendors, and Delivery Men

Another example of the *gap* and *eul* relationship is evident in the link between delivery men, who are extensively utilized, food vendors, and their clients. In this triad, consumers of delivery food remain at the top of the hierarchy. This privileged position results from their role as consumers with the resources to pay for the food they order, including delivery costs. Food vendors retain some power because of their ability to hire, fire, and pay the salary of delivery men. However, food vendors have less power than customers because they provide a service in exchange for the money consumers can afford to pay for it.

Delivery men are at the bottom tier of this chain because their role depends entirely on the other two parties. In such a position, delivery men receive pressure from clients and food vendors, but they cannot apply pressure on them. Given their advantaged position in the triad, consumers can demand on-time food delivery. They expect restauranteurs, as well as delivery people, to be efficient. They can apply pressure on vendors, and in turn, vendors pressure delivery men to make the deliveries as fast as possible regardless of how many traffic rules they must break or whether they risk their own lives or the lives of others in the process. Once again, the concept of efficiency is present in this triad. The issue of food delivery accidents is discussed in detail in Chapter Three.

Based on the discussion above, it is evident that in the *gap* and *eul* relationship, the pressure flows in the same direction as the movement of money. Therefore, it is safe to assume that in these examples, money determines who is on top and who is at the bottom of the association. Even though the *gap* and *eul* relationship pattern resembles similar situations in other capitalist countries, the difference is in the higher degree of intensity that appears to exist in Korean society. This higher intensity may very well be related to the ubiquitous fierce competition. In the "nut rage" case, the flight attendant had to excel in a brutally competitive environment to attain his job. In contrast, the Korean Airlines owner's daughter gained her high-level position through her relationship with the company owner—her father. It is safe to assume that she did not have to compete with others for her title. Her privileged position with the company will continue even after the owner dies since it is widespread practice for the ownership of a *chaebol* or any company, privately- or publicly owned, regardless of its size, to be transferred to the next generation along with the corresponding socioeconomic status.

We discuss the *gap* and *eul* relationship between contracting companies and subcontractors in Chapter Eight. The remaining chapters show the pervasive nature of the cultural and behavioral patterns discussed in this chapter.

Match-making Clubs

Competitiveness and efficiency coexist as complementing traits, even in the social aspect of Korean society. There are many match-making clubs that interested men and women can access to find their ideal mate. Club operators happily accept applications from clients with detailed personal and family information. Matchmakers corroborate these facts through an interview with the candidate. Then, they convert this information to numerical values to generate a ranking system, which they use to evaluate and categorize the client quickly and efficiently. This ranking enables matchmaking club operators to identify potential candidates for an individual. Below is a sample of information items collected from clients. It is worth noting that although the data for men and women are similar, there is a subtle difference between them.

Sample Information Collected from Male Clients
- Profession and education
- Income and property ownership
- Family wealth, responsibilities, and socioeconomic status
- Appearance (i.e., looks, height, and weight)
- Age and marriage history

Sample Information Collected from Female Clients
- Appearance (i.e., looks, height, and weight)
- Age and marriage history
- Profession and education
- Family background (e.g., father's occupation)

The materialistic nature of the information collected from clients is worth noting. These questionnaires reflect cultural aspects embedded in Korean society. The data obtained from male clients have a financial bias. For example, property ownership is an indicator of economic stability and wealth. Therefore, family wealth is an essential factor for male clients. On the one hand, historically, in Korean society, sons have inherited most of the family assets. On the other hand, family background, such as a father's occupation, indicates financial status or family prestige and reputation attributed to a female client.

Based on the information items listed above, this screening system is more thorough than dating services in the United States. Korean matchmakers are more direct and pose questions beyond the dating service queries in the U.S. American dating systems show details about potential candidates that match the criteria identified by the client. The client then selects the possible candidates for dating. This trial-and-error system could be lengthy and, thus, possibly inefficient.

Conversely, Korean matchmakers determine whom the client can contact based on the candidates' evaluation and rank. This system is more efficient because it significantly reduces and sometimes eliminates the trial-and-error period. The matchmaker achieves this by pre-screening both the client and the potential candidate to determine the viability of the match based on their rank. In other words, the matchmaker will introduce a likely candidate and a client if their respective ranks match. Conversely, a matchmaker will not introduce a client to a potential candidate from a higher or lower tier because that would open the door to a mismatch, thus wasting time.

Adopting New Trends

As stated earlier, because of the competitive nature of Korean society, the tendency to conform and the desire to differentiate from one another represent a dichotomy Koreans aspire to navigate successfully. The competitive environment, particularly in discerning an individual's socioeconomic status of an individual may explain why when a new trend surfaces, whether in the economy, in fashion, or on social media, the trendsetters or early adopters seem to gravitate in the same direction. This behavior pattern holds until the latest trend has been generally adopted. When a new pattern is in vogue, the urge to stand out, be different, and be better than others, including family and friends, becomes the driving force of individual and group behavior.

Because the fundamental tendency to conform promotes homogeneity and harmony but discourages individuality, Koreans find themselves in a quandary—they want to simultaneously conform to group norms and differentiate themselves from the pack. Those with financial means tend to differentiate themselves by acquiring material possessions. These include items like a more expensive car or apartment, more stylish clothing, eating in a more costly or fashionable restaurant, or shopping or hanging out in a newer or more prestigious mall in a more upscale neighborhood. However, once that trend is generally adopted, people switch and find a new material possession, interest, place, or activity that sets them apart. Restaurants seem to fall victim to this process. New specialty restaurants that engage in an effective promotional campaign have the potential to attract a sufficiently large clientele to generate initial success. Still, the large crowds can fade rapidly once the novelty effect wears off.

The popularity of and subsequent blasé attitude toward fusion Mexican Korean food provides a revealing example of this pattern of early adopters establishing a new trend to distinguish themselves from the masses and then moving to a new area of interest once the novelty wears off or the fad is adopted more universally.

A Business Initiative Illustrates Koreans' Tendency to Adopt New Trends

In 2011, three Korean Americans decided to open a fusion Mexican Korean restaurant called Vatos Urban Tacos in Itaewon, a multicultural, foreign-friendly area of Seoul where 20,000 foreigners reside. In 1997, Itaewon was designated as a special tourist zone.[19] "Travelers [and Korean residents] can taste authentic cuisine and experience culture from around the globe on the World Food Street where there are 40 restaurants operated by foreigners."[20] In addition, to international food, visitors, as well as locals, can enjoy shops, bars, and clubs. On weekends, Itaewon is exceptionally crowded with foreigners, locals, and American servicemembers who gather to shop, eat, and party in this diverse environment.

The restaurant was a tremendous success due primarily to its location and the target audience—foreigners who were familiar with and enjoyed Korean and Mexican cuisine and Koreans who had savored Mexican food in the U.S. The Korean early adopters had traveled or studied in the United States; therefore, their socioeconomic status is assumed to be proportional to those who could afford to travel or study abroad. Other Koreans who had never been to the United States and had never tried Mexican food saw this as an opportunity to appear as having a higher socioeconomic status, so they visited the restaurant to try the food. In a comparable situation, early adopters in the U.S. would not necessarily be considered of a higher socioeconomic status.

Eventually, the owners opened at least three other restaurants in very strategic districts of Seoul: Yongsan-gu, the fashionable Sinsa-dong district, and Songpa-gu. In addition, many Korean entrepreneurs impressed with Vatos Urban Tacos's success tried duplicating the experience. Suddenly, Mexican restaurants in Seoul became commonplace. However, once the trend became mundane, fusion Mexican Korean food lost the "special" quality and novelty perception. The food was no longer considered trendy, so it lost its attractiveness outside Vatos Urban Tacos. No other Mexican restaurant in Seoul has been able to match its success. CNN reports that the "waits can take up to three hours on weekends."[21]

To complete the story, the owners of Vatos Urban Tacos eventually took the experience to market internationally. They opened a restaurant in Singapore and another in the Philippines.

The Shake Shack Phenomenon

The Shake Shack phenomenon exemplifies the tendency to differentiate from others superficially. On July 22, 2016, amid high anticipation, the high-end burger chain opened its first restaurant in the affluent Gangnam district in the south end of Seoul. This business venture was possible thanks to an exclusive contract with SPC Group, the nation's largest bakery company. On the opening day of the Shake Shack location, people lined up for hours in the sweltering summer heat. Some reported waiting an entire night to ensure they were among the first to savor the taste of the burgers, fries, and shakes. The *Korea Times* reported that approximately 1,500 people waited two to three hours to taste the American premium burger.

The Korean reaction to this franchise exemplifies their desire to differentiate themselves from the crowd, fascination with novelty, and longing to emphasize or emulate a higher socioeconomic status. On the surface, the attitude vis-à-vis the opening of the first Shake Shack restaurant in Seoul would be no more than a typical reaction to novelty. However, the behavioral patterns become evident when analyzed through a social lens.

First, Koreans do not like waiting in line, especially for food. Throughout the country, high-quality food is readily available due to the oversaturation of restaurants that prepare foods of all types and emphasize efficiency.

American fast food, specifically pizza and hamburgers, is readily available thanks to the proliferation of American fast-food chains such as Pizza Hut, Papa John's, McDonald's, and Burger King. However, these restaurants established a foothold so long ago that Koreans no longer consider them a novelty. According to *Modern Seoul*, McDonald's opened its first restaurant in Seoul in 1988.[22]

Second, in today's experiential culture, Koreans in their 20s and 30s have vigorously embraced social media, just as millennials worldwide have. One of the activities that increases their visibility is the practice of food photo sharing. Consequently, the opportunity to be a part of a new trend that includes enduring a two- or three-hour wait in the blistering summer heat to taste a quality prime burger, which only a select group can experience, boosts the photographer's social prestige tremendously. Consequently, the long wait itself becomes a social event. Given these conditions, social media contributes enormously to the Shake Shack novelty phenomenon. Thanks to social media, these trendsetters post pictures of themselves and friends on their web pages. For some, it is an opportunity to inform or remind their friends and acquaintances that the taste of Shake Shack burgers brings back memories of the first time they experienced them in New York. In their minds, traveling in the U.S. makes them "unique."

Third, the prices charged by the more traditional burger chains range within the amount of money Koreans usually spend on lunch, which is around 8,000-10,000 Korean won (~$6.80-$8.50). By comparison, a no-frills outing at a Shake Shack restaurant in Gangnam might include a basic single Shack burger for 6,900 Korean won, basic fries for 3,900, a regular fountain soda for 2,700, and a basic shake for 5,900, which would add up to 19,400 Korean won (~$16.50).

Customers feel that they are set apart from the crowd by paying two or three times the amount they spend for lunch. It is a status symbol they underscore through their selfies. The long delay in the heat and humidity of the middle of summer is an additional benefit in showcasing the experience. It shows that the burgers are worth the price and the wait. It is fashionable. It is expensive by Korean standards. Therefore, it is trendy.

The Shake Shack phenomenon has expanded to other parts of Seoul. It will eventually open in different cities since, according to NPR (National Public Radio), the SPC Group plans to open as many as 25 Shake Shack restaurants in Korea by 2025.[23] The novelty eventually will wear out; other trendy, expensive restaurants will pop up, and the early adopters will be the first to move on while the rest will continue to try to catch up.

A Korean's Explanation of the Contradiction between Conformity and Differentiation

A Korean friend of mine explained the dichotomy of wanting to conform to social norms and simultaneously taking action that accentuates differences, which, in essence, shows the competitive aspect of the culture by saying: "We all look the same. We all have black hair and slanted eyes. Therefore, we want to be better than or at least look different from, and trendier than, everyone else. Aside from fashion, that is one reason why the young dye their hair of a different color: women are attracted to super expensive (*myung-poom*) items such as cosmetics, jewelry, and luxury handbags by Louis Vuitton, Hermès, and Chanel, and men gravitate toward expensive cars."[24]

My friend went on to say that these expensive handbags are such a vital status symbol for Korean women that some will purchase the bags even though their salary is not commensurate with the cost of the expensive items. The difference between Korea and the United States is the degree or intensity of this practice. Specifically, it is common for Korean women to become experts in designer bags to such a degree that they can identify the specifications associated with an item, including the price, whether it is a new or classic design, and how rare the item is. In addition, one of the most popular topics among women is precisely luxury designer bags.

News 1 published eye-opening statistics regarding 2017 worldwide luxury bag sales, indicating that Korea held the number four position behind much more populous countries: the United States, China, and Japan.

Table 2: 2017 Luxury Handbag Market[25]

Rank	Country	Sales in Trillion Korean Won*
1	United States	16.9
2	China	6.3
3	Japan	6.2
4	Korea	3.2
5	France	3.0

* Excludes Duty-Free Shop and Black-Market Sales

The news source claims spending on luxury handbags in Korea for 2017 would be number two worldwide if duty-free shop sales were included.[26] This point becomes even more emphatic given the population difference between Korea and the United States. In 2017, at fifty million, the Korean population was one-sixth of that of the United States at 326 million.[27]

Fashion Trends

The recent intense popularity of The North Face activewear among young people is another excellent example of this tendency toward finding a material possession to differentiate oneself from the masses. Not long ago, wearing The North Face apparel became popular among the well-to-do, especially the children who would do anything to convince their parents to purchase clothing items, particularly jackets, with this manufacturer's logo. The popularity of this brand name spread like wildfire. It became the latest craze among the masses who go hiking on weekends and holidays and even among individuals of a lower socioeconomic status. When this fad spread to the middle class, wearing the attire lost its glamour. Consequently, people at the upper echelons of the socioeconomic ladder, and eventually those below, moved on to wearing other brands. This is not to say that the brand name became unpopular. On the contrary, it remains a status symbol, but it has undoubtedly lost some of the appeal it had when it first became popular.

After the 2018 winter season, Discovery Expedition's Leicester model was the most popular brand of bench coats, or "long padding coats," as they are often called in Korea. Discovery Expedition, the brand name of a Korean clothing company, sold 200,000 Leicester model bench coats in the winter of 2018. The Exploring model of bench coats by North Face came in second with an estimated 100,000 units sold.[28] It is quite possible that Korean nationalism also had something to do with the discrepancy in the sale of these two coats since Discovery Expedition is a Korean brand and North Face is American.

Bench coats are thick and stuffed with materials like duck-down feathers. The term "long padding" became widely used in Korea only after the "PyeongChang long padding" – a bench coat sold as official merchandise of the PyeongChang Winter Games – attracted significant media attention after people lined up for hours outside department stores to purchase one of these limited-edition coats.[29]

The long-padding coat became the latest winter fashion among middle and high school students in the fall of 2016. With temperatures dropping in November, one could spot these trendy coats on the streets. They became even more popular in the fall of 2017 as the fad continued to spread among teenagers. Koreans, especially teenagers, tend to gravitate toward contemporary

Figure 2: North Face's Exploring and Discovery Expedition's "Leicester" Bench Coat[30]

trends with high intensity. This tendency is magnified particularly with cloth-ing because of the social pressure, even from one's own family, to wear the latest styles. It is common for a person's relatives to point out directly that the clothes they are wearing are out of style. In the case of long-padding coats, teenagers who did not want to stand out in their school or among their friends pressured their parents to purchase these coats that ranged in price between 50,000 Korean won (KRW) (~$47) and one million KRW (~ $935); however, apparently, only those that cost above 200,000 KRW (~ $187) could satisfy the fashion-conscious youth.

This fashion consciousness undoubtedly places a burden on parents who already have financial pressures associated with private education costs. Korean parents assume the full economic responsibility for raising their children, and they usually prefer that their children not work so they can focus on their studies. However, suppose a child desires an expensive item the parents cannot afford. In that case, the teenager may take the initiative to obtain a temporary part-time job to purchase the item.

Teenagers around the world tend to be fashion-conscious; however, among Korean youth, there is the added cultural pressure and desire to blend in or conform to group norms. Because of their uniformity, these long-padding coats have a social significance for Koreans who find "comfort in uniformity rather than individuality."[31] Not surprisingly, the official 2018 PyeongChang Winter Olympics long-padding coats, released on October 26, 2017, flew off the shelves. They came only in three colors—black, white, and gray and cost 149,000 Korean Won (KRW) (~$137 U.S. dollars). They sold out within two weeks of their release. People camped out the night before outside the stores that advertised the PyeongChang padded coats to ensure they could purchase one.

- What are the cultural and behavioral patterns that helped Korea rise from the ashes after the Korean War?
- The concept of sacrifice runs deep in the collective psyche of the Korean people.
- Conformity to social norms is congruent with the cultural concepts of unity and harmony.
- The terms *gap* and *eul* differentiate between two parties: one with money, influence, authority, or power and one without them.

CHAPTER THREE

How Everyday Life Reflects Efficiency

How I Familiarized Myself with the Korean Culture

To balance my observations of the culture and people, I traveled extensively. Although I visited cities such as Seoul, Busan, Daejeon, Incheon, Yeosu, Mokpo, Pohang, Suwon, Jeju City, and Tongyeong on many occasions during the five years I resided in the country, I spent a large portion of the time in two relatively small cities: Jukjeon and Jeonju. I lived in Jukjeon, a comparatively new city just south of Seoul in Gyeonggi Province, for one year. Jeonju is the capital of Jeollabuk-do in North Jeolla Province, a relatively small city of 663,000 residents located in the Southwest area of the country.[1] This city is dwarfed by metropolitan areas such as Seoul, home to 10 million people, Busan, over three million, and Incheon and Daegu, with over two million each. Consequently, many Koreans living in big cities regard Jeonju as provincial.

A Korean friend who lived in one of the large cities once asked me if there was a Paris Baguette shop in Jeonju. Paris Baguette is a popular chain of ubiquitous bakery stores. The answer was: "Of course there is." This relatively innocent but telling question reveals the attitude that people living in the big cities have toward smaller towns. Jeonju attracts thousands of Korean tourists from as far away as Incheon and Seoul on weekends, holidays, and in the summer to its primary tourist attraction, Hanok (Traditional Korean) Village. Regardless, the city is considered rural. This attitude remains despite the city's nomination to UNESCO's Creative Cities Network for Gastronomy in 2012. The perceptions of the big city citizens are largely accurate since Jeonju's two most dominant industries are tourism and hospitality and agriculture.

I lived in Jeonju for four years. Confirming UNESCO's designation, the city is viewed by many as a gastronomical center for its home-style cooking handed down from one generation to the next. The limited transportation to and from different cities during my stay contributed to the town's rural reputation. Routes between Jeonju and Seoul were particularly challenging. Only a handful of KTX (Korea Train eXpress) trains per week passed through Jeonju. However, the situation has since changed. As of this writing, four KTX trains travel daily from Seoul to Jeonju, and four return to the capital. With high-speed trains traveling 300 kilometers (186.4 miles) per hour, KTX is considered the most comfortable, convenient, efficient, and fastest way to get around Korea.[2]

The official KORAIL (Korea Railroad Corporation) website describes KTX as follows:

> High-speed rail service has not only reduced the travel time to anywhere in South Korea to less than 3 hours, causing a dramatic change in people's life-style, but also had a significant social, economic, and cultural impact. High-speed rail is emerging as a new transport means for the future, equipped with state-of-the-art technologies that ensure a fast, safe, comfortable, and environment-friendly ride.[3]

Because of my extensive knowledge of the city, my observations of everyday life have a Jeonju flavor. However, these observations also apply to other parts of the country. Nevertheless, some of these experiences may have been more or less pronounced in Jeonju than in other cities.

Regarding transportation, I had access to a car while working in Korea to facilitate going to and from work five days per week and simplify my travels throughout the country. For example, on weekends, I visited large and medium-sized cities such as Busan, Gunsan, Gwangju, Iksan, Incheon, Mokpo, Pohang, Pyeongchang, Seoul, Suwon, Tongyeong, and Yeosu. In addition, I traveled to small cities and towns, including Gimje, Gochang, Im Sil, Jinan, Jumunjin, Namhae, Namwon, Nonsan, Seocheon, Sunchang, and Suncheon, as well as Buddhist temples in the mountains. I also visited Jeju Island several times and attended education conferences in Seoul and Incheon.

Throughout my travels, I continued to observe people's behavior. Invariably, two qualities that permeate my observations are the emphasis on efficiency for efficiency's sake and the constant quest to circumvent established rules, policies, or laws for convenience or to achieve quick financial returns. We present these observations through stories, anecdotes, and substantial evidence. Below are some behavioral patterns I noted in everyday life. Some of these observations may appear trivial to the casual observer; however, they represent a microcosm of pervasive behavioral patterns in society.

The Eating Experience

Having had over 3,000 meals in public (i.e., in restaurants or the university cafeteria) during my stay, I had the opportunity to make valuable observations about the eating habits of Koreans. This exercise prompted me to reflect on the eating habits of Westerners so that I might compare and contrast the two. This process helped identify eating habits that appear to be cultural in nature.

The most obvious observation is that, in Korean cuisine, an array of side dishes complements the main course. These side dishes are usually served before or simultaneously with the main course. Among other items, they consist of small layers of plain scrambled eggs, assorted vegetables, including green onions, fried in batter in the shape of a pizza, and a large variety of marinated vegetables with spices, such as garlic, red pepper, green onions, sesame oil and seeds, rice vinegar, ginger, and fish oil. These side dishes are like a painter's palette that adds to the variety of colors, but most importantly, the rainbow of flavors that partakers are free to sample in the sequence or combination of their choice. To say that Koreans genuinely enjoy their food is an understatement. They eat with gusto and savor the variety of flavors and consistency of each component. They innately know what side dish to choose and how much to mix with a small portion of the main course to maximize their enjoyment. The eating experience is such an iconic element of Korean culture that it plays an integral role in dramas.

Efficiency vs. Socialization during Meals

Koreans view lunch and dinner very differently. They approach lunch with a more efficient attitude. Therefore, when eating out, every facet, from traveling to and from the restaurant to ordering the food, being served, and paying the check, is approached with this mindset. Even if eating out with co-workers, the expectation is to return to work promptly within an hour. Even though a similar attitude toward the lunch hour may exist in other capitalist countries, the main difference is the degree of intensity of this attitude. Everyone is mindful and respectful of the time constraint. Lunch is a short break from work to recharge the body with some nourishment to make it to the end of a long workday. A minimal amount of socializing is possible. This tradition of utilizing one's time efficiently during the lunch hour appears to have originated during the economic expansion period between the 1960s and 1980s, which seems to coincide with the beginning of the *pali pali* culture as well: "A great many Koreans had to work hard and long hours to attain the goal of high growth, shortening their lunch and dinner breaks."[4]

An example of efficient use of time during meals, but particularly at lunch, is calling the restaurant beforehand and placing the order over the phone for the group members. Doing so ensures that the table is reserved and set ahead of time and the food is prepared and served just before or as the party arrives at the restaurant. This proactive action guarantees that party members can consume their meals immediately. No time is wasted.

However, whether with family, friends, or co-workers, dinner is an opportunity to socialize, unwind, enjoy a meal, and most likely some drinks, such as beer and *soju*. Without the time constraints of lunch, dinner lets participants drop the efficiency mindset. Thus, the ambiance is more relaxed. It is common practice for these dinners to last two or three hours. Because occasionally socializing with co-workers at the end of the day is expected to maintain good morale and interpersonal relations in the unit or company, some employees feel pressured. Despite this feeling, they participate out of concern of being ostracized if they do not. The sense of being imposed upon is not unfounded, for Koreans put in some of the most prolonged work hours in the world. The OECD (Organization for Economic Cooperation and Development) data discussed in more detail in Chapter Seven supports this assertion. Tagging additional hours for a social dinner to an already long workday feels like an imposition on employees' personal time. This tradition is less of a concern now than it used to be because a law was passed in 2018 limiting the work week to 52 hours. Working people in other capitalist countries, such as the United States, also occasionally have dinner with co-workers. However, the difference is that the frequency and pressure to participate are higher in Korea.

Sharing food amongst Koreans is a charming, humanistic behavior. Food sharing has a deeper meaning than the mere act of eating together. It represents communal solidarity, which supports the concepts of unity, conformity, and harmony. We discuss these cultural attributes in Chapter Two. Whether eating in pairs or as a group, the participants share the main courses and the accompanying side dishes. Everyone digs in with zest, enjoying every bite while being careful not to appear too eager or selfish or eat faster or larger quantities than the rest of the group as a sign of consideration and respect for the others. It is common for family members, friends, and very close individuals to take a piece of food from either the main course or side dishes with their chopsticks and place it on another person's plate or even offer to put it in their mouth as a sign of affection. The receiver accepts the gesture, and they may reciprocate.

In the West, when eating out as a group, the individualistic qualities of the culture are evident because individuals do what they usually do. When they place their order, they instruct the server precisely how they want their food prepared. It is not surprising to hear Westerners declare that they are following a vegetarian or special diet. Therefore, they require very different food from the rest of their party. Americans, for example, believe that individuals exercise their intrinsic right to be different when they point out their dietary needs in a social situation. The idea of reaching a consensus on a group order is unimaginable, depending on the party.

The Conformity and Efficiency Concepts in Group Meals

This scenario is very different in Korean society. The conformity and efficiency concepts are evident when small or large groups eat together. The party may have a brief discussion about the menu options. Still, individuals will be agreeable about what to order and yield to the group's wishes or defer to one participant. This person might be the senior member or one who is most familiar with the menu choices offered by the restaurant. Individuals cannot imagine ordering something unique or different from the rest of the group.

Although following a vegetarian diet is not unheard of in Korea, collective wishes take precedence when eating out in a group. Furthermore, Korean food typically contains many vegetables, particularly among side dishes. Therefore, it is easy for vegetarians to satisfy their hunger and adhere to their diet in a group outing without much fanfare.

In the scenario described above, the idea of conformity is present. The efficiency concept is easily explained by the fact that group consensus facilitates placing, taking, preparing, and serving the order. Therefore, it is smooth sailing for the group leader placing the order, the server taking it, the cook or chef preparing it, and the server serving it. Everyone performs their role efficiently.

The situation is notably similar when ordering in, whether at home or the office, and whether ordering one or several dishes. The concept of sharing remains prominent, and individuality is nonexistent. The advantage of Korean food is that the main course is ordinarily garnished with side dishes that complement or enhance the flavor of the main course. People decide which side dishes to enjoy and in what order, thus maximizing the enjoyment of individual and combined flavors.

The concepts of uniformity, conformity, and efficiency regarding food are learned at an early age. When eating at home, families share meals: Everyone eats the same dishes. In other words, the concept of preparing different dishes for individuals does not exist. By contrast, it is common in America to prepare various dishes for specific family members based on diet or preference. In Korea, individual family members would not dream of requesting unique dishes made especially for them. The food-sharing concept continues from preschool to university, the armed services, and the workplace. If the school provides lunch, the menu options are limited. If students bring their lunch from home, they share the side dishes with their friends.

I observed similar patterns in student behavior in the high school where I worked. For example, if a group of students ordered food delivered to the school, they all ordered the same item from the menu. The food was catered whenever the school administration scheduled an activity during lunch. Moreover, whether the group was large or small, the students' absolute preference was to ensure that everyone ate the same dish, even when given the choice of two. The concepts of uniformity, conformity, and efficiency also ruled the day during overnight field trips, whether dining in a restaurant or having a cookout.

One of the teachers at the school where I worked followed a strict vegan diet. She encountered no difficulty dining in restaurants, alone, with other Westerners, or in the university cafeteria; she could select whatever she wanted. However, when the school administration provided food for on-campus meetings during business hours, the administrative staff had difficulty remembering to order a vegan meal for her. Doing so meant they had to order her a unique (read: different) meal. This course of action would represent a departure from the norm. It is much more efficient to place a lunch order for a group if everyone is eating the same dish, so is taking the order and preparing it. Therefore, she would likely have to skip a meal whenever the administration provided lunch. Even though the staff was aware of her dietary needs, most of the time, they still ordered the same lunch for her that they ordered for everyone else. Thus, the concept of uniformity was ingrained in the minds of the administrative staff. Consequently, it was difficult for them to remember that one faculty member had special needs.

Food Delivery

Koreans have embraced the concept of "fast food." It is part of the culture. In Korea, "fast food" is indeed fast, especially the delivery. For efficiency-minded

Koreans, food delivery has been pervasive for many years. It was in vogue in this country before Domino's Pizza, Uber Eats, and Grubhub became popular in the U.S. In Korea, even McDonald's delivers! While researching this book segment, I found many fascinating stories about food delivery. This concept was first introduced during the Joseon Dynasty (1392-1897). According to *Korean Culture and Information Service (KOCIS),*

> The earliest Korean food delivery on record is *naengmyun* cold buckwheat noodles in soup in the Joseon [E]ra (1392-1910). In his book, the scholar Hwang Yun-seok (1729-1791) mentions that he ordered *naengmyun* for lunch with his colleagues [...] the day after the state examination. This was in July 1768. It appears that *naengmyun*, a delicacy enjoyed in the royal court, had gained popularity among noblemen, leading to the introduction of a delivery service. In Lee Yu-won's book, it is recorded that King Sunjo (r. 1800-1834) of Joseon ordered his servants to buy cold noodles and bring [them] back to the palace while moon-watching with his officials in the early years of his reign. In later times, food delivery expanded to various soups and noodles in the 1930s, and delivery became a common thing.[5]

The port of Incheon, located approximately 34 kilometers or 21 miles west-southwest of Seoul, officially opened in 1883.[6] The opening of the port attracted Chinese immigrants, particularly to the city of Incheon, until approximately 1910 when Korea came under Japanese rule. During this period, the Chinese population increased from about 200 in 1883 to 12,000 in 1910.[7] The food culture underwent a renaissance because of the multicultural ambiance. Two dishes that became favorites were *jajangmyun*, a Korean-style Chinese noodle dish with black bean paste, and *naengmyun*, buckwheat noodles in a chilled broth. By mid-century, *jajangmyun* had become "one of the most popular foods among the general public."[8]

A fascinating report about food delivery came from the latter part of the Joseon Era. It revolves around a dish called *hyojonggaeng*. The story depicts not only Koreans' art of cooking and their love for food but also priceless cultural details that identify a nation:

> Korea's earliest known record [...] [of] commercial food delivery service is [...] *hyojonggaeng*, meaning 'soup eaten to chase away a hangover at daybreak when the bell announces the lifting of [the] curfew.' [The modern-day version of this soup is *haejangkook* (해장국).] In the book Haedong jukji ('Bamboo Branch Lyrics of Korea') published in 1925, Choe Yeongneon, a scholar and calligrapher

during the later years of the Joseon Dynasty, wrote about this hearty soup: 'People in Gwangju (a county south of Seoul, in Gyeonggi Province) are known to be good at cooking *hyojonggaeng*. They put cabbage hearts, bean sprouts, pine mushrooms, shiitake mushrooms, beef ribs, sea cucumbers, and abalones into water mixed with thick soybean paste, and boil them all day. At night they wrap [...] the soup pots in padded blankets so they [can] be transported to Seoul. There, the soup pots are delivered to the residences of senior government officials around the time when the morning bell rings. Pots would still be warm, and the soup was highly prized as a hangover cure.'[9]

In the 1990s, the food delivery business became commercialized and expanded widely. The proliferation of fried chicken restaurants and pizza franchises contributed to this growth: "The food delivery market grew exponentially from this point."[10] As of 2019, "the volume of the food delivery market [...] is estimated at around KRW 15 trillion (about $13 million) per year."[11]

Contributing factors to the astronomical growth of the food delivery business include extreme weather conditions, particularly in the summer, and Koreans' appreciation for convenience. Why bother to walk or drive in the pouring rain or sweltering heat when you can have the food delivered to your home, school, or place of employment? Other factors that made it possible include the economic expansion between the 1960s and 1980s and the *pali pali* culture.[12] Indeed, "food delivery was able to firmly take root thanks to the existence of many densely populated urbanized areas and the age-old custom of enjoying late-night snacks...."[13]

In the 1990s, when food delivery began to take off, customers placed their orders by phone. They already considered the method convenient. However, mobile apps make the process even more convenient by providing customers with "various complimentary services, like providing user feedback, along with payment functions and offers of special discounts."[14]

Some food delivery services operate 24/7, 365 days a year, including holidays, so if someone gets hungry in the middle of the night, no problem! Delivery men on motorcycles will do whatever it takes to deliver the food to the customer as quickly as possible. Pedestrians know this, so they stay away from the bicycle/motorcycle-designated section of the sidewalk. These delivery men do their job fast because restauranteurs and their customers expect it. Since being efficient is part of the fabric of Korean culture, they demand that the food be delivered quickly. The question is, at what cost?

If you live in Korea, food delivery is the perfect alternative when you are in a hurry, do not have time to cook, or do not feel like preparing a meal. You will save cooking time, effort, and aggravation by ordering from the comfort of your home, school, or office. Why cook at home when you can have Chinese or Korean food delivered fast to your door? Other foods available for delivery are fried chicken, pasta, salads, Big Macs, Whoppers, Domino's Pizza, and hamburgers from Lotteria, a Korean fast-food chain. Furthermore, the cost of a meal is generally the same whether eating out or having it delivered at home or the office. Budget-conscious Koreans have done the math and figured that fixing a home-cooked dinner is more expensive than having it delivered. You do not even have to tip the delivery person since tipping is not customary. Moreover, food delivery services will pick up the dishes after you finish your meal. In summary, today, food delivery services in Korea are efficient, convenient, and reasonably priced.

To establish where Korea stands regarding food delivery, we emphasize two concepts: Food delivery and technology integration into the process. Undoubtedly, the food delivery concept and its commercialization have been entrenched in the culture longer than in the West.

Clearly, technology is also being utilized in other countries to simplify and make food delivery more convenient. However, given the long history of the concept in Korea, the infusion of technology into the process, its convenience, and widespread utilization, other countries, particularly in the West, are just beginning to catch up.

The Driving Experience

Based on my observation, police officers' responsibilities include traffic control at intersections, particularly during rush hour, at festivals in various cities, and crowd control during demonstrations. Those are the three scenarios where I noticed a uniformed police presence. During my five-year stay in the country, I only saw one police officer issuing a traffic citation to a driver who had passed a red light at an intersection. Maximum speed laws are efficiently enforced, mainly with cameras strategically located at crossroads and various intervals on highways. These cameras have a dual function: They act as radars and capture the image of the car, its license plate, and the face of the driver who breaks the speed limit law.

I did not see a single patrol car enforcing speed limits during my extensive travels on city streets and highways. Whether the speed limit is 60, 70, 80, 90, 100, 110, or 120 kilometers per hour (kph), this information is readily visible on the GPS (Global Positioning System) available on nearly all cars on the road.

The Utilization of Technology for Divergent Purposes

Koreans maximize technology for efficiency's sake via speed-tracking cameras, GPS systems on cars that alert drivers where they are located, and dashcam recorders for evidence gathering in accident investigations. We discuss automation and its impact on the economy in Chapter Ten.

We use GPS to navigate from one place to another, find the fastest or least traveled route, and locate areas of interest. An exceptional efficiency-driven advantage of the Korean GPS is that the system also warns drivers of an impending speed-enforcement camera. This capability prompts them to maintain the posted speed limit while the car is within the camera's viewfinder. However, drivers have learned to game the speed monitoring system.

As I drove on city streets and highways, I noticed that efficiency-minded drivers slowed down just in time for their vehicles to go through the camera range, where the system calibrated their speed. However, as soon as they cleared the camera, their speed reached 20 to 40 kph faster than the posted limit. Another less frequent practice of impatient drivers who wish to avoid speeding citations is to pass slower traffic at high speeds on the far right or shoulder side of the road. These opportunistic drivers pass on the far right instead of the left lane, whether there is a legal lane or not. Such action prevents them from being detected by the infamous speed-tracking cameras. This blatant disregard for laws meant to maintain order and promote traffic safety underscores the emphasis on efficiency, gaining an advantage over law-abiding and safety-conscious citizens, and the underlying belief that rules are meant to be broken. Also, the penalty for speeding is not harsh enough to deter drivers from exceeding posted speed limits.

Average drivers and government officials know that the existing national speed limit enforcement system is inefficient. As a result, aggressive drivers game the system. The government has begun to utilize a technique commonly referred to in Korean as 구간단속, loosely translated as "Speed Control System for a Stretch of Road." In addition to monitoring speeds at designated spots, it can average speeds over stretches of road. By tracking license plate numbers, this system calculates the distance traveled by individual drivers, the elapsed time, and the speed average on a given stretch of road. A traffic citation is issued and mailed to the driver's home if a driver averages a speed above the limit.

This new method appears more effective than the one currently in place. In 2015, I noticed this new and improved system employed on expressways near and around Seoul. The government has also vowed to deploy new police officers for traffic enforcement duties. The officers will focus primarily on enforcing speed limits. As of this writing, it is unknown how many police or highway patrol officers have been or will be designated under the new measure. Both initiatives are long overdue and send a message loud and clear to the people, indicating that the government is serious about improving road safety.

I felt fortunate that my car was equipped with a GPS and a dashcam recorder—one to help me with directions and the other to gather evidence in case of an accident. I heard horror stories from my colleagues who had witnessed drivers scream at each other and beat each other up over an accident. I also carried an international driver's license to ensure my driving in Korea was legal.

Some of the most blatant traffic violations I witnessed would be considered rude at the very least, if not outright dangerous maneuvers, when performed in the West. This assertion does not mean that drivers in the West do not break traffic laws; they do. Once again, efficiency seemed to be the motivator behind these driving patterns. For example, on a two-lane road where drivers in the far-right lane can either go straight or turn right at an intersection, they are expected to turn right or speed up and merge left to go straight and clear the lane to avoid causing a delay for others wanting to swing right. These drivers are forced to make one of these moves even though they have the right to be in that lane. This precarious situation is exacerbated if they happen to be caught by a red light. If anyone obstructs the right lane when drivers wanting to turn right are present, those behind them will use their horns to ensure that the message, "You are blocking my way!" comes across loud and clear.

Food Delivery Accidents

Some of the most daring drivers are food delivery employees. These delivery people ride a motorcycle and carry the merchandise in a box attached to the back of the vehicle. A research study by Chung, Song, and Yoon explains the reason motorcycles are the preferred mode of transportation for food delivery in Korea, as opposed to the U.S., where the favored method is a car:

> [Q]uick service delivery requires high speeds on congested roads and easy accessibility on narrow ones. Accordingly, the use of motorcycles for delivery purpose[s] is perceived by the industry to be the best mode of transportation,

[…] [mainly] because of their relatively easy accessibility and low cost of travel, especially in the Seoul metropolitan area with its highly congested roadways as well as a comparatively high portion of narrow alleys.[15]

The article goes on to describe the driving patterns of some food delivery drivers as follows:

Motorcyclists in the delivery industry often commit traffic violations during delivery, such as improperly weaving through traffic, crossing the centerline, driving over the speed limit, [and] violating traffic signals.…[16]

Also, it is a widely accepted practice for delivery people to drive on sidewalks and crosswalks or break numerous other traffic laws. As a result, it is not uncommon for these drivers to be implicated in serious accidents involving injuries. Consequently, they place their own lives and the lives of others at risk more often than the average driver. The research article quoted above provides some statistics that may give the reader a more concrete idea of the seriousness of the problem:

The fatality rate for motorcycle crashes is about 12% of the fatality rate for road traffic crashes, which is considered to be high […] [However,] motorcycle crashes account for only 5% of road traffic crashes in South Korea.[17]

However, some non-fatal crashes involving motorcycles go unreported. Therefore, the latter statistic mentioned above may be artificially low. The problem with traffic accidents involving delivery men may be more severe than the figures show. Food delivery business owners employ temporary workers to make deliveries to save money. The business liability insurance may not cover temporary workers' accidents in such cases. The delivery men may choose to use their insurance coverage instead. If they use their insurance, food delivery accidents may not be reported as such. Therefore, they are not accounted for in food delivery accident statistics.

In some cases, delivery drivers may want to avoid involving their insurance company for fear that their insurance premiums will increase. In other instances, delivery men may not have insurance at all. It is common for drivers involved in accidents to settle them in cash whether they have insurance or not. This practice also distorts accident statistics.

Korean society has been wrestling with this potentially dangerous situation for years without much success. How many accidents and casualties must occur for Koreans to finally realize that the efficiency they demand and take for granted comes at a very high price?

These food delivery accidents are not the fault of one group alone. All three groups—restaurant owners, delivery men, and clients—are partly responsible. A cultural mindset change must occur to eradicate this potentially dangerous situation. Efficiency for efficiency's sake, convenience, or short-term financial gains must be balanced with safety.

Naver and Trending Topics

Naver, one of Korea's most popular internet portals, was founded on June 2, 1999.[18] It includes widely used services such as search engine capabilities, news, email, and community services, including blogs, cafes, and rankings of real-time trending topics. In 2018, Naver ranked 34 on *Forbes'* Top 100 Digital Companies list.[19] Also, it was ranked number nine the same year on *Forbes'* World's Most Innovative Companies list.[20]

Naver's real-time trending topics service has become a phenomenon unique to Korean culture. The company presents general trending topics and breaks them down by age category. The phenomenon underscores the emphasis on efficiency. It is common for Koreans to ask each other, "What is the number one trending topic?" When people pose this question, Koreans know precisely that the question refers to Naver's number one real-time trending topic. In other words, Koreans identify the number one trending topic by visiting the Naver website. As a result, it becomes the "topic du jour," or more precisely, the topic of the moment, thus "cutting to the chase" efficiently and eliminating wasted time and effort. The real-time nature of the trending topics reflects the ephemeral quality of issues in vogue, the fickle nature, and the tendency to gravitate toward fads. By contrast, United States websites do not break down the trending topics by age category. Additionally, people do not ask each other, "What is the number one trending topic?" expecting others to know what they are talking about.

My Experience with the Medical Profession

As a resident in Korea, I had the opportunity to visit large hospitals and small clinics to receive medical attention. The affordability of the services was astonishing. For example, as of the time of this writing, the cost of a liver ultrasound test in Korea is less than $100 without medical insurance. By comparison, in the U.S., a similar test costs $390 on average, according to New Choice Health, Inc.[21]

The major hospital I visited most frequently was associated with a national university. As such, it was a research institution consisting of approximately 40 departments. The efficiency with which the staff addressed many patients' needs was most impressive. This efficacy is facilitated through the strategic use of technology. For example, the self-service machines in the lobby issue numbers directing patients to the appropriate window for processing purposes. They also facilitate the payment for scheduled services, including doctor's visits and lab tests. Finally, they even generate the patient's prescription after completing all services. Naturally, these self-service devices enable patients to enjoy prompt, efficient customer service.

In the above scenario, once patients complete the initial processing in the lobby, they proceed to the designated unit. Departments employ a digitized system to manage intake and facilitate the processing of large numbers of patients. Once patients check in at the receptionist's desk, the automated system displays their names and the order in which the doctor will see them. Patients feel satisfied because they enjoy efficient customer service. This enables them to maximize their wait time, as they know approximately when the doctor will see them. The system also informs nurses and doctors of the exact order of patients.

Whenever I visited the hospital, I was amazed by the multitude of patients throughout the facility and in each unit. Walking into a specific department, I saw several dozen patients sitting in the waiting room. A few were lined up in front of the receptionist's desk at each end of the floor. Even though there was always a long wait, physicians saw patients in an orderly fashion. Once patients checked in with the receptionist, they waited for their names to appear on a screen in front of the doctor's office. Instead of being escorted to an examination room, each patient met with the physician in their office for a few minutes. The doctors did not need to walk around to different examination rooms. They simply stayed in their offices, seeing one patient after another. The emphasis on efficiency was evident.

Although the number of patients seemed overwhelming, technology enabled the staff to process everyone efficiently in an orderly and timely manner. Equally efficient was the process I experienced from a patient's perspective. In three hours, I underwent several blood tests, an ultrasound, and a visit with the physician. When I entered the doctor's office, the test results were already in the system. Thus, we could reference them during my examination.

My experience in this hospital was typical practice and not an aberration. When I visited other hospitals and clinics, I found that they similarly used technology to provide patients with a seamless and efficient service.

Although Korea is a trendsetter regarding implementing automation to enhance efficiency and provide better customer service, other countries are also making inroads. The COVID-19 pandemic accelerated technology adoption in fields such as business, hospitality, and medicine. In the U.S., for example, hospitals and other healthcare providers are making doctors accessible to patients via teleconferences. Also, patients can manage their health care online by making doctor appointments, communicating with their doctors via email, tracking their medications and changes to their medical records, such as blood test results, and even paying their medical bills.

When does efficiency reach the breaking point in the medical profession?

On March 2, 2018, KBS, one of Korea's largest broadcasting companies, televised a story about the country's emphasis on efficiency in relation to the medical profession. The segment focused on the concern over the number of patients assigned to nurses. The School of Nursing at Seoul National University provided the statistics presented during the broadcast. According to the data quoted during this segment, nurses in Korea are assigned 43.6 patients on average, eight times more than in the U.S., where the average is 5.3 and five times more than in the United Kingdom at 8.6. The news segment also reported that a joint study between Chonbuk National University and Ulsan University found insufficient nurses responsible for approximately 9.2% of total medical complications. These complications might have been avoided if nurses had fewer patients assigned to them.[22] However, efficiently utilizing medical professionals and facilities in Korea helps keep medical costs significantly affordable.

"Love Motels"

"Love motels" are ubiquitous throughout Korea. Guests can rent a room for three to four hours during the day or in the evening for a romantic rendezvous or for sleeping during the night. When I first visited Korea, my Korean friends correctly assumed I was unaware of the love motel concept. Therefore, they wanted to alert me to avoid accidentally finding myself in an uncomfortable situation.

When making accommodation reservations in Korea, travelers need to know whether they are booking a motel for sleep or a romantic rendezvous. Fortunately, love motels do not come up when searching for motels on the Internet. Therefore, foreigners should only be concerned if they resort to finding a place to stay on the go. This is not an issue for locals since they are familiar with the concept and can tell the difference between the two types of accommodations. Love motels are relatively less expensive than regular motels. Also, in many instances, they specify that the check-in time for the evening is after 8:00 or 9:00 p.m. or later. Finally, guest reviews are usually very explicit and alert the reader if the facility they are reviewing is a love motel. When renting a room for a few hours during the day, a guest pays the day rate, which is lower than the night rate. Usually, guests checking in after about 8:00 p.m. or those planning to stay overnight must pay the night rate.

The business model used by love motel operators is an example of the emphasis on efficiency found in most facets of Korean culture. This business model is financially efficient for both management and guests. It maximizes room availability for motel owners and managers. They can rent the same room to several guests in one day, thus maximizing revenue per room. It is economical for guests because they only pay for the time they use the space.

Construction

As a result of my extended stay in Jeonju, most of my Korean friends were Jeonju-born residents, including my urologist and a farmer whom I met through my yoga class. They taught me that the city had changed significantly in the last ten years. This transformation was fueled by the conversion of farms into apartment buildings, "officetels" (a word combining "office" + "hotel," indicating efficiency or convenience apartments), villas, and the accompanying shopping areas and restaurant rows. This expansive development facilitated new neighborhoods such as Shin-shi-ga-ji (New Town) and Hyuk-shin-do-si (Innovation City). The rapid pace of expansion continued even while I lived in the city.

Since I am an avid walker, I had the opportunity to walk on the paths on either side of the river, which cuts through various neighborhoods. One of the activities that caught my eye during my daily strolls was in and around construction sites. Projects were completed relatively quickly. Furthermore,

I noticed that many, if not most, construction sites were in operation seven days per week, including Saturdays and Sundays, and even in late evenings. I noted this as peculiar. I do not know whether the workers were working longer than regular shifts or were being paid overtime. They may have been on a rotating schedule or covered the site by overlapping shifts. In the West, construction workers begin their workday early in the morning and complete their assignments in the early afternoon. Also, they take Saturdays and Sundays off. Not so in Korea. Koreans have the distinction of being among the leaders in the world in the number of hours worked.[23]

When I made the above observations, my concern was the potential for mistakes or accidents due to the apparent tight schedules, long hours, and a seven-day-long work week. It is common knowledge that the body and brain must rest to function optimally. This observation is a prelude to discussing man-made and industrial accidents in chapters seven and eight, respectively.

In the West, it is common for construction companies, project owners, and developers to agree to an incentive for the construction company and the workers if the project is completed on time or early. I am unaware of whether this tradition is common practice in construction contracts in Korea. If this incentive is customary, it partially explains the long hours and emphasis on efficiency. However, even this financial incentive, if it exists in Korean construction contracts, should not preclude construction workers from taking Sundays off.

Swing Doors

A subtle and mundane exchange between strangers happens when two individuals reach a swing door either from the same or opposite direction. In the West, if two people approach a door in the same direction, one behind the other, invariably, the person in front will hold it out of courtesy until the individual behind them grabs the handle. This social collaboration facilitates the safe passage of both people. I found that Koreans react differently in similar situations. On many occasions, I anticipated that people walking through a swing door in front of me would hold it long enough for me to grab the handle. Instead, I ended up with a swing door practically hitting me in the face.

Conversely, if I happened to open a door and someone walking in the opposite direction noticed, they quickly accelerated the pace. They went through the door before I did to take advantage of the fact that it was held open briefly.

Some may view the latter example as related to rudeness; however, it is more related to efficiency. Thus, the underlying value of efficiency is omnipresent even in the most common facets of daily life, including this random encounter between two people.

Respect for Other People's Property

Coming from a country in the West, where people must safeguard their personal belongings in public places, life in Korea was like a breath of fresh air. There, individuals show honesty and respect for other people's property. Some of my colleagues and I, and many of the students at the school where I taught, used public transportation, either local or inter-city buses, taxis, and occasionally trains. It was common for students to forget some of their belongings, including their cell phones, wallets, textbooks, or their backpacks, in a taxi or bus. Occasionally, this would happen to teachers as well. When these unfortunate instances occurred, the school staff would intercede on their behalf and call the bus or taxi company to inquire about the objects left behind. Every time this happened, the items were returned, or the owner was directed where to retrieve them. Occasionally, a taxi driver would drive back to the school to return the items. Even wallets would be returned with the money still in them.

A Sense of Personal Safety at School

While working in Korea, I experienced a sense of personal safety and security that was less common in all the years I worked in education in the United States. The fact that guns are not allowed in Korea contributed to this feeling. Also, school shootings are associated with American but not Korean schools. This does not mean the school where I taught did not have discipline cases. The few issues we had were mild compared to those in U.S. schools. A colleague who taught at the same American school and eventually obtained a job in another Asian country recently emailed me, reminiscing about "the innocent, kind Korean students."[24] This comment reflects Koreans' high regard for the teaching profession as opposed to some Western countries where respect for teachers is generally a thing of the past.

The common thread among most of the observations in this chapter is the concept of efficiency in everyday life. The reason for including them is to show the pervasiveness of efficiency. The remaining chapters will show that the construct has a positive and a negative impact on society and the economy. The non-efficiency-related observations, where a humanistic aspect is the driving force, such as respect for other people's property, demonstrate that not everything is about efficiency in everyday life.

- People living in metropolitan areas undervalue provincial regions.
- With its high-speed trains, the KTX (Korea Train eXpress) system reflects the emphasis on efficiency.
- To say that Koreans genuinely enjoy their food is an understatement. They eat with gusto and savor the variety of flavors.
- The concept of food delivery was first introduced during the Joseon dynasty (1392-1897).
- Koreans maximize technology for efficiency's sake through speed-tracking cameras, GPS systems, and dashboard video cameras.

Unintended Consequences of the Overemphasis on Private Schooling and the Democratization of Higher Education

The Role of Education

Since the end of the Korean War, the distinct characteristics of the industrious, entrepreneurial, goal-oriented, practical, and sacrificial Korean people have contributed enormously to the nation's macroeconomic and technological advancements. Equally crucial for the Miracle on the Han River is the tremendous value Koreans place on education and efficiency. They view education and efficiency as the keys to success for individuals in the country's highly competitive environment. As alluded to earlier, education is one of the pillars of Korean culture. Thus, it is emphasized from elementary to graduate school. The strong emphasis on education extends to private instruction to a higher degree than in other countries.

The promotion of education as an efficient formula or a panacea for future financial well-being has turned Korea into a country with one of the highest literacy rates and one of the most highly educated populations in the world. The nation has embraced the concept that education represents an escape from poverty and a way to maintain or improve one's socio-economic status.

The emphasis on education has its roots in Confucian principles. Similarly, the reliance on testing dates back to the civil service exam, extensively utilized in the Joseon era (1392-1897). It was established in 958 AD by King Gwangjong. Its primary purpose was to select and appoint government officials based on merit rather than hereditary privileges. The exam aimed to ensure that individuals entering the civil service were qualified and knowledgeable, contributing to a more effective and competent bureaucracy. Influenced by Confucian principles, this system emphasized education, ethical conduct, and administrative skills as essential criteria for government positions.

As in other countries, education in Korea is crucial in determining success in the job market and eventual financial security and wealth. With a population of over 51.6 million in Korea, the road to financial success includes the best elementary through high school education, leading to prestigious universities and top-level jobs in major corporations.[1] For example, semiconductor manufacturing, the biggest income generator in Korea, demands a solid academic foundation in highly advanced sciences such as chemistry, physics, engineering, and computer science. The educational preparation for these fields requires extensive, arduous work, sacrifice, and a long-term commitment. However, the good news is that the trail is well-delineated. It is sprinkled with clearly identified markers and directional signs that point students toward job security and financial success.

Literacy Rate – Two Different Generations

Korea has one of the highest literacy rates in the world. To support this statement, I will provide pertinent figures from the National Center for Education Statistics (NCES), an entity within the U.S. Department of Education and the Institute of Education Sciences. These statistics are collected from OECD data provided by member nations. Per the NCES, in 2021, Korea distinguished itself by having the highest level of high school completion in the 25 to 34 age group (those born between 1987 and 1996) among 36 of the 38 OECD member nations reporting data in this category. While the average high school completion rate for OECD countries in this age category was 86%, Korea's rate was an astonishing 98%.[2] Not surprisingly, however, the high school completion rate for the 55 to 64 age group was only 72%.[3] These two statistics reflect Korea's emphasis on education after the Korean War, especially since the 1980s. During this period, Korea also experienced the democratization of higher education and an impressive increase in the country's productivity as measured by GDP.

The Democratization of Higher Education

Among OECD nations, Korea has been uniquely effective at democratizing higher education. Consequently, besides having a high literacy rate, it has one of the highest percentages of individuals with postsecondary degrees worldwide. According to NCES, for 2021, Korea is fourth behind Canada, Japan, and Ireland among OECD countries regarding the portion of the population 25 to 64 years old with any postsecondary degree at 52% or 12 percentage points higher than the OECD average of 40%.[4] Thirty-seven of the 38 OECD member nations provided data in this category. Korea's percentage in this category more than doubled from 24% in 2000 to the 52% mentioned above in 2021. This remarkable increase is due to the democratization of higher education that began in the early 1980s and continues to the present.

NCES further breaks down the postsecondary degree data presented above into two age groups: 25 to 34 and 55 to 64. The data for Korea further underscore the enormous achievement difference between the two generations and pinpoint the beginning of the democratization of higher education. Specifically, for 2021, the country holds the top spot among OECD nations submitting data on the percentage of the population who had attained any postsecondary degree, with an impressive 69% in the 25 to 34 age group (those born between 1987 and 1996).[5] By contrast, the 55 to 64 age group (those born between 1957 and 1966) attained an expectedly dismal 26% in the same category.[6] The relatively unimpressive attainment of any postsecondary degree by the 55 to 64 age group is not surprising, given that the people who constitute this cohort were born in the years following the Korean War. No other country in the OECD comes close to matching the vast 43-point differential between the two age groups. The OECD member nation that comes in second to Korea's impressive variance between the two age groups is the small country of Luxembourg, with 31 points. These data also provide further evidence of the astonishing economic recovery after the Korean War, education's central role in the Miracle on the Han River, and the success of the democratization of higher education.

The percentage of individuals aged 25 to 64 who possess a postsecondary degree will likely increase over the next few years. Furthermore, it will undoubtedly continue to outpace the average of OECD nations by a wide margin. According to an article published in the *Korea JoongAng Daily* on January 23, 2017, "69.8 percent of Korean high school graduates continued their studies at colleges as of last year [2016]. Even though the number of college-degree seekers has been declining in the country, the figure is still higher than the OECD average of 41 percent."[7] Statista confirmed that the percentage of high school graduates attending university from 2013 to 2022 ranged between 68.9% and 73.3%. The latter figure was reached in 2021 and 2022.[8] That almost 70% of Korean high school graduates transition to university is an astounding statistic. It is a testament to Koreans' value of education, which is viewed as the road to financial security, economic prosperity, and prestige.

A Road Well Traveled

The trajectory to financial stability is a well-traveled path. Those students with the most robust support network have the best chance to succeed and attain the coveted financial rewards that can ensure a repeat of the cycle for the next generation. Korean parents have proven that they are willing to sacrifice everything for their children's education. The parents themselves are the essential elements of the student's support network. They are ready to make drastic decisions to ensure their children can compete for a spot at a top-tier university. These decisions include spending a sizable portion of their family income, depleting their savings, and borrowing money. Relatives, family friends, and acquaintances who have navigated the passage successfully can provide advice or function as sounding boards when students need to make critical decisions.

Families with financial means can avail themselves of *hagwons* and private tutors. The latter represents the most expensive option. *Hagwon* instructors and private tutors have the subject matter expertise and test preparation skillset to share with students. Students can stand a chance in the brutally competitive university admission process with this support.

The Good Mother Role

Like all societies, Korea has its share of cultural role models whose purpose is to inspire the populace to be good citizens and achieve success. Every Korean child learns the folk tale about Han Seok Bong, a well-known calligrapher from the Joseon era (1392-1897) whose mother sold rice cakes for a living. She is considered an ideal mother because she sacrificed for her son and raised him well. The fact that she sold rice cakes for a living indicates that she was not a typical full-time homemaker because she needed to work to support her son. Despite her limited means, she sent him to a Buddhist temple to study calligraphy with the masters so he could become as proficient as possible.

Initially, his studies were supposed to last ten years, but he returned home after three years, believing he had nothing more to learn from the masters. His mother knew better and wanted to teach him a lesson on humility, so she challenged him to a contest in which he would write letters, and she would cut rice cake. He agreed. As they went about their respective tasks, she blew out the candle, and they were left to continue the contest in the dark. When finished, they reviewed each other's performance. They found that his letters were crooked, the sizes did not match, and they were difficult to discern, whereas the rice cake pieces she had cut were the same size.

Realizing his judgment error and understanding the humility lesson, Han Seok Bong returned to the temple to study for seven more years. Subsequently, he returned to his hometown. Eventually, his reputation as a calligrapher became widely known throughout the land, even as far away as China.

Han Seok Bong's mother personifies the "good mother" standard. Traditionally, the "good mother" is expected to do everything within her power for her children's success. In modern-day Korea, "good mothers" sacrifice their retirement money to cover their children's private education costs. Also, it is common for some middle-aged mothers to procure employment to afford their children's *hagwon* and personal tutor costs. "Good mothers" consult their extensive network of friends to recommend the best private education providers for their children. Suppose the mother's friends hold a given *hagwon* or private tutor in high esteem. In that case, that institute or tutor will more likely receive the nod from the family. Decision-making is usually reached through consensus, as social pressure plays a significant role.

Suppose a mother is wealthy, assertive, and influential enough. In that case, she may be allowed to join the informal network of mothers at her child's school. She may be considered a *chima baram* (치맛바람) (skirt wind) if she is aggressive enough. This term refers to an assertive mother looking after her children's well-being and using her influence to tip the scales on their behalf. In English, the expression "helicopter mom," "overly protective mom," or an "overly involved mom" who hovers over her children may be considered the closest equivalent to *chima baram*.

This function is viewed as a mother's role because, traditionally, women did not have access to the workplace. Therefore, they stayed home to care for the family, specifically the children, both within and outside the home, ensuring their future success had a solid foundation. Today, the *chima baram's* responsibilities include ensuring that her children attend the best *hagwon* and that the parents hire the best private tutors. Doing so will increase her children's likelihood of admission to a top university. The *chima baram's* network is instrumental in screening cram schools and private tutors.

In the process of connecting herself with her child's school network, the *chima baram* identifies the most influential group member or informal leader known as *dwagee-o-ma* [돼지엄마] (translated as mother pig followed by her piglets). This individual has the authority to determine who can join the group. Because of the nature of the university admission process, mothers' network groups remain purposely small to share invaluable information only with an exclusive group of typically wealthy mothers. These networks are particularly prevalent in Gangnam, possibly Korea's most affluent area. Psy made Gangnam world-famous with his 2012 hit single and video "Gangnam Style." In his song and video, Psy pokes fun at the posh district for its emphasis on a high-status lifestyle, which includes luxury high-rises, fancy cars, high-tech medical tourism, high rents, and upscale shopping and dining.

Education as the Path to Financial Success

Following the Korean War, people in the upper echelons of the socioeconomic ladder viewed education as a means to maintain their status. Conversely, education was a way to escape poverty for those at the lower levels. Older generations, including baby boomers, trusted the Korean education system that claims to reward academic preparation and hard work, including long hours of costly private education outside of the regular school curriculum. It worked for them. For previous generations, educational preparation and diligence did provide an avenue to level the playing field for individuals from families with limited resources. Traditionally, a baccalaureate degree from a reputable university opened the door to the "dream job" with a high salary and job security in one of the conglomerates. Having achieved success, previous generations wanted their children to follow in their footsteps so they, too, could have respectable careers. They envisioned that once their children accomplished this goal, they could care for them in their golden years.

However, since the latter part of the 20th century, individuals from the less privileged socioeconomic ranks have discovered that the well-traveled path that people used to rely upon for access to elite universities and eventually "dream jobs" in the *chaebols* does not yield the same results it once did. That path is less dependable nowadays than it was for previous generations. Even a bachelor's degree from a top-tier university no longer guarantees an "ideal job" in one of the *chaebols*.

University graduates face this reality despite years of dedication, hard work at school, long hours of private education after school, and family financial sacrifices. This new reality is one of the unintended consequences of the extraordinarily successful push for the democratization of higher education. This national effort has taken the existing competitive environment to a higher level.

The Education and Socioeconomic Cycle

Figure 1 below depicts the Korean education and socioeconomic cycle from elementary school to eventual wealth and parenthood for those at the top of the pyramid. For those who find themselves in the bottom portion of the pyramid

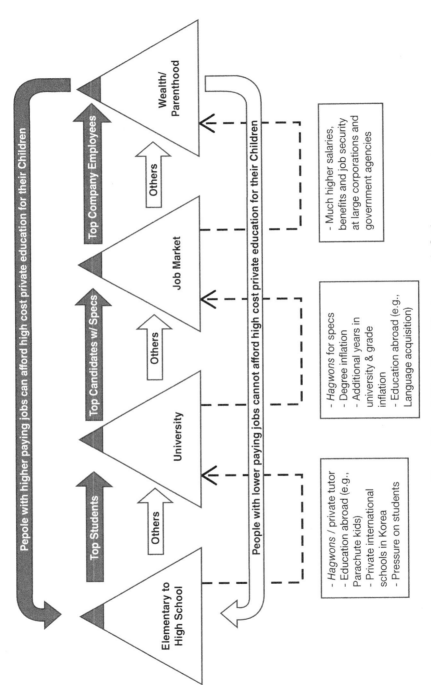

Figure 1: Korea's Education and Socioeconomic Cycle

from the start, breaking into the top section is challenging, if not impossible. Of course, there are exceptions. For example, students with creative talent, extraordinary academic ability, or an exceptional entrepreneurial spirit can transcend this traditional flow. The narrative following the chart describes the realities, conditions, and consequences of each stage in the cycle.

The Role of Private Education

A discussion about Korean education would be incomplete without mentioning the role of private education in the culture. Private education focuses on enrichment, supplemental instruction, and test preparation. These services are provided via *hagwons* and private tutoring. As we explain in Chapter Two, *hagwons* are after-school academies or "cram schools" that families utilize extensively to address their children's academic needs. Private tutors may be university students, professors, *hagwon* instructors, or professional tutors. These individuals are generally hired at a premium salary primarily for subject matter tutoring and test preparation. However, they also provide training in areas such as language, art, and music. Tutoring sessions may be one-on-one. Alternatively, one tutor may work with a small group of students. Children begin utilizing these services at a young age and continue through high school. Therefore, tutees come from all levels of education—elementary, middle, and senior high school. Middle and high school students are heavy users of subject matter tutoring. As expected, high schoolers frequently utilize private tutoring for test preparation. Depending on their needs and family's financial resources, they may receive subject matter tutoring in one, two, three, or more courses.

Government entities conduct surveys and maintain statistics on the estimated cost of private education for the entire country, the cost of private education as a percentage of household income, the per capita expenditures, and the participation rate at each stratum in education. However, critics argue that statistics on private education costs and participation rates are highly conservative. Some published statistics are presented here to give the reader an idea of the significance of private education in Korean culture. However, we caution the reader to view the cited figures with an open mind. Furthermore, consider the critics' argument, as well.

The Cost of Private Education

A realistic expenditure figure on private supplemental education in Korea must include the cost of both *hagwons* and tutoring. Government statistics reported by the *Chosun Ilbo* on March 27, 2017, indicate that "spending on private crammers reached W18 trillion [~ $16 billion] last year [2016], up 1.3 percent compared to 2015. The total rose even though student numbers dwindled from 6.08 million to 5.88 million amid the shrinking birthrate."[9] However, the total expenditures on private crammers are significantly higher if the cost of private tutors is included. The article specifies: "The state-run Korea Development Institute estimates that parents spend more than W30 trillion [~ $26.7 billion] a year on extracurricular tuition if private tutoring and overseas language courses are included."[10]

Based on the article cited above, expenditure figures on private education aside from the money spent on *hagwons* are only estimates whose accuracy is questionable. Regarding estimates on the portion of household income spent on private education, the *Independent* reported that Korean "parents […] spend around 22% of their household income on education and educational service [….] It is one of the highest proportions of household [spending] on education among developed nations."[11] However, the article fails to specify its source and whether this figure represents either expenditures on *hagwons* or private tutoring or both. Therefore, critics who claim that estimates of private education expenditures are underestimated may also question this number.

The perception that private education is the most efficient and effective way to prepare students for the grueling Korean university admission process forms part of the culture's fabric. As expected, given the figures quoted above, the per capita private education expenditures have increased significantly. Such has been the case since 2007, the first year the Korean Statistical Information Service (KOSIS) collected, tabulated, and published the annual private education spending survey results.[12] On March 17, 2018, the *Korea Herald* reported that monthly expenditures on private education increased by 33% in the ten years from 2007 to 2017. The article asserts that "households spent a monthly average of 384,000 won [U.S. $359] per child on private tutoring in 2017, up from 288,000 won [~ $268] in 2007, according to a survey by South Korea's statistics agency and the education ministry."[13]

Absent concrete data on private education expenditures before 2007, other factors should be considered as possible indicators that the per capita expenditure increases began before 2007. One of those factors is the development of Gangnam district in Seoul, which eventually attracted some of the country's best and most costly private schools and *hagwons*. Gangnam remained underdeveloped until the early 1980s.[14]

Since then, however, the area's development trajectory parallels the country's economic expansion. In addition, the unprecedented growth in GDP and GNI per capita also began in the mid-1980s. Furthermore, the infrastructure build-up for the Summer 1988 Olympics contributed to the economic expansion and, most likely, GDP and GNI per capita. This would have made it feasible for parents to increase spending on private education for their children. Finally, the outstanding 70% attainment of any postsecondary degree in 2021 by the 25 to 34 age group born from 1987 to 1996 is the most direct indicator of increased spending on private education, including test preparation.[15] In conclusion, Young Lee and I agree that given the indicators discussed, it is likely that the increased spending on private education began in the mid-1980s.

Naturally, the per capita spending on private education increases in the higher grades as students approach the university admission process. The above-cited article breaks down the average cost of private education by level:

> Monthly expenditures on private education reached 515,000 won [~ $466] per high school student in 2017, up 43.5 percent from 2007.
>
> Corresponding data per middle school students rose 39.5 percent to 438,000 won [~ $396] over a decade, and that for elementary school students rose 19.9 percent to 307,000 won [~ $278].[16]

We reiterate that the figures quoted above are averages. Therefore, some families spend more and others less. The location of a specific *hagwon* is critical in determining the cost. A family whose child attends a *hagwon* in Gangnam should expect to pay much more than the average price estimate since it is the district with the highest cost of living. It is also where some of the most expensive *hagwons* are. Despite the expense, some families purposely move to Gangam to provide their children with the best private education possible.

Critics who claim that the published statistics on private education spending in Korea are highly conservative appear to have a compelling case. They state that private tutors are required to register for income tax purposes. Therefore, critics claim that many, if not most, tutors do not register. Thus, they argue that the actual number of tutors and their earnings are unknown. Assuming these arguments are accurate, participation rates and private tutoring cost estimates are generally unreliable. Critics point to the fact that most, if not all, private tutor transactions are conducted in the form of cash, which is difficult, if not impossible, to track. Also, *hagwons* must register as businesses, whereas private tutors do not. Therefore, the information related to this expensive education alternative remains opaque.

Another issue is the cost of private tutoring. Several factors, such as location, student-to-tutor ratio, tutor experience, education level, and reputation, determine this cost. At the time of publication, the current monthly rate for subject matter private tutoring ranged between the equivalent of $300 and $1,000. For example, the monthly cost of private tutoring for a math class twice weekly for a non-professional tutor is between $600 and $1,200 for a professional tutor. Therefore, if a high school student requires private tutoring in three subject areas, the total monthly cost would be the equivalent of $1,800 by a non-professional and $3,600 by a professional. The high tutorial costs and the practice of paying cash for these services support the critics' argument that the published participation rates and private education costs contradict reality. The reason is that cash payments for tutoring are most likely not reported. The fact is that parents are willing to spend as much money as necessary to give their children an edge in the university admission process. Therefore, considering only the amounts being reported paints an incomplete picture.

Private Education Viewed as an Efficient Investment and a Way to Get an Edge

A critical question is: Why are Korean families willing to spend so much on after-school supplemental, enrichment education, and test preparation? The driving forces behind *hagwon* education and private tutoring are the extraordinarily competitive university admission process, concern for the children's future, and desire for financial success and social status.

First, jobs at major corporations in Korea are difficult to find. Large companies usually only consider those candidates who graduate from top-tier universities. Therefore, high school students are under a great deal of pressure from parents and themselves to be admitted to one of the best universities in the country.

The obsession with and struggle to obtain a degree from a top-level university was recently reflected in the JTBC cable network production of the popular Korean drama *SKY Castle* (스카이 캐슬). The title includes the acronym symbolizing three top institutions of higher learning: Seoul National University, Korea University, and Yonsei University. JTBC broadcasted the show weekly from November 2018 until February 2019. The drama is a perfect example of art imitating life. The plot developed around wealthy parents who use every trick in the book to ensure their children obtain admission into the School of Medicine at Seoul National University.

Director Jo Hyun-tak did not shy away from showing the dark side of the country's education hype on the show. During a press conference [in November 2018], he said viewers might experience different emotions as they see people trying all methods and pulling every string to send their children off to the best universities.[17]

The show gained such popularity that from December 10 to 16, 2018, it became the most talked about drama on social media.[18] Furthermore, "ahead of the series finale, [...] its most popular episode had been watched by 23 percent of South Korea's entire subscription television audience, the highest such rating ever achieved by a drama."[19]

The show gained unprecedented popularity primarily because Koreans identify with the plotlines. They include expensive supplemental private education, grueling student schedules, and strategies parents use to give their children an advantage in university admission. Some plotlines "are inspired by real-life events, including a high school teacher's arrest [in 2018] on charges of stealing exam papers for his own daughters."[20]

Other plotlines include the "hiring [of] illegal help from a law professor to write an application cover letter to a college entrance coordinator that costs over 100 million won [~$86,349] a year to hire."[21] A "college entrance coordinator" is a consultant or "coach" whom parents contract to ensure their child gains admission to the best university possible. Students can attain this goal by taking the correct steps in preparation for the admission application process. The proper steps include ensuring that the student follows an academically challenging schedule, receives top grades, and earns a high score on the *Suneung* test. To achieve the highest possible grades and university entrance exam scores, the college entrance coordinator ascertains that the student attends the best *hagwons* and receives the best tutoring possible.

Second, Korean parents lack confidence that the Korean education system will provide their children with the necessary high-level preparation to be competitive when applying to top-tier universities. Often, it is the *hagwon* education and private tutoring that make the difference in university acceptance. In other words, private education costs represent an efficient investment in the children's future. Students who are denied admission to top-tier universities and graduate from less selective institutions have a lower probability of successfully competing for jobs at the country's conglomerates. Their chances of being hired by major corporations like Samsung, LG, Hyundai, and POSCO are reduced significantly.

Third, Korean parents view their children's private education as a necessity rather than a luxury. They consider the cost an investment in their children's future and their own. Consequently, parents are willing to spend family savings on their children's private education costs. When the savings are insufficient, parents are even willing to borrow money to afford the prohibitive cost of private education for their children.

The Gap Between the Haves and Have-nots

Despite this zeal for private education, the gap in participation between children from low- and high-income families has widened significantly in recent years. The article in the *Korea Herald* quoted above specifies that private education participation rates among children from low-income families (defined here as families with a monthly income of two to three million Korean won ~ $1,809-$2,714) fell sharply over the ten years between 2007 and 2017.[22] This trend is of particular concern since the possibility of a crossover between the top and bottom portions of the pyramid in the Education and Socioeconomic Cycle is minimal to nonexistent as it stands. This sharp decline will likely worsen matters for students from lower socioeconomic backgrounds. The decrease in the private education participation rate of children from low-income families ensures that the status quo is maintained. The system favors top students from wealthy families from elementary school through university and, eventually, the job market. Given this survival-of-the-fittest system, children from high-income families have a definite advantage because their parents can afford expensive *hagwons* and private tutors. The *Korea Herald* article cites the following participation rates for 2017 compared to 2007:

Table 1: Private Education Participation Rates – 2007 and 2017*[23]

	2007	2017
Children from high-income Families[a]	92.7%	80.8%
Children from Low-Income Families[b]	77%	58.3%

*Note:
a. High-income families: monthly income = 6-7 million Korean won (~$5,427-$6,332).
b. Low-income families: monthly income = 2-3 million Korean won (~$1,809-$2,714).

The Teaching-to-the-Test Environment and Its Profound Impact on Student Learning and Behavior

Private education providers, from *hagwon* instructors to private tutors, have infused the element of efficiency into private education. *Hagwons* specializing in test preparation, be it the *Suneung,* SAT, ACT, TOEFL, TOEIC, or other tests, use the most efficient approach possible. They teach to the test by giving students extensive test practice through strategically selected items from previously published test forms, projecting the types of questions on a given test, and teaching students shortcuts to answer questions quickly and efficiently. They also provide pointers on how students may best manage their test time. Time-saving techniques include identifying the best answer choice by utilizing a process of elimination, thus avoiding working out the solution to a math problem. Instead, the student decides when it is advantageous to guess the answer. The emphasis is on efficiency through rote memorization, repetition, and test practice, not creativity, critical thinking, or self-expression. An article published by the BBC (British Broadcasting Corporation) titled "South Korea's Schools: Long Days, High Results" asserts that the "relentless focus on education has resulted in formidable exam performers."[24]

Test preparation providers in other countries indeed use similar techniques. However, two fundamental differences are the extent to which these services are utilized and the degree to which these strategies are applied in other circumstances.

This extensive exposure to test preparation, or the teaching-to-the-test approach, profoundly impacts student learning processes and behavior. Unfortunately, the element in the culture that has given students an advantage in a highly competitive university admissions environment has produced some undesirable unintended consequences. Strategies espoused by test-preparation providers perpetuate a mentality that relies heavily on efficiency. These strategies have become deeply ingrained in everyday life, as we will see in Chapter Nine's discussion about the national reaction to catastrophes.

Being avid users of rating systems for efficiency's sake, Koreans often refer to their star *hagwon* instructors and private tutors as "tweezer teachers" (족집게 선생님). This term identifies those who have the best test preparation strategies. In other words, they can coach students to select the correct answers to multiple-choice questions most efficiently. They are exceptionally skilled at anticipating the types of questions appearing on specific tests such as the *Suneung.*

For example, the instructors can anticipate the questions regarding a passage in a reading comprehension section of an examination. In other words, they pinpoint the questions students should study for the test. Effective "tweezer teachers" conduct an item analysis of past *Suneung* tests. Through this analysis, they screen not only for concepts that have been assessed previously but also how frequently a vocabulary word, mathematical problem, or concept is included on the test. After this item analysis, "tweezer teachers" determine whether a specific vocabulary word, mathematical problem, or concept will be on the next test. Based on this item analysis, they advise students on what to study. "Tweezer teachers" have reached celebrity status in test preparation. *Hagwons* with this specialty use their star teachers' images on billboards and advertising campaigns.

Hagwons Specializing in English Instruction

Some *hagwons* provide students with a more individually tailored supplemental, enrichment, or test preparation program. Therefore, I cannot emphasize enough that not all *hagwons* are created equal or share the same purpose. Consequently, they employ different strategies. Performance-oriented *hagwons* that teach art and music are in a separate category. In the previous section, the discussion centered on *hagwons* that provide test preparation. This section will focus on *hagwons* specializing in English instruction, including skills such as conversation and grammar or a combination thereof.

English instruction begins in elementary school. Since Korean parents want their children to be proficient in the language, students begin attending English instruction at an early age. The emphasis on learning the language persists throughout middle and senior high school and university. Eventually, this emphasis continues in the workplace because of globalization spearheaded by multinational corporations, which are the backbone of the Korean economy. Consequently, besides the established English education, Chinese language instruction is rapidly gaining popularity.

The range of reasons individuals wish to improve their English proficiency is as wide as their diverse backgrounds. Some of the reasons are:

- to prepare for a test;
- to strengthen conversational skills for professional purposes;
- to fulfill a personal interest;
- to gain a more solid grammar foundation and vocabulary expansion.

Before they joined the American school where I worked, some of my colleagues had been employed as English conversation instructors in *hagwons*. They reported that instructors used a "cookie-cutter" approach with all classes. One curriculum is established for each proficiency level, a textbook is chosen, and the instructor is told to lead the course. Because the demand for English instruction is so high, *hagwon* directors do not have the luxury of selecting the most prepared or qualified instructors. Also, they cannot possibly fill all the teaching positions with native English speakers. Therefore, in many instances, they hire Korean instructors whose command of the English language is questionable, particularly their oral communication. It would also be unrealistic to expect *hagwons* to attract only certificated or credentialed ("credentialed" hereafter) teachers from English-speaking countries because they commonly issue one-year contracts. These temporary assignments would not be attractive to credentialed teachers because they would prefer a tenure-track position.

Also, teachers already tenured in their home country would not find these positions compelling enough to leave their posts since they would cease contributing to their retirement system. The exception to this likelihood would be young, recent graduates from teacher education programs with little or no teaching experience, who have an adventurous spirit, or who cannot land a teaching job and are most likely paying off student loans. Other primary candidates would be recent baccalaureate recipients in similar situations who are adventurous and welcome the idea of working and traveling simultaneously. This is not to say that Korea has no mature foreign teachers. They certainly exist. Many start their teaching career in Korea, fall in love with the country, and remain there for many years.

Although the situation seems to be improving, initially, the preferred qualification for hiring was exclusively to be a native speaker from a country where the official language is English. Candidates from a country with historical ties to the United Kingdom (e.g., Australia, Canada, Ireland, New Zealand, South Africa, and the United States) received priority consideration for linguistic reasons, regardless of the applicant's college major. Increasingly, a bachelor's degree is required. However, a teaching credential is not in most instances, but it helps. Consequently, many candidates flocking to these positions are young college graduates with a bachelor's degree but no teacher education preparation or teaching experience. Thus, most of these recruits may lack the necessary pedagogical knowledge to implement an effective teaching methodology based on the educational needs of the students. They may also be deficient in classroom management skills essential to a conducive learning environment. Classes in *hagwons* vary in size depending on several factors, including subject matter, grade level, and location. However, they are smaller than regular classes in the Korean and American education systems.

Some of my colleagues who had worked in *hagwons* complained that the students were disrespectful and unruly. This disruptiveness calls for effective classroom management, a skill some *hagwon* instructors may be missing due to their lack of training. In some cases, they protested that their role was reduced to that of a babysitter. Another complaint from former *hagwon* instructors was the lack of support from the administration in disciplinary matters. They found that the administration sided with the students and parents instead of backing the instructors on discipline-related issues. The *hagwons* maintained high enrollment by valuing the student perspective at the expense of the teacher's authority. This attitude rendered the instructors powerless, with little to no authority and an inability to implement high academic standards and enforce proper behavior. Fights between students were commonplace, especially among children in middle school (6th, 7th, and 8th grade). Regarding fighting between students, the administration held that fights represent differences between individuals, and the students themselves should resolve the issue. Finally, former *hagwon* instructors complained about not receiving payment on time.

Because of these poor working conditions, credentialed teachers did not last long in these *hagwons*. They soon applied for and successfully moved to international schools. Again, Young Lee and I want to reiterate that not all *hagwons* are created equal; therefore, the above complaints do not apply to all *hagwons*. The situation in Gangnam, where the quality of supplemental enrichment education and test preparation is considered the best, is the exception to the rule. The school where I was employed enrolled some students who had attended outstanding *hagwons* that specialized in providing training in the performing arts. These students' talents were nurtured and developed to high proficiency levels.

Long Hours, Sleep Deprivation, and Stress

Frequently, *hagwons* continue class until 10:00 p.m., 11:00 p.m., or even midnight, Monday through Friday. Some even operate on Saturday, depending on the school level (e.g., elementary, middle, or senior high school) and location. Per the BBC, in 2008, a 10:00 p.m. curfew was established for *hagwons* in Seoul. However, cities have no uniformity; they apply different restrictions.[25]

After attending *hagwons*, students go home and do their homework for their day classes, which forces them to stay awake until the wee hours of the morning. Consequently, these very same students are understandably exhausted and sleep-deprived. Considering the high stress levels, competition, and sleep deprivation among students, it is no surprise that "intentional harm" (read: suicide) was the leading cause of death among youth aged 9 to 24 from 2007 to 2017, according to *Statistics Korea*.[26] Young Lee and I recognize that a cause-and-effect relationship between a high suicide rate and any specific factors needs to be extensively studied before establishing such a connection. Said research is beyond the scope of this book. However, the conditions described above appear to be contributing factors, even if the extant evidence is insufficient to prove a direct cause. Critics may argue that the link between intentional harm and school-related stress has not been established through research. However, the potential correlation is difficult to ignore. Even though the correlation is not established, the aligning factors suggest that some relationship must exist. These dismaying statistics beg the question, is Korean society taking these figures seriously?

In addition to the high levels of stress and sleep deprivation among students, research has shown that 50% of Korean youths are dissatisfied with their lives. Among other things, they have expressed shallow happiness levels and identified school as the cause of stress. In addition, surveys have shown that they spend very little time outdoors. Similarly, they spend little time engaged in physical activity. Given these signs, experts are clamoring for parents and schools to lighten the burden on youngsters and give them more free time and opportunities to engage in activities. See Chapter Six for an in-depth discussion and statistics on the above topics.

Alternatives to *Hagwons* and Private Tutors

An alternative for high-income parents is enrolling their children in an international school. This option particularly benefits students who intend to apply to Western universities. It exposes them to a Western style of education, thus facilitating their academic and social adjustment, which is critical to student success.

Moreover, in this environment, students can associate with others who have attended either middle or high school abroad and thus possess a relatively good command of the English language. English fluency is critical for students competing against native speakers in an academic environment. Technically, a student who wishes to attend an international high school must have attended school abroad previously.

Korean parents recognize the long-term benefits for children who graduate from an international school. However, the zeal to capitalize on these benefits, regardless of cost and means, drives some families to procure forged documents indicating that the students have attended school outside Korea. These forged documents, they hope, will enable their children to attend one of these highly sought-after international schools. Fraud cases such as these have surfaced occasionally in the media in major cities where these institutions are usually located. The media attention that international schools have received is one reason they have been a source of controversy. Critics portray them as providing children of high-income families with an unfair advantage. The question of fairness and equal treatment is a source of consternation in Korean society, primarily because of the competitive environment.

Parachute Kids

Sending children to study in the United States or other English-speaking countries is another popular, albeit expensive, choice for wealthy parents who can afford thousands of dollars in monthly expenses. These include travel, tuition, room and board, and other incidentals. The motivating factor for paying these fees is ensuring that their children qualify for admission into a university abroad, preferably in an English-speaking country.

These "international students" are commonly known as "parachute kids." They attend international schools at all grade levels, from elementary to high school. China has the largest high school student delegation to the United States. According to a report titled *Globally Mobile Youth—Trends in International Secondary Students in the United States, 2013-2016* published by IIE (Institute of International Education), there were a total of 81,981 international students enrolled in U.S. high schools in the fall of 2016.[27] The top six countries sending children to the United States were China, South Korea, Vietnam, Mexico, Japan, and Canada, in that order. The fact that Korea, with just over 51 million people, is among these much larger countries regarding the number of students enrolled in U.S. high schools speaks volumes about the emphasis Korean parents place on education.[28 and 29] The statistics reveal the perceived importance of acquiring a high school education and subsequently a baccalaureate from a U.S. university. Korean parents know full well that utilizing this strategy will give their children an edge in the university admission application process and, eventually, in the job market.

Sending students to study high school in the U.S. is feasible for Korean parents, especially if the family has relatives living in the U.S. who are willing to host their child. However, a lack of relatives in the U.S. is not an obstacle, especially for wealthy parents. It is common for families that send their children to study in the U.S. to place them with a Korean or non-Korean family willing to provide room and board and varying levels of supervision for a substantial fee.

However, for those who do not have relatives already living in the U.S., it is common for Korean mothers to accompany their children while they study abroad. As stated earlier, this is a costly proposition. Splitting the family requires sufficient income to pay the student's tuition, travel, and living expenses for the child and the mother and maintain two homes, one in Korea and another abroad. These families are generally known as "wild geese families" in reference to the migration quality of wild geese and the long distances that these families must travel. In this arrangement, the father stays behind in Korea, working to generate enough money to make this strategy possible. These fathers are commonly referred to in Korean as *gireogi appa* (Korean: 기러기 아빠, "goose dad"). Even though the U.S. is the destination of choice, Korean families flock to other English-speaking countries such as Australia, Canada, New Zealand, the UK, and the Philippines.

At least four students in the institute where I taught had previously attended school in Australia or the Philippines. After studying abroad for only one year, at least three of those four students returned to Korea speaking English more fluently with an Australian or Filipino accent. I make this observation to show how impressionable children are and how quickly they adapt to their environment, not to judge whether speaking English with an accent is good or bad. Their experience in an English-speaking country contributed enormously to their improved performance on their return to the American school in Korea.

These observations speak volumes in favor of an immersion environment. In such a setting, students must listen to and speak the target language in and out of class. It is safe to presume that these students' improved academic performance was due to their educational experience in an English-speaking country instead of the American school in Korea, where their English exposure was only during class. They reverted to using Korean outside of class. Also, living outside Korea for a year gave these students more self-confidence socially and academically. Admittedly, these examples are anecdotal, and the number of students involved is relatively small. However, they attribute linguistic, academic, and self-esteem advantages to studying in a country where the target language is also the official language of instruction.

According to an article that appeared in the Australian Broadcasting Corporation (ABC) on June 15, 2015, "…an estimated 20,000 families […] leave South Korea each year to go and live in an English-speaking country" to enable their children to acquire an English-language education.[30] Parachute kids have several tremendously advantageous options once they attend high school in an English-speaking country. These are viable only if they compile a respectable academic record, including the appropriate courses, a high grade point average, the required SAT or ACT, and possibly the TOEFL test scores.

Suppose they do not graduate from a foreign high school. In that case, one option is to enroll them in a prestigious private international high school in Korea, giving them a leg up in the Korean university admission process. Alternatively, if they graduate from high school in the U.S., they could apply for admission to a university in the United States or another English-speaking country. A common belief is that completing high school in the U.S. gives students an edge in the admission process for American universities. If they follow this formula, they should play it safe by considering institutions at different tiers to ensure admission somewhere, even if they receive multiple acceptance letters. Otherwise, they could apply for admission to a prestigious university in Korea with the understanding that acceptance is not guaranteed. This option is less viable because the estrangement from Korean education limits their exposure to an academic environment in the Korean language. Linguistic deficiencies often develop even if students deliberately attempt to maintain exposure to the Korean language in their private lives while living outside of Korea.

The option of sending children to study abroad, even when accompanied by their mother, presents various challenges for all parties concerned. These include separation anxiety, stress, loneliness, depression, and inadequate nutrition. The issues become more severe if the children are not academically, socially, or psychologically prepared to adjust to the new environment.

College Admission Coaching

Parents of students who wish to study abroad generally recognize that they must seek university admission expertise outside the school system to increase the probability of their children's acceptance. The exception to this rule is if the student attends an international school, where these services are usually provided. The demand for this type of support has prompted entrepreneurs to provide college admission consulting services or coaching for a fee. This consulting service is analogous to *hagwons* or private tutors since the services purportedly give students an edge in university admission. These services may include guidance in choosing the appropriate high school courses, test preparation and test-taking advice, information about university selection and the admission application process, college admission research and specific college or university suggestions, and practical assistance with the application process.

The efficacy of these consultants is uneven, especially when advising seniors and their families on admission to U.S. universities. To be effective, college admission consultants must be thoroughly familiar with admission requirements, the application processes, the programmatic strengths, and the idiosyncrasies of universities and their campuses. In addition, consultants must ascertain the applicant's academic strengths, deficiencies, and preferences. Most importantly, the consultant must guide the applicant through a strategic plan to ensure admission to several institutions based on the student's academic and extracurricular record. Then, the applicant and the family can select from these options.

Unfortunately, there are ethical issues related to consulting services. A valid question is, How misguided are some of these services? Rumors indicate that some consultants complete the applications and even write the required essays for the applicants. Do students who obtain assistance with the essay-writing process have an unfair advantage over students who lack this support? Suppose universities in the U.S. rely upon essays as one of several factors determining academic potential and eventual eligibility for admission. Are admission decisions being made on false premises regarding some international students who hire unscrupulous university admission consultants?

Korean students are keenly aware of the sacrifice and financial stress that their parents face because of the prohibitive cost of their private education. They are also conscious of their need to deliver their parents' desired result: acceptance by a prestigious university. Consequently, the students themselves are under enormous stress. As a result, some students resort to "intentional harm." They are particularly vulnerable to this psychological distress when admission to a reputable university fails to come to fruition. They are also understandably susceptible to a feeling of failure under such conditions. It is not surprising that this previously mentioned intentional harm was the leading cause of death among youth aged 9 to 24 from 2007 to 2017.[31]

University Education Abroad

Obtaining a bachelor's degree from a reputable university abroad is considered an attractive option, albeit expensive, to stand a chance of attending a postgraduate program in fields such as medicine, engineering, and computer science. It can also help land the "dream" white-collar job, possibly in a conglomerate. Some employers, particularly global companies, give applicants bonus points in the hiring process if they have earned a degree from a reputable university abroad, particularly in English-speaking countries. Korean global companies commonly recruit Korean graduates directly from U.S. university campuses. Frequently, job announcements include a statement indicating that the company is explicitly searching for Korean applicants who graduated from a university in the United States.

It is advantageous for teaching position candidates at Korean universities to have a bachelor's, a master's, or a doctorate from a university in an English-speaking country. One advantage is the extensive exposure to academic writing in English. This experience is helpful since Korean universities require professors to publish research papers in English journals to obtain tenure. Also, the ability to teach in English can earn candidates extra points in the job application process. Furthermore, university professors who teach in English usually receive additional compensation.

Anecdotally, a Korean friend who had earned a bachelor's degree from a Korean university decided to apply for a doctoral program in the United States. After she earned her degree, she applied unsuccessfully for a teaching position at several universities in the U.S. Then, she applied for a similar job at a top-tier university in Korea. Her application was successful after the first attempt. She received additional compensation for teaching some major classes in English. Subsequently, she was granted tenure after she published research papers in English journals.

Studying abroad appeals especially to students who have excelled academically or have not earned the necessary test scores or grades to be admitted by a top-tier university in Korea, provided their parents have the financial means to pay for it. Parents are willing to sacrifice to pay for their children's tuition, travel, living, and incidental expenses. These expenses often add up to several thousands of dollars per month. Parents rely on their savings or borrow money from family members or banks to cover these costs. However, they must consider the high tuition, room and board, travel and incidental expenses, and the fact that a bachelor's degree requires at least a four-year commitment. Education abroad, especially in the U.S., remains a viable option only for wealthy parents.

Academic Competition, Degree Inflation, and Disenchantment

Bachelor's degree holders, including top-tier university graduates, find it increasingly difficult to procure employment. Even though large companies give these applicants priority consideration, a job is not guaranteed. Some graduates recognize that a bachelor's degree does not ensure employment, nor does it necessarily provide them with the needed entry-level skills. Therefore, even some top-tier university students enroll in career and technical education programs, usually after completing a bachelor's degree, to obtain practical skills and the corresponding certifications for entry-level jobs. Thus, they may add technical skills or licenses to their resumé. These include a computer operation license, CPA (Certified Public Accountant) license, Korean stenographer certificate, barista license, culinary license, and foreign language training. Koreans refer to these add-on certificates as "specs" (specifications) on their resumé. The purpose of this practice is to stand out from their peers in the job-hunting process. They do this out of desperation and to become more competitive in the job market, not necessarily to perform these jobs and utilize those skills.

The relevance of these added "specs" on an individual's resumé is highly questionable. If, on the one hand, prospective employers are taking these additional, sometimes superfluous, "specs" into consideration when making hiring decisions, then the bar for job-filling decisions is being raised artificially and with no rhyme or reason. If, on the other hand, prospective employers are disregarding these "specs," then the whole exercise of taking classes and completing certificate or license requirements to add these skill sets to a resumé is wasted effort, time, and money. This additional exercise to pad one's credentials results from the brutal competition for jobs and the pervasive degree inflation that the democratization of higher education engenders. However, this initiative by university graduates, as well-intentioned as it is, exacerbates the situation.

Additionally, the myth that a university degree is a panacea for future economic success, the universal expectation that individuals graduate from university, and the democratization of higher education contribute to a de-emphasis of and stigma toward career and technical education. The result contributes toward a substantial degree inflation and unemployment or underemployment of overqualified individuals.

The country's education level is unusually elevated because of the high percentage of bachelor's and higher degree holders. The reality is that the economy cannot absorb the excess of "highly educated" individuals. Consequently, those unable to secure a position in their specialty have the painful choice of being unemployed or underemployed, in other words, being without a job or settling for one at minimum wage that requires less than their academic preparation. Those who choose to be unemployed over working in the service industry out of pride, shame, or any number of reasons end up relying on their families for financial support. The situation is similarly devastating for the self-esteem of those who wish to be employed but cannot secure a job months or even years after graduation, despite any additional certifications and test scores, on account of being overqualified for the available jobs and the oversupply of candidates.

A Rude Awakening

We have established that one of the motivations for Korean students is to land one of the highly coveted jobs in a *chaebol*, providing them with inherent financial security and prestige. These jobs are considered compensation for the time, effort, money, and sacrifices made by students and parents alike from when children enter elementary school until they graduate from university. The fierce competition for jobs resulting from the democratization of higher education has caused an awakening. In reality, job openings in large corporations are limited, and these companies can only accommodate some university graduates. Even top-tier university graduates do not have a clear path to one of those jobs. Many have difficulty securing a position anywhere, let alone in the nation's conglomerates. Therefore, young Koreans are devastated by and frustrated with the economy's inability to create sufficient, well-paying permanent jobs to accommodate the number of university graduates annually. It is essential to clarify that the designation of "permanent jobs" excludes contingent full-time jobs that are allowed for a maximum of two years. The insufficient number of desirable permanent positions in government and major corporations has contributed enormously to the competitive nature of Korean society.

Disenchanted students are beginning to discover the fallacy that a bachelor's degree guarantees a place in the job market and, thus, financial security. A case in point is a graduate from the university that had jurisdiction over the institute where I worked. He graduated in 2018, and five years later, in 2023, he could still not secure a job. Below is a description of his experience in his own words.

My college days weren't so happy… During these days, I was very impatient and anxious, and I [wasted a lot of time], and I was terrified. Of course!! I [still] have a lot of fears.

I don't remember much about my 20s after graduation. Maybe it's because every day [was] the same. In the years after graduation, I lost a lot, I gained a lot. To be honest, I lived a very pessimistic life after graduation.

Employment is… It's like a big wall and trauma for me. As soon as I graduated, I felt like an unnecessary garbage in society, and no matter how hard I tried,

I couldn't even get an interview. Confidence was lost, so I was more and more betting on getting a license [b]ecause I never wanted to face that fear again.

Every day when I lost my passion was like death to me, but I walked on the road. I didn't even know where I was going with a scary heart. Now that I think about it, I wonder what I was so afraid of. I guess the fear came too far when the [guard] rails that others had laid were [out of control]. I realized that I was too swayed by other people's words. You can't do this; you can't do that [....]

I graduated from university, but it wasn't the level [required by companies], and I took a step back and got several certificates, but it was not easy to [stand] a chance [at getting a job]. I have completed the TOEIC and have acquired other qualifications. I still can't find a job, but I'm satisfied now because my efforts are reaping the results.

I really appreciate heaven because I don't believe in myself, and my parents don't believe in me [....] I feel at ease because I know that everything is not meaningless. But even if I don't get a job in the second half of this year [2023], it doesn't mean my life is over. Stop being stubborn and try [for] another job.

My mind is much more stable than before, and I've achieved my goal to some extent. I'm only going to study until this year. Three years is enough! I'm trying to find another way. The end of the test doesn't mean my life is over, so I think it's courage[ous] to give up on that.

So I'm trying to move forward little by little. These days, I'm starting to exercise again [, which] I stopped doing, and I keep doing it because I feel like my confidence is coming back little by little.

Well... now I'm thinking about how to live [....] What do I do... Well... I think it's the moment to choose something again.

I'm really scared.

I don't think the last time I studied was wasteful, I hope these memories give me a little courage in my future choices.[32]

In reading the young man's description of his life experience and given the uncertainties and disappointments with a competitive system that was supposed to allow him to enjoy a "normal life," I sense the fear, stress, anxiety, and unavoidable low self-esteem and self-doubt. However, in the end, he finds the strength to muster a ray of hope for the future and the will to try something new to forge ahead and make something of himself.

He deserves much credit for not losing hope and not resorting to self-harm as the answer to a desperate situation. It is evident that he has been trying to carry on without much of a support system. Reading between the lines, I also sense his disappointment with the consensus-building practice. It did not prove effective for him to listen to other people's opinions. He seems to realize it is best to follow one's instincts when making life-changing decisions.

Update: I am immensely pleased to report that this young man finally landed his first job in January 2024, six years after receiving his baccalaureate degree. He acknowledges in his message that the difficult times he lived through have made him stronger. Also, a sense of relief is evident. At last, the weight he had been carrying on his shoulders since 2018 has finally been lifted.

The Impact of the Democratization of Higher Education on Employment

One cannot underestimate the effect of the democratization of higher education on employment. Data published in the *Munhwa Ilbo* indicates that in 1990, 20% of staffers working at large corporations with at least 500 employees had a bachelor's degree. By 2015, that figure had skyrocketed to 60%.[33]

The negative impact of degree inflation is felt especially at the higher echelons of education by those holding master's or doctoral degrees. According to the article cited above, 1.13 million individuals have a master's, a doctoral degree, or both. The employment market, however, can only accommodate 250,000 people with such degrees. Consequently, there is an excess of 880,000 advanced degree holders, clearly revealing a surplus of overqualified individuals.

Contributing to this degree inflation are individuals who, for one reason or another, cannot find a job after obtaining their bachelor's degree. Desperate, they return to education if their parents can afford to pay for graduate school costs. The assumption is that these postgraduate degrees will increase the chances of landing the "dream job." Unfortunately, the unintended consequences further exacerbate the degree inflation in the country. Understandably, this situation causes a great deal of consternation and frustration for individuals who cannot secure a job after all the time, effort, money, and sacrifice invested in obtaining a postgraduate degree. In the article cited above, Kim Ahn-kook, a senior researcher at the Vocational Competency Development Center, suggests that a modification in people's approach to higher education is needed.[34] Kim points out that this surplus of overqualified individuals is a wasteful and inefficient use of resources. Furthermore, he underscores the short-term consequences discussed in this section: unemployment and underemployment.

The gravity of the persistent degree inflation is evident in a May 2018 Korean National Statistics Office (NSO) report titled *Labor Force Population Research*. Based on the reported data, the number of unemployed citizens who graduated from four-year universities has reached a record high. According to the report, the number of unemployed workers holding a bachelor's degree or higher in May 2018 was 402,000. This figure represents a year-to-year increase of 76,000 from 2017.[35] The 2018 numbers are the highest ever since such statistics were first recorded in June 1999.[36] The number of unemployed workers with a bachelor's or higher degree represents 35.8% of the total unemployed population, which is 1,121,000.[37]

If the number of unemployed individuals with a two-year vocational college degree is included, the percentage of unemployed with a higher education degree is a staggering 48.8%.[38] In comparison, in May 2000, the number of unemployed with a bachelor's or higher degree comprised only 14.2% of the total unemployed.[39] Therefore, the proportion of unemployed with a bachelor's degree to the total unemployed increased 2.5 times in 18 years. As of May 2018, the total labor force population, employed and unemployed, with at least a bachelor's degree, was 9.32 million. This figure has also increased about 2.5 times from 3.79 million in May 2000.[40]

Such an increase is due to the degree inflation caused by the democratization of higher education and the insufficient number of jobs for individuals with bachelor's degrees. This situation exacerbates the extreme competition in the job market. As a result of these dire unemployment conditions, some young people have become weary of the socioeconomic challenges facing Koreans, the competitive nature of Korean society, and the sacrifices students and their families must make to have a fair chance in a system that appears to favor the rich. Some of these weary young people refer to Korea as *Hell Joseon* in reference to the Joseon era (1392-1897). Utilizing this term, they reject some of the values that present-day Korea represents. This topic is discussed more in-depth in Chapter Ten.

Those students who gain admission into middle-tier or third-tier universities know their chances of being hired by a major corporation are practically nonexistent. They hope they can secure a job at a small or mid-sized company with significantly lower wages, benefits, and job security than expected. As a result, the quality of life that these conditions generate is not up to their standards. Also, many young people feel that such a competitive environment is not conducive to raising their future children. Therefore, their attitude and outlook reflect low self-esteem and a feeling of resignation.

A Korean colleague who teaches at a lower-tier university confided that many students at these universities are ill-prepared and have an entitlement attitude. They often expect to pass courses despite doing the least work possible. Students who do practically no work, attend class unprepared, put their heads down on their desks, and sleep during class expect to receive passing grades. And they often do. Faculty are aware of the uphill battle students face in these universities. Consequently, they attempt to give them a leg up by awarding better grades than they deserve, thus exacerbating the grade inflation problem. In other words, both parties contribute to academic mediocrity.

Furthermore, university non-tenured faculties are at the mercy of student evaluations for job security, particularly faculty at the instructor or adjunct (part-time) level. It is not uncommon for faculty in their probationary period, instructors and adjunct professors, to award students a higher grade than they deserve in exchange for positive evaluations. Because job security for non-tenured teachers depends heavily on student evaluations, historically, grade inflation has existed at middle- and third-tier universities. As a result, the Ministry of Education has mandated that universities impose maximum percentages allowed for letter grades.

For example, the university with jurisdiction over the high school where I worked implemented a policy restricting the awarding of "A" and "B" grades. The regulation established that no more than 40% of final grades be "A" and 60% "B" for non-major classes of 19 or fewer students. For non-major courses of 20 or more students, the maximum percentage allowed of As is 30%, and the combination of As and Bs cannot exceed 70%. These artificially imposed grade percentage restrictions raise questions on two counts: First, the reality of academic freedom that the teaching profession is universally characterized by, and second, the universal belief that a grading system should recognize merit, not seat time.

Grade Inflation

During their university stay, students often repeat the courses where they earned poor marks to improve their academic records, thus contributing further to grade inflation. Subsequently, once a course is repeated satisfactorily, the more recent grade is posted on the official transcript, and the original mark is expunged. This record-keeping practice gives the student an artificially higher grade point average. It also conceals the fact that the student repeated specific courses. Deleting grades from official transcripts would be considered unconventional in the West because they are supposed to reflect reality.

Consequently, when courses are repeated, the original grade remains on the transcript along with the new grade. Regarding the calculation of the grade point average, some institutions average out the two grades, and others only consider the latest grade. In either case, the transcript clearly indicates that the course was repeated.

Some university students volunteer for or participate in internships to distinguish their resumés. As indicated earlier, others augment their academic or professional certifications, known in Korea as "specs," by completing certificate requirements beyond their degrees. The motivating factor is the belief that these additional qualifications will make them more competitive in the job search process.

By supplementing their academic and professional backgrounds, students can extend their university stay by one or two years beyond the traditional four-year sojourn. Even though prolonged university stays take the pressure off the job market by delaying the graduates' job search, they come with an expensive price tag. This includes additional living expenses, enrollment, tuition fees, and possibly *hagwon* costs. When the program involves foreign language training, travel, tuition, and living expenses represent additional costs if it takes place in another country. These practices artificially raise the bar for job applicants and make the competition even more brutal. Simultaneously, universities serve as "holding tanks" for the job market while students add qualifications to their resumés. The question is, how relevant are these additional certifications if they are unrelated to the individual's major or minor?

While applying for jobs, some university seniors delay graduation to maintain their student status, even after completing their course requirements. They believe their chances of success in the job search are better as students than as graduates. Assuming this belief is correct, the children of wealthy parents have yet another advantage over students whose parents have limited resources. Extending the time at university requires families to incur additional expenses. Those who are cynical about the competitive nature of Korean society and refer to the country as *Hell Joseon* may view this practice of extending university stays as another point of contention.

In other capitalist societies, the wealthy can also gain an advantage over others by virtue of their privileged position, money, and social connections. However, any edge is magnified in a country like Korea, where university degree attainment is so high, job creation cannot accommodate the annual number of graduates, and the competition for jobs is grueling.

Furthermore, Korean universities themselves permit this gaming of the system. In contrast, universities in the United States, particularly state-funded institutions, do not allow extended stays once students complete their graduation requirements. In this case, the premise is that space at universities is limited, and they want to provide an educational opportunity to as many people as possible.

- As in other countries, education in Korea plays a crucial role in determining future success in the job market and financial security.
- Among OECD nations, Korea has been uniquely effective at democratizing higher education. Consequently, besides having a high literacy rate, it has one of the highest percentages of individuals with postsecondary degrees.
- The successful drive to democratize higher education has had unintended consequences.
- For baby boomers, education represented the means to maintain a high socioeconomic status or to escape poverty. However, this path is not as secure as it once was.
- The reliance on private education in Korea is unprecedented among OECD nations.
- According to the BBC (British Broadcasting Corporation), the "relentless focus on education has resulted in formidable exam performers."[24]

CHAPTER FIVE

A School as a Microcosm of Society and Culture

Profile of an American High School

This chapter examines the students' behavioral patterns and learning behaviors at the American high school where I taught. First, describing the school's profile is essential to provide the context of this educational setting. The institute was accredited by the Western Association of Schools and Colleges (WASC), making it a bona fide American high school and facilitating students' application to U.S. colleges and universities. At the beginning of my tenure, during the 2012-2013 academic year, all the students were of Korean descent. They hailed from various parts of Korea, including large cities like Seoul, Busan, and Daejeon. Some came from the Korean education system, and others had attended a school in a Western country where the language of instruction was English, such as the U.S., Canada, or Australia. Three years later, in the fall of 2015, only a few non-Koreans enrolled. These non-Koreans had lived in the country long enough to communicate fluently in Korean and blend in with the rest of the student population. Therefore, their presence did not disrupt the harmony and homogeneity of the student body.

The school was co-ed. Boarding facilities were available for students, whether their families lived in or outside Jeonju. The percentage of boarding students fluctuated annually between 40% and 50% of the total population, typically less than 100. Many students enrolled primarily for exposure to a Western style of education, to improve their English language proficiency, and to gain admission into a reputable university. Their options included Korea, the United States, Canada, Singapore, and the United Kingdom.

Instructors were native speakers of English. Most of us received teacher preparation training in the United States or Canada. Some had prior experience teaching in the Korean education system, others had taught in *hagwons*, and others had neither. A Korean administrator who spoke Korean and

English and a bilingual-bicultural American principal shared the administrative duties.

My Professional Experience with Korean Students

This four-year phase of my professional experience was not my first exposure to Korean students. Previously, I was a teacher and guidance counselor in California for 15 years. I taught at a high school in a city considered a port of entry for recent immigrants. Even though there were waves of immigrants from various parts of the world, most incoming students were from Korea. Subsequently, I had the opportunity to provide academic counseling for ten years at a reputable community college with a high percentage of recent Korean immigrants. Many transferred to major universities in and out of California. Some, however, had trouble adjusting to a Western style of education. These difficulties were made apparent by their less-than-stellar academic performance.

The observations below about the learning behaviors of Korean students are based on my professional training, 28 years of professional experience, and input from colleagues in various disciplines. These colleagues were in the United States and the American high school where I worked in Korea. Through my professional training and experience, I have learned that several dynamics influence students' attitudes in a learning environment. These dynamics are intrinsic, environmental, and sociocultural. Examples of these dynamics include the students' motivational level, prior exposure to learning stimuli such as books and computers, their parents' educational level, their home environment, and the pedagogical approaches to which they are exposed (e.g., teacher-, student-, or learning-centered). Yet, some students exhibit an attitude conducive to learning even when some factors are less than ideal.

Because of the relatively small number of students and the unique characteristics of this school, it is critical to avoid making generalized assumptions about Korean students based on a small sample. The context of the educational experience is undoubtedly an influential factor in student behavior. Consequently, the environment of an American high school may evoke different results from a Korean school.

The teachers at the school delivered the instruction in English, except in world language classes like Chinese and Spanish. Thus, the staff attempted to emulate an American environment with English instruction facilitated by Western educators, a Westernized code of conduct, and the corresponding expectations.

However, one would expect culture-biased behavioral patterns to reflect society. In other words, it would not be surprising if the students' Korean upbringing influenced their behavior even though they were immersed in a simulation of an American setting. It would be natural for student behavior to reflect their culture in a similar situation regardless of their background. Therefore, their behavior could mirror values embedded in the Korean culture even as they operate in a different environment.

Students' Behavioral and Learning Patterns

My colleagues and I observed behavioral and learning patterns among the students we worked with. Initially, pupils seemed uncomfortable in a student-centered environment. Not surprisingly, those who had prior exposure to a Western style of education seemed comfortable in this setting. Those without exposure hesitated when allowed to operate in a participatory environment. In other words, they were more comfortable with a teacher-centered approach. In such a setting, students can sit at their desks and listen to the teacher's lecture while taking notes and subsequently studying them to restate the information on a test. Most students showed remarkable improvement as they became more proficient in English, more comfortable, even adept, in a participatory environment, and simultaneously more aware of teacher expectations. However, those accustomed to a teacher-centric approach found old habits difficult to overcome.

Students' Reaction to Open-ended Questions

Students who had attended the Korean education system before transferring to this American high school initially had trouble adapting to the more interactive methodologies. For example, students initially "froze" when asked open-ended questions or allowed to practice independent thinking. They froze even when there were no linguistic impediments to responding. They assumed incorrectly that all the correct answers had to come from the teacher rather than the students. Also, they were more comfortable being fed the responses by their instructors than actively participating in the learning process. The concept of open-ended questions appeared to be new to them. In other words, they were being asked to become independent thinkers with little preparation for this Westernized learning environment.

Gradually, as teachers used this approach while encouraging students to pose questions and express their opinions, they became more skilled. They posed not merely average but incisive questions. This development usually coincided with the students' improved command of English and critical thinking skills.

In an article appearing in the *Korea Herald*, Professor Justin Fendos, an educational researcher at Dongseo University, made similar observations about the lack of independent thinking and creativity among Korean students at the university level. Professor Fendos states: "There is no scientific proof that South Korean students are less creative than their Western counterparts; the main reason for this [assumption] is the lack of a reliable assessment that can quantify creativity."[1] Nevertheless, he shares that anecdotally, he and his colleagues

> have frequently observed a significant difference between Korean university students and foreign peers when they are put together into groups and asked to solve problems. The Korean students simply aren't good at solving problems they haven't experienced before and will often gape in amazement at the speed and ease with which their foreign colleagues can think up new solutions.
>
> Assuming this difference is real, a conclusion both I and the Korean government agree on, it becomes paramount to identify the causes. When one studies the common experiences of Korean students, one thing becomes obvious immediately: the fact that creativity is largely discouraged in Korean classrooms at virtually every level.
>
> Throughout primary school, Korean students are socialized to be submissive and do what teachers tell them.[2]

Fortunately, the learning style and social skills Professor Fendos and his colleagues have identified as lacking in the Korean students' repertoire can be developed and mastered if nurtured. We discuss techniques that help promote them later in this chapter.

The hesitation to ask questions in class has cultural roots. In the West, students are encouraged to pose questions, a sign of intellectual curiosity and critical and independent thinking. Asking individual questions is opposed to the Korean concepts of unity and harmony, achieved when all students behave similarly. Based on the Korean paradigm, a student asking questions disrupts the unity and harmony of the classroom. Students learn early on to ask questions during a teacher's lecture only if they are considered top-notch students. When one such student asks a question, the harmony is maintained by the concentrated attention of their classmates. Through their attention, they honor the questioner, who has earned the unspoken right to pose questions based on their academic prowess, and the teacher, the provider of knowledge and wisdom. By withholding questions, students avoid "wasting" both the teacher's and their classmates' time, a concept related to efficiency. If only the best students ask questions, the entire group benefits and maximizes class time. This behavior pattern is further explained by the motto 대를 위한 소의 희생, which means "For the large, sacrifice the small" or "Each individual should act or sacrifice for the benefit of the group." We discuss the concept of sacrifice in more detail in Chapter Two.

Group Projects

When assigned group projects, individuals had to be cajoled into participating, let alone taking leadership roles, to ensure that the group accomplished its objectives. The lack of initiative was exacerbated by the lackadaisical attitude of group members who would rather have one or two students do all the work than participate and contribute to the learning. To counteract this tendency, teachers would assign specific tasks to individual group members and allocate individual and group grades to make everyone accountable. After a semester or two, students would become acculturated to a more participatory learning environment and an accountability system that held them responsible for their performance.

This attitude is not unique to Korean students. As with other observed behavior, the difference is in its pervasiveness. People associate this behavior with laziness or apathy in different educational settings. However, in the Korean context, this behavior appears to relate to the efficiency element.

Students who relinquish their responsibilities to others recognize that by doing so, the most capable will carry the heavy part of the group project. As a result, the group will reap the benefits by receiving a higher grade. However, those students who abrogate responsibility benefit the least from the learning process. In contrast, those who actively participate will benefit the most. The latter expand their critical thinking ability, develop or enhance their leadership and social skills, and strengthen their self-esteem.

One of the missions of education is to prepare students to become productive members of society regardless of their chosen profession. Educators who allow pupils to shirk responsibility do students on both sides of this dichotomy a disservice. The inherent message to those who relinquish their responsibilities is that they can get by in life with the bare minimum. Conversely, permitting students who take the initiative to carry the entire workload instills an unhealthy attitude vis-à-vis their learning. It also allows them to escape the challenges of collaborating with a team by doing what they always do: doing it themselves. By providing a safe environment where all are able and required to participate in the learning and discovery process, students recognize how stimulating it can be while contributing to the group's success. Along the way, they learn to accept responsibility by sharing the workload equally. Also, their self-esteem and self-confidence are enhanced because they discover that their contributions matter.

Multiple-choice vs. Other Types of Tests

In their behavioral habits, Korean students display a quality that permeates the culture: the tendency to be efficient. They prefer multiple-choice over essays, short answers, and fill-in-the-blank questions. Multiple-choice tests, by nature, are easier to prepare for since they lend themselves to rote memorization and repetition. Conversely, fill-in-the-blanks, open-ended, short-answer, and essay questions align with critical and independent thinking skills. Two simple reasons explain the students' preference: They can answer multiple-choice questions much faster than they can answer other questions. Furthermore, they can earn higher scores on multiple-choice exams than on other tests since the former are less proficient at identifying the student's deficiencies. Therefore, the student preference for multiple choice questions over others is congruent within the Korean cultural context.

Teachers noted this tendency in most subjects. However, it was of utmost concern in mathematics and science courses, where showing the step-by-step process of arriving at the correct answer is a highly valued skill. This is particularly important in higher-level classes, such as AP (Advanced Placement), which emphasize critical thinking and research-based curricula. Also, inquiry-based learning and experiments are essential to the learning process in these courses.

The emphasis placed on education from an early age is one reason Korea has advanced so dramatically in science and technology since the end of the Korean War. Education and culture go together. Therefore, observing the cultural stress on efficiency and the overemphasis on multiple-choice questions and standardized tests is unsurprising.

The observed student habits and learning patterns are likely reinforced by the teaching and learning methodology employed by private tutors and *hagwon* instructors specializing in test preparation. In such an environment, learning relies exclusively on repetition, rote memorization, and teaching to the test. The teachers' primary goal is to instruct students to maximize their test time by answering questions quickly and efficiently and giving them lots of practice with test questions.

Realistically, tutors and *hagwon* instructors do what they are paid to do. They coach students on the most efficient strategies to approach a test to obtain the highest possible score. This practice is not unique to Korea. We reiterate that, as with many other behavioral patterns observed among Koreans and discussed in this book, what is unusual is the degree of intensity and pervasiveness of the behavior, which could be a byproduct of the desire to be the best at everything due to the competitive environment.

Is the learning culture espoused by *hagwons* and private tutors bleeding into other areas of society?

This setting has little opportunity to promote creativity, independent thinking, inquiry-based, and collaborative learning. The unintended effect of employing this teaching methodology in the universally used *hagwons* and by private tutors may be enabling the resulting learning strategy in other contexts. The transference of this learning strategy is happening whether it is the most effective for long-term assimilation or is educationally sound.

If the *hagwon* learning culture is bleeding into other areas of society, the "goose that laid the golden eggs," or *hagwons* and private tutors that make higher education accessible, negatively impact students' learning ability. Students and parents must recognize that the skills needed in an academic testing environment differ from those leading to success in a practical educational setting. Such an environment thrives on creativity, critical and independent thinking, and inquiry-based and collaborative learning.

Some observed behavioral and learning patterns are also present in other settings and cultural contexts. However, they seem more pronounced in the Korean culture. It is difficult, if not impossible, to assign a direct cause-and-effect relationship, such as attributing a behavioral pattern to culture rather than prior education experience or even a lack of interest or motivation, not to mention the stress and anxiety caused by being in a different educational environment and dealing with language acquisition challenges. A combination of causes could be considered a distinct possibility. However, it is more important to recognize the existence of specific problematic, unfavorable behavioral patterns, and devise a plan to eradicate them or, at the very least, counteract their negative impact on learning.

Is it possible to eradicate counterproductive behavioral and learning patterns?

From a pedagogical perspective, it is possible to eradicate these counterproductive behavioral patterns without considering cultural influences by meeting students "where they are" regarding their critical thinking and learning ability. First, students can be exposed to experiences supported by their learning preferences to give them a taste of success and build their self-confidence. If teachers gradually introduce more challenging activities, students will learn to build critical thinking and enhance their communication and social skills. Suppose instructors gradually increase the activities' difficulty level while moving pupils toward desired behaviors, such as collaborative and problem-based learning. Then, they may offset the negative impact of efficiency-based learning behaviors, focusing on short-term gains. Students may even discover the joy of learning.

Teachers must incorporate specific and clear rubrics into the grading system and make them explicit to ensure students understand the instructor's expectations. The teacher grades the student's individual and group contributions separately within the collaborative and problem-based learning paradigm. This practice fosters active student participation in all stages of the group project. The grading should be fair and include a reward mechanism to be effective. The reward system promotes positive behavior and academic achievement. Adopting productive behavioral patterns will enable students to acquire the skills needed to succeed in a demanding educational setting, including higher education, and eventually in the workplace.

In this American school, teachers espoused specific values ingrained in Western culture. For example, businesses and industries in the United States seek employees who are team players but also independent thinkers and learners. As such, schools need to develop creative individuals with the necessary critical thinking and social skills to function effectively in an environment where teamwork is essential.

Pedagogy

Although instructors could use the lecture method, they only partially relied on it. It was one of a multitude of strategies available to them. I include this discussion about the teaching and learning methodologies espoused by instructors to contrast them with those employed at test-preparation *hagwons*. The purpose is to emphasize the participatory classroom environment and present the discussion as a backdrop for some of the adjustment difficulties experienced by new students coming from the Korean education system.

Teachers had several methodologies at their disposal to deliver the instruction, including individual and group projects, the Socratic and lecture methods, collaborative and problem-based learning, class discussion, scaffolding, research, and laboratory experiments in science classes. The strategy selection depended on several factors, including the subject matter, the course level, and the students' command of the English language.

Students' Emphasis on Efficiency and Their Adjustment to a New Paradigm

As a result of the competitive nature of the education system and the emphasis on efficiency, Korean students have developed a tendency to work out solutions to mathematical problems on multiple-choice tests by making a few calculations on scratch paper or in the margin of the exam, considering the options, and choosing the answer through a process of elimination without going through the entire step-by-step methodical procedure. While this may result in identifying the correct answer, students can succeed on a test without being able to explain how to calculate the problems.

Because of their training, the Western mathematics teachers employed by this school encouraged pupils to demonstrate the step-by-step process of arriving at the correct answer on paper. This practice enabled students to show their analytical thinking process. Instructors were aware of the students' emphasis on efficiency and wanted to help them develop their analytical thinking. Consequently, they awarded students partial credit for showing the steps for solving a problem. The students would receive the credit even if the final answer were incorrect due to a mathematical miscalculation.

Since the environment was interactive, teachers encouraged pupils to use the blackboard to show their peers the steps necessary to solve a problem. This demonstration reinforced the method to the rest of the class while improving students' communication skills and self-confidence. These techniques benefitted all students, mainly those planning to attend a Western university. Practicing these skills helped them assimilate more quickly to a Western style of education at the university level.

OTHER OBSERVED STUDENT BEHAVIOR

Cramming

Students tended to "cram" for tests and subsequently "dump" the information, thus purposefully "washing away" or forgetting most of what they learned before a test. The theory behind this process is the incorrect assumption that they have no more use for that information after the test. Students believe they must "make room" in their short-term memory for new material instead of viewing the learning as building blocks. Students at the school where I taught may have invented their own euphemism by referring to this process as "brainwashing." On several occasions, while discussing a new concept related to a topic we had studied previously and tested on, students had no recollection of the subject matter. When I reminded them that we had already covered the material and had been evaluated on it, they quickly explained that because they had already been tested, they had forgotten it. Once again, this behavioral pattern also exists in other cultural contexts. However, given the extent to which Korean students use cramming, it appears to be driven by the cultural emphasis on efficiency.

Sleeping in Class

Students brought other habits from their previous experience that were more deeply ingrained and consequently more difficult to eradicate than learning patterns. One of those habits was putting their heads on their desks to rest or nap during and between classes. Those new to the school incorrectly assumed that teachers would condone the practice. However, they soon found out that it was not. First, the school had a policy that discouraged sleeping in class. Second, the relatively small class size made it impossible for any student who fell asleep to go undetected. If students put their heads down, teachers would instruct them to sit up. Instructors would wake them up if they fell asleep in class and issue a warning. When the attitude persisted, teachers either assigned detention or lowered the students' participation grade in the course or both. In chronic cases, the administration contacted parents to determine whether a health issue was involved.

As indicated earlier, most students came directly from the Korean education system. Even if only some of them habitually put their heads down on their desks, the logical assumption is that this behavior was allowed in their previous experience. Assuming this observation is accurate, three factors are possible contributors. First, the average class size in Korean schools is much larger than at the school where I taught; therefore, it is easier for students to engage in this activity without being noticed. Second, when class size is an issue, there is a tendency to use less interactive teaching strategies, such as the lecture method, to cover the required material. If used extensively, this method exhausts the students physically and mentally because of physical inactivity and a short attention span. Third, teachers in Korean schools may take a more indulgent attitude regarding this behavior because they know the students' grueling schedules. We discuss extensively the topic of demanding student schedules in Chapter Four. Instructors at the American school employ a grading system that includes a small but significant percentage assigned to class participation. Naturally, students cannot participate if they fall asleep in class.

Students' Workload

Since this was an American high school, participating in *hagwons* was unnecessary. However, students enrolled in seven classes instead of six, as is customary in California public high schools. Furthermore, students were required to participate in a sport or a co-curricular activity after completing their seven daily classes. Physical activities were in place instead of a physical education program because the facilities were under the university's jurisdiction. Therefore, offering all physical activities at once was more feasible than dispersing them throughout the day. Also, the size of the student body made it impractical to provide a physical education program. The sports activities included basketball, fitness, golf, soccer, volleyball, and tennis. The co-curricular activities covered SAT preparation, AP mathematics and AP science preparation, Model United Nations, and Yearbook. These activities ended just before dinner, meaning the students had a much longer school day than High school students on American soil. The consolation was that even though their day was long, it was shorter than that of their counterparts in Korean schools. The constant battle with some students' somnolence may reflect the excessively long school day.

Discipline

The administration assigned supervisors to the boys' and the girls' sides of the dorm. Occasionally, however, there were some after-school disciplinary cases. Some of these infractions include individuals or small student groups playing video games in their dorm rooms during study time and slipping out of the dorm to smoke or consume alcoholic beverages. It is essential to note that the institute was a boarding school, but most Korean high schools are not. The residency factor could make a difference in supervision, concentration, and discipline level.

Young Lee and I recognize that the discipline issues described in this section are not necessarily typical of students enrolled in Korean high schools. Therefore, this behavior should not be generalized to other high school students.

Smoking among Teenagers

According to a study by *Statistics Korea*, the smoking and drinking rates for middle and high school students in 2014 were 9.2% and 16.7%, respectively.[3]

By 2017, according to the *Korean Statistical Information Service*, the percentage of smokers dropped to 3.0% and 9.2% for middle and high school students, respectively.[4] Interestingly, the downward trend in smoking for middle and high school students parallels the drop in overall tobacco use for the entire country. According to OECD data, the percentage of daily smokers for Koreans aged 15 years and older was 20% in 2014 and 17.5% in 2017.[5] This decrease in smoking may be related to the national sentiment toward tobacco during the same period. The adoption of smoking ban laws throughout the country reflects this feeling. Specifically in Seoul, where smoking was prohibited in 17,500 public areas and 23,900 indoor locations were designated smoke-free zones.[6]

Despite the impressive number of non-smoking and smoke-free zones in Seoul, the World Health Organization (WHO) cited Korea for "not properly implementing policies on protecting, enforcing bans and raising taxes, according to the WHO Report on the Global Tobacco Epidemic 2017."[7] The WHO recommended that Korea intensify its policies. "In September [2017], the World Health Organization recommended [that] South Korea adopt more stringent regulations to ban cigarette smoking in public places and restrict tobacco advertising and promotions."[8] The recurring issue with the lack of stringent regulations and enforcement of existing laws will become more apparent in Chapters Seven and Eight about accidents.

Boarding Students' Sleeping Habits

The poor sleeping habits of some of the boarding students caused them to wake up just in time to shower or wash their face, brush their teeth, get dressed, and walk to their first-period class, thus missing the most important meal of the day: breakfast. Meal costs were included in the tuition and expenses fees package selected by the parents at the start of the school year. Boarding students' parents could include meal costs in the fees package. An element of efficiency appears to be present in this seemingly ordinary activity. Skipping breakfast allowed students to sleep more to compensate for the time spent studying or playing computer games late into the night. The lack of nutrition in the morning exacerbated the students' sleepiness until lunch. Per a social survey conducted by *Statistics Korea*, in 2016, only 57.7% of youth aged 13 to 24 ate breakfast.[9] Not surprisingly, when this figure is further disaggregated, the younger population aged 13 to 19 showed a higher percentage who ate breakfast, 67.6%, versus those aged 20 to 24 at 45.8%.[10]

Commuting students may have been in a better situation since they had more personal attention, structure, and supervision at home. Their sleeping habits were supposedly more regular and adequate, and they came to school with full stomachs. However, some may have been worse off if their home environment was overly structured and strictly supervised.

The Payoff Window

Most students eventually overcame the learning challenges and counterproductive behavioral patterns described in this chapter and successfully adapted to an American style of education. Some adjusted quickly, and others took longer. However, the result is that a substantial number of graduates were admitted to a university in the United States, Canada, Korea, and other parts of the world. Some seniors who gained admission to a university in the United States received scholarships based on their academic accomplishments and potential. It was heartwarming to see deserving graduating seniors receive a well-earned scholarship. The awards ranged from $20,000 to $25,000 in several instances.

Adapting to and successfully functioning in a new learning and cultural environment is challenging. However, those students with clear objectives who showed adaptability and invested time, effort, and hard work, in the end, received a well-deserved compensation.

- Initially, students froze at the prospect of practicing their independent and critical thinking skills. They assumed incorrectly that all the answers had to come from the teacher rather than the students.
- Asking individual questions in class is opposed to the Korean concepts of unity and harmony, which are achieved when all students behave similarly.
- The teaching and learning methodology employed by private tutors and *hagwon* instructors specializing in test preparation may reinforce the counterproductive student habits and learning patterns observed in the classroom.
- Those students who had clear objectives, showed adaptability, and invested time, effort, and hard work, in the end, received a well-deserved compensation.

CHAPTER SIX

The View from 30,000 Feet

President Barack Obama praised the Korean education system several times during his administration. The President and former Education Secretary Arne Duncan often asked why American education could not be more like the Korean model.

The answer has its roots in the divergent historical, social, economic, and cultural factors unique to Korea and the United States, respectively. Neither President Obama nor Secretary Duncan implied that the U.S. should duplicate everything about the Korean education system. Duplication would be challenging on account of the above factors and because Korea's homogeneity contrasts with U.S. diversity. The prevailing cultural and ethnic diversity permeating the United States would make adopting the Korean education model impossible. One such difference is the Western emphasis on individuality as opposed to the Korean stress on unity, harmony, conformity, and consensus building, which we discuss at length in Chapter Two.

In the West, parents, teachers, and other adults praise and reward children from a young age for their accomplishments, independent thinking, the pursuit of uniqueness, standing out, and asking relevant and incisive questions. This uniqueness runs the gamut from their clothes to their chosen career or profession. Also, even among siblings, children are given choices from the food they eat to the talents they cultivate, be it in academics, sports, or the arts. By and large, Western parents realize that happy and healthy children require a balance between study and play.

In several public speeches, Duncan and the President identified elements of the Korean education system that they felt the U.S. should emulate despite the cultural differences. Because people at these levels often speak in soundbites, they do not provide much detail or evidence for their rationale. Following is a brief discussion of the points they found admirable about Korean education. Subsequently, we present an in-depth analysis of Korean society's more prominent education elements to explain possible outcomes and behavioral patterns learned at an early age and adopted as a part of the modus operandi of individuals within the overarching Korean cultural context. Then, we apply the principles of these behavioral patterns to everyday life.

Last but certainly not least are the challenges that the different organizational structures of education in each country would pose in adopting the Korean model. In the U.S., education is a state function. Therefore, it is considered a decentralized model, whereas the Korean organizational structure is a "centralized decentralization" or "decentralized centralization." The Ministry of Education has the authority to set the national curriculum standards and policies for education. However, the regional and local offices have some autonomy and responsibility for implementing and managing the education system in their respective areas. Furthermore, schools and teachers have some discretion and flexibility in adapting the curriculum and instruction to meet the needs and interests of their students.

A bird's-eye view looks different from the ground. Although it may seem simple for the President to suggest that Americans "adopt" elements of Korean education, the model has evolved as a unique embodiment of each nation's cultural values.

Seriousness about Education

Secretary Duncan believed that the Korean sense of educational purpose is rooted in policy and culture. In a 2014 speech, he commented on the policy aspect of Korea's seriousness about education: "Korea is serious about developing and rewarding great teachers. That means recruiting top college graduates into teaching, training them effectively for the job, and making sure vulnerable students have strong teachers."[1]

He then went on to compare U.S. and Korean practice vis-à-vis teacher recruitment, teacher pay, and teacher training:

> In the United States, a significant proportion of new teachers come from the bottom third of their college class, and most new teachers say their training didn't prepare them for the realities of the classroom. So, underprepared teachers enter our children's classrooms every year, and low-income and minority kids get far more than their share of ineffective teachers.
>
> In contrast, in South Korea, elementary teachers are selected from the top 5 percent of their high school cohort. Teachers there get six months of training after they start their jobs. They are paid well, and the best receive bonus pay and designation as "master teachers."

In Korea, according to an international study, students from low-income families are actually more likely than students from rich families to have high-quality teachers.

Why? Because teachers get extra pay and career rewards for working with the neediest kids. Their children who need more, get more. Our children who need more get less.[2]

After reading these comments, I, as an educator, am left with more questions than answers. For example, to compare apples to apples, it would be enlightening to find out whether new Korean teachers feel that their teacher training prepares them for the realities of the classroom. If it does, why do they receive six months of training after they start their assignment? Their response should then be compared to American teachers' responses to understand how well teacher training prepares educators. However, ensuring that survey protocols are identical or similar does not go far enough.

Consideration must be given to school and classroom conditions in Korea and the U.S. As an example, delinquency and violence appear to be more prominent in U.S. schools for several reasons, some of which are cultural, including the legalized gun policy in the United States. This policy does not exist in Korea. Examples of guns and violence only scratch the surface regarding the differences in the cultural context for teachers in each country. Therefore, teacher training beyond the delivery of instruction and classroom management must be different and address societal needs. Besides, societies are dynamic. Consequently, teacher training programs cannot prepare instructors for every eventuality.

For example, a student shot himself before his teacher and classmates at a California high school where I taught. I am confident that the instructor underwent teacher training, but did the training prepare her for that situation? Probably not. Therefore, because of the dynamic nature of societies, it is better to provide ongoing training in addition to that offered by teacher education programs to meet the needs of a changing community.

Parental Involvement

During his tenure, Secretary Duncan was fond of relating a story from 2009 when President Obama met with then-Korean President Lee Myung-Bak (2008-2013). Reportedly, President Obama asked his Korean counterpart what his biggest challenge was in education. Lee responded that parents in Korea are too demanding. Even the "poorest Korean parents demanded a first-class education for their children, and he [President Lee] was having to spend millions of dollars each year to teach English to students in first grade because his parents won't let him wait until second grade."[3]

The quote above fails to tell the audience that the primary motivator for "poor" Korean parents to demand a "first-class education" is the gruelingly competitive environment of the country in general and the university admission process in particular. As previously mentioned, this admission process ultimately links to the brutally competitive nature of the job market. Therefore, by "demanding a first-class education," "poor parents" are advocating for their children. These parents want to ensure their children have a fair chance to compete against those from families with the financial means to pay for top-quality *hagwons* and private tutors. The parents' desire for their children to succeed in this ruthless environment is understandable.

Therefore, the constant advocacy push-pull between wealthy parents and those with lesser means amounts to a process of upping the ante. For example, suppose public schools offer English language instruction beginning in the fourth grade. In that case, wealthy parents will ensure their children receive private English education earlier to secure a head start over other students. At that point, parents who cannot afford to pay for private English language instruction will demand that the government offer English education earlier than the fourth grade. Once the government agrees to subsidize English language instruction starting in the third grade, the competitive nature of the culture will likely motivate wealthy parents to pay for the same in the second grade or earlier. And so on. Viewed from a different perspective, if parents do not "demand a first-class education," their children would be significantly disadvantaged in this highly competitive environment. After all, their children's success determines, at the very least, the comfort level and, at most, the economic survival of the next generation.

An example of this fierce advocacy for their children involves the father of a student at the American high school where I taught. He insisted that his son be scheduled for physics the semester after transitioning from the ESL program into regular classes. The father was insistent, even though his son was not ready at that particular juncture to succeed academically in such a high-level course. The only argument this father finally listened to was the explanation about the rationale behind prerequisites and the sequential order of mathematics and science courses.

After completing the appropriate prerequisites, his son would be more likely to succeed in physics. Some of the student's teachers reported that he exhibited some concerning behavioral patterns. For example, his science teacher noticed that he studied using two chemistry textbooks literally side by side: one in

English issued by the school and another he purchased in Korean. This study habit demanded more time than using only one textbook. Evidently, he was under pressure to do well in chemistry class.

Moreover, teachers noted that he often fell asleep during class. This was most likely a sign that he was not getting enough sleep even though he was a commuting student living at home under the supervision of his parents. It is also conceivable that living at home under parental control applied additional pressure on him to perform at the highest possible level. Furthermore, teachers observed that he appeared detached from his peers; he kept to himself and did not take the initiative to associate with others. These symptoms gave us a reason to be concerned about the student's well-being.

Many similar examples come to mind, whereby parents insisted that their children be placed in higher-level classes than their academic preparation stipulated. This happened even when their children did not have the command of the English language required to succeed in a rigorous academic program. The parents insisted on driving their students beyond their educational limitations at a particular time in their development. The parents' concern that their children would fall behind others in the same age group prompted their insistence. They feared that their children would be disadvantaged academically for the foreseeable future.

I realize that the situation was unique. The American private school represents a small sample of Korean parents. Therefore, caution should be used when applying these generalizations to the entire Korean population. However, based on my observations, the parents at this school were very much involved in their children's education as advocates. At times, parents were so relentless in their desire for their children's academic advancement that yielding to their wishes would have been detrimental to the students and the educational program's integrity. From my perspective, the nation's competitive environment and the desire to provide their children with an advantage were at the root of what seems to be purely a "parental involvement" attribute on the surface.

Respect for Teachers

In his State of the Union Address on January 25, 2011, President Obama alluded to the respect accorded to teachers in Korea as a quality that the American education system should emulate. He stated:

> After parents, the biggest impact on a child's success comes from the man or woman at the front of the classroom. In South Korea, teachers are known as

"nation builders." Here in America, it's time we treated the people who educate our children with the same level of respect. We want to reward good teachers and stop making excuses for bad ones.[4]

The President delivered a similar message in various other speeches, including an address at Kenmore Middle School in Arlington, Virginia, on March 14, 2011.

The respect for teachers that President Obama refers to applies to both individuals and the profession. It includes an acknowledgment of teachers' contributions to the education of the nation's youth, as well as a compensation level that is commensurate with or at least relative to other professions.[5]

This concept is more evident in the President's remarks on the launch of the ConnectHome Initiative at Durant High School in Durant, Oklahoma, on July 15, 2015. He stated, "[T]hey [South Koreans] pay their teachers the way they pay their doctors – and they consider education to be at the highest rung of the professions."[6]

Young Lee and I agree that in Korea, teaching is considered "the highest rung of the professions," which contrasts with how people perceive the practice in the United States. Koreans have a high regard for the profession partly due to cultural reasons and because of its inherent job security, the competitive nature of the field, and the difficulty in landing a tenure-track position. The cultural reasons are based on Confucian ideology, which shaped Korea's politics, society, culture, and education during the Joseon Era (1392-1897). Confucianism was also the basis for the establishment of a scholarly tradition.

However, elementary and secondary teaching positions are not regarded as well-paid jobs despite the profession's high esteem. Even if accurate, the statement, "They pay their teachers the way they pay their doctors," is misleading to an American audience. Their point of reference is that U.S. doctors are well-paid; however, their Korean peers are not as well compensated.

Traditionally, doctors have been at or near the top of the best-paid jobs in the United States. According to *U.S. News and World Report*, physicians rank 6th on the list of best-paid jobs for 2018. They are paid $196,380 on average.[7] Other medical specialists rank even higher on the pay scale. However, teachers do not even make the top twenty-five best-paid jobs list. Historically, they have not received lofty salaries, considering the amount of academic preparation and dedicated time the profession requires.

The point here is not that teachers ought to be paid at the same level as doctors but to point out the cultural context for each of the two countries and the dissonance between President Obama's statement and the image it conjures in the minds of his American audience. When Americans hear, "they [Koreans] pay their teachers the way they pay their doctors," the logical assumption is that Korean instructors must have high salaries because they are paid at the same level as doctors. This assumption is incorrect since Korean doctors are not as well compensated as their American counterparts.[8]

Higher Expectations of Students

Regarding the perception that Korean parents and schools place higher expectations on students than their American counterparts, President Obama and Secretary Duncan agreed. In a speech delivered on January 13, 2014, to the National Assessment Governing Board's Education Summit for Parent Leaders, Secretary Duncan referenced the poor performance of students on standardized tests in the United States relative to other countries. For example, he indicated, "America now ranks 22nd in math skills and 14th in reading among industrialized countries—and our achievement gaps are not narrowing."[9] The Secretary also alluded to the precipitous decrease in college completion rates, which saw the U.S. drop from the number one position to number 12 in the time frame of one generation.[10] Interestingly, the U.S. was replaced as the number one country in the college completion rate category by none other than Korea.[11]

As a result of these sobering statistics, Secretary Duncan took the opportunity to underscore the significant differences between American and Korean education that, in his opinion, tipped the balance in favor of Korean students in the achievement gaps. The Secretary identified the demands placed upon Korean students as one of the factors contributing to their achievement edge. He reiterated the following:

> South Korea—and a few other countries—are offering students more and demanding more than many American districts and schools do. And the results are showing in our kids' learning and in their opportunities to succeed, and in staggeringly large achievement gaps in this country.[12]

Since his audience was composed primarily of parent leaders, the Secretary repeatedly stated his theme of demanding more from schools, teachers, and students throughout his speech. His theme undoubtedly resonated with his audience. However, Secretary Duncan clarified that he was not proposing that the U.S. should imitate everything Korea does in education. He noted without going into detail that in Korea, "the pressure to study can get out of hand."[13]

However, the tone of his speech is in the context of: "Why can't American education be more like its Korean counterpart?" Clearly, this is the message when he reiterates to his audience that "we need to act on what we know about countries that are out-educating us."[14]

Although he conceded that Korean students are exhausted, he did not mention that "intentional harm" among 9 to 24 years of age has been the leading cause of death for some years.[15] "Intentional harm" may result from the pressure placed upon students.

Also, notably absent from Secretary Duncan's remarks was the high percentage of families' income directed toward private supplemental education and test preparation. Nor did he mention that this emphasis on test preparation has made Korean students outstanding test takers. Another notable omission from his remarks is the Achilles' heel of the Korean education system, which parents have complained about: the lack of emphasis on creativity.

This concern is magnified if private education through *hagwons* and personal tutors is included in the mix, given their emphasis on repetition, rote memorization, and test practice. Finally, when the Secretary singled out Korea's accomplishment as the country with the highest college completion rate, he neglected to acknowledge the vulnerabilities of the democratization of higher education, which has caused an oversupply of overeducated individuals with a bachelor's degree or higher. At a personal level, there is an emotional impact on overqualified graduates who cannot obtain a job proportionate to their educational credentials or, worse yet, cannot secure a job at all.

Public speeches by government leaders and other dignitaries have a purpose. Some are meant to convince the public, sway public opinion, or advocate for a program, idea, or belief. The portrayal of Korean education described by President Obama and Secretary Duncan focuses almost exclusively on the positive aspects and understates the vulnerabilities of Korean education. It is an oversimplified and incomplete image captured from a high altitude where contrasts are nonexistent, and details are considered inconsequential. The danger for an uninformed public is to be swayed by arguments based on incomplete and superficial representations.

This argument about the effectiveness of Korean education is akin to tourists posting pictures of magnificent places they visited during their trip abroad and excluding photos of the not-so-appealing places. Depending on where the viewers live and their financial resources, those representations may compel them to visit or wish they could live there. Also, posting only photos limits the travelers' ability to share details such as the sounds and smells that did not entirely agree with them or the insects that bit them. Consequently, the viewers will have an incomplete image of those places unless they have been there themselves.

Longer Hours of Instruction and the Impact on Students

President Obama believed that one of the reasons Korean education has an advantage over its American counterpart is the difference in the amount of time Korean children spend "in school." In his remarks to the Hispanic Chamber of Commerce delivered on March 10, 2009, President Obama lauded the Korean education system for requiring students to spend more time in the classroom than in American schools. His comments about the antiquated calendar of the American education system compared to its counterpart make a compelling case from an American audience perspective but not from a Korean outlook, as we will see following his remarks.

> We can no longer afford an academic calendar designed for when America was a nation of farmers who needed their children at home plowing the land at the end of each day. That calendar may have once made sense, but today it puts us at a competitive disadvantage. Our children – listen to this – our children spend over a month less in school than children in South Korea – every year. That's no way to prepare them for a 21st century economy. That's why I'm calling for us not only to expand effective after-school programs but to rethink the school day to incorporate more time – whether during the summer or through expanded-day programs for children who need it....
>
> The challenges of a new century demand more time in the classroom. If they can do that in South Korea, we can do it right here in the United States of America.[16]

Many Koreans reacted swiftly in disbelief to the President's comments, suggesting that the U.S. look to their country's education as a model to emulate. One day after the President's remarks, on March 11, 2009, their reaction was summed up in a piercing statement in an article appearing in the *Korea Times*:

> Obama's remarks came as a surprise to many South Koreans as the country's education system has been under constant public criticism due to its lack of creativity and heavy dependence on private tutoring.[17]

Korean students indeed attend classes for more hours than their American counterparts. However, it is also true that many of these additional classes are supplemental to those provided by the Korean education system. As a result of the extended hours in "crammers" and tutorial sessions, Korean students give up activities that otherwise would constitute a balanced teenage life.

The unfortunate "intentional harm" figures cited earlier are not surprising, given that since at least 2010, Korean school-aged youngsters have scored poorly on satisfaction surveys compared to their counterparts in other OECD (Organization for Economic Cooperation and Development) countries.[18]

In 2010, the *Chosun Ilbo* reported that

> Children and adolescents in Korea are the least satisfied with their lives among 26 member countries of the OECD. According to a survey released on Tuesday by a research center affiliated with Yonsei University and a foundation named for educator Pang Jong-hwan, only 53.9 percent of 5,435 schoolchildren from fourth grade to 12th said they were satisfied with their lives. That means one in two Korean children and adolescents are dissatisfied.[19]

The article specifies: "The greatest source of stress was school work, followed by physical appearance and problems with parents."[20]

Five years later, in 2015, the *Chosun Ilbo* reported that:

> A whopping 50.3 percent of Korean kids are stressed about their studies, the highest proportion among 30 countries surveyed, according to an analysis by Kim Mi-sook of the Korea Institute for Health and Social Affairs [...]
>
> Only 18.5 percent of kids in Korea said they are "very happy" at school. Korea comes fifth from the bottom [...]
>
> The happiest kids were in Ireland (42.5 percent), Romania (41.6 percent), Lithuania (39.0 percent), Norway (38.8 percent), and the Netherlands (38.4 percent).[21]

The article quotes Kim Mi-sook, the analyst, as saying,

> We need to lighten their [the students'] burden of study and give youngsters more free time and more things to do with it [...] We should also learn what we can from countries like the Netherlands, where kids are happy and perform remarkably well.[22]

Spending excessive time studying in *hagwons* or with private tutors beyond regular school hours has turned Korean students into sedentary people at an early age. In 2016, the *Chosun Ilbo* reported that Korean youngsters spend only half an hour a day outdoors.

> Korean children spend only 34 minutes outdoors a day on average, a survey shows. That is a mere third of the time spent outside by their counterparts in the U.S. (1 hour and 59 minutes) and Canada (1 hour and 40 minutes).
> The Environment Ministry surveyed 8,000 children and adolescents [...]
> Korean children between three and nine years of age spend most of their time indoors, going to crammers, playing games, or watching TV.[23]

The reported unhappiness or dissatisfaction pattern and the lack of exercise by Korean teenagers appear in statistics as late as 2017 when the *Chosun Ilbo* published the results of worldwide surveys conducted among 15-year-olds. The article reports that

> Korean teenagers rank at the top in the OECD when it comes to academic performance but are among the unhappiest in the club of rich countries. They also start private tuition earlier than in any other country, suggesting that public education is failing them, talk less to their parents and spend the least time exercising....
> Compared to 48 countries, including non-OECD member nations, they still ranked at the bottom....
> They start trudging to crammers at the age of nine, sooner than anywhere else. The average age was 11....
> But they spend very little time engaged in physical activities, with only 46.3 percent playing a sport either before or after school, ranking at the bottom. One out of five does not spend even a day exercising the minimum of 60 minutes, like walking and cycling....[24]

In conclusion, as noted earlier, Korean students spend more time in the classroom than their American counterparts. However, they dedicate much extra classroom time to supplemental enrichment education and test preparation. Consequently, they are likely better test takers than American students.

What is the cost of this imbalanced lifestyle? Based on the factors that Young Lee and I have examined, Korean students pay dearly for their academic accomplishments by being among the most dissatisfied children with their lives in OECD countries. They are also some of the most stressed about their studies.

This pattern is not new but has gained momentum in recent years based on self-harm counseling data. According to the *Chosun Ilbo*:

> Self-harm is on the rise among Korean teenagers, suggesting that stress levels are rising in the country's brutally competitive education environment.
>
> The Ministry of Gender Equality and Family analyzed records from 230 youth counseling and welfare centers across the country and found that counseling for self-harm rose from 4,000 in 2015 to 28,000 last year [2018].[25]

Preparing for Exams vs. Preparing for University

The cultural reliance on testing makes students proficient at cramming. Consequently, retaining learned material past a specific test is more challenging because the incentive is no longer there. Although students everywhere use cramming before a test, Koreans have taken the technique to new heights. For example, in Chapter Five, I described the "brainwashing" method that students at the American school where I taught used to "make room" for new material in the short-term memory part of their brains. This process involves discarding or forgetting everything learned for an exam as soon as it is over.

Also, as discussed in Chapter Five, Korean students are adept at picking the correct answers on multiple-choice tests but very poor at demonstrating the step-by-step process of arriving at the solution, a highly coveted skill in American high schools and universities. In an article written by Alan Singer and published in *HuffPost*, he shared the experience of Clay Burell, an American humanities teacher living in Korea, who reports that

> Korean students are forced to study in 'hagwons' – private night, weekend, and summer classes with an overwhelming emphasis on learning English. The Korean Education Ministry estimates that as a percentage of GDP, South Korean parents spend four times more on average on private education than their counterparts in any major economy. [As discussed earlier, this figure may be underestimated because most parents pay cash for private tutors. Therefore, these payments are not reported in government-generated statistics.] Most of what they study is 'worksheet-based, scripted, and devoted to passing college examination tests, the SAT, TOEFL, and all the other tests these classes teach to.' What Burell finds ironic is that despite this investment and high test scores, Korean students are notoriously poor at reading, writing, and speaking English. In other words, they can't use what they are supposed to have learned and what they test well at.[26]

This unfortunate result may be related to *hagwon* instructors' and private tutors' teaching techniques and the students' cramming and dumping habits. Efficiency is the driving force behind these strategies. Suppose the link between the methods and the result exists. Then, the disconnect that Alan Singer points to between obtaining high scores on standardized tests and English language acquisition, which ends up failing at the practical level, is an indictment of the *hagwon* instructors' and tutors' methodology and the students' cramming and dumping approach.

Alan Singer argues that "years of extra tutoring prepares Korean students for college entrance exams but not for acquiring a college education."[27] The author quotes Dr. Samuel Kim's research on American university dropouts to support his argument. According to Singer, Dr. Kim is a senior research scholar at the East Asian Institute at Columbia University. He reports that

> 44% of Korean students who enter 'top' American universities drop out before graduating. This is much higher than the dropout rate for students from China (25%), India (21%), and even the 34% dropout rate for American students at the same universities.[28]

The lesson from observations, testimonials, and statistics in this and previous chapters about education in Korea is that the skills needed to succeed in a testing environment are only a subset of those required to thrive in a practical university setting. The reality is that learning continues after students complete a university entrance examination, receive their exam score, or accept their admission offer from their dream school. The building blocks of the learning process continue accumulating, and the joy of learning reaches a higher dimension once students begin their college experience. Students who prepare for both will maximize their learning and adapt more quickly to any learning situation.

The assumption that one education system is better than another requires an in-depth analysis that includes identifying appropriate, culture-bias-free objective criteria. The fact that Korean students are good test-takers does not imply that the Korean education system is better than its American counterpart. This is particularly true, given that a significant aspect of Korean education is the extensive utilization of private education that relies heavily on repetition, test practice, and memorization. Therefore, it is unsurprising that Korean students perform well on multiple-choice tests. The "cram academies" and private tutors focusing on test preparation generally appear to be excellently elevating the students' test-taking ability. However, this skill represents only one aspect of the entire education spectrum. The most enduring portion of education is the experiential piece. It occurs in a safe academic environment where students can exercise their individuality while excelling in a collaborative setting and are comfortable with experimentation. This environment promotes a hunger for discovery, learning, and boundless creativity.

Suppose "cram schools" prepare students for the test-taking portion of education but not for the experiential piece. Is the rest of the Korean formal education preparing students for the experiential component? Suppose university admissions staff and others use multiple-choice test results to compare student performance. Then we must ask ourselves: What role do test practice and teaching-to-the-test play in temporarily influencing test scores? Are test practice and teaching-to-the-test the most effective methodologies? Do they promote long-term retention? Do standardized test results truly reflect students' potential for success in an academic setting? Or do they reflect students' ability to retain information and facts in short-term memory? Is the movement in the U.S. to minimize or eliminate the utilization of standardized test scores for admission purposes justified? Do we espouse a system that emphasizes rote memorization as its primary method of teaching and learning? Or do we embrace a system that fosters creativity, critical and independent thinking, self-expression, and problem-solving?

The fact that Korean families spend more money on private education with an emphasis on test preparation than their American counterparts does not necessarily translate to better-prepared students for higher education. This is especially true when the system values creativity, critical and independent thinking, collaborative learning, and the discovery process.

When comparing two countries' education systems, one must consider the many variables influencing student performance. In comparing the Korean and American education systems, the two most glaring differences are as follows: First, the amount of time, money, and effort spent on private education in Korea. Second, the Korean education system comprises students from a homogeneous society, language, and culture. In contrast, American students are as heterogeneous as can be. Korean students come from different socioeconomic backgrounds, just like their American peers. However, in addition to having diverse socioeconomic backgrounds, their American counterparts report to school with a wide range of learning behaviors and, most importantly, varied levels of exposure to the mainstream culture and the language of instruction.

These differences can help or hinder students' success even before they cross the threshold of the kindergarten school gate, thus potentially perpetuating social inequality. However, the fact that a middle school student can succeed in the American education system despite beginning with enormous socio-cultural disadvantages is a testament to access and equity. These disadvantages include a lack of knowledge of the English language and Anglo-Saxon culture. That child eventually learned English and French, earned a doctoral degree, and became a successful higher education administrator. Besides illustrating access and equity, this success story exemplifies the power of determination, dedication, love for learning, and mentoring from those who saw a diamond in the rough. That student is me. My chances of replicating this feat would be minimal to nonexistent in the Korean education system, which favors children from families that can afford expensive private supplemental instruction.

- During his administration, President Obama praised the Korean education system several times and wondered why U.S. education could not be more like the Korean model.
- According to Korean President Lee Myung-Bak (2008-2013), his biggest educational challenge was that parents in Korea are too demanding. Even the "poorest Korean parents [demand] a first-class education for their children."[3]
- Spending excessive time studying in *hagwons* or with private tutors beyond regular school hours has turned Korean students into sedentary human beings at a very young age.
- The preparation and skills needed to succeed in a testing environment differ significantly from those required to thrive in a university setting.

CHAPTER SEVEN

Why Are There so Many Man-Made Accidents?

Efficiency

Today, our world is undergoing profound changes. Many of these changes have emerged due to advancements in technology. Volumes have been written about technology's impact on our lives; therefore, I will not go into detail here. Suffice it to say that the Digital Revolution's profound impact on humankind is akin to the Industrial Revolution's. The fundamental difference is that the influence of the former is more profound and ubiquitous. It is influencing humanity at a more personal level, thus changing how we work, live, and think. Technology has both forced and enabled industries from business to health care, banking, tourism and hospitality, entertainment, and education to assess and rethink their operational processes.

As we incorporate technology into our daily lives, we become so comfortable and accustomed to it that we take it for granted. When ATMs were first introduced, some of us distrusted them. Concerns about the machine's ability to conduct a secure, private transaction delayed our acceptance of the new devices. Now, for better or worse, we have embraced even the smartphone, which we use for every aspect of our lives. Despite the very same privacy concerns, we use our smartphones to select our commute, monitor our bank accounts, pulse, physical activity, and the quality of our sleep, conduct financial transactions, plan our day based on weather forecasts, and decide where to shop, eat, and take a vacation. Technology has made everything that touches our lives more convenient and accessible, thus making us more efficient.

Korean culture, of all cultures, recognizes the value of efficiency. I dare say that efficiency is a way of life for Koreans, as evidenced by the pervasive *pali pali* culture. In Korea, efficiency is everywhere, from how students answer math problems to the use of student rankings for top-tier university admission and major corporation prospects, from driving habits to the saturation of love motels, and from fast-food delivery to restaurant dining.

Work Ethic

One of the practices that caught my attention in Korean culture is the work ethic. Generally, Koreans work six days per week. Furthermore, it is common for entrepreneurs and small business owners to work seven days per week. One Sunday, I experienced a drain problem in my apartment. I called a handyman to resolve the issue. He came and promptly took care of the situation and did not even charge me overtime for a Sunday visit. I had a similar event with my telecommunications service under similar circumstances. In my experience, a weekend service visit like this would be unheard of in the United States.

According to the Organization for Economic Cooperation and Development (OECD), in 2017, Koreans were second only to Mexicans in the number of hours they worked per year, with an average of 2,024 to Mexico's 2,257. By comparison, Americans and Japanese averaged 1,780 and 1,710 hours, respectively. The average working hours of the 35 OECD countries reporting data was 1,759. Therefore, Koreans worked 265 more hours than the average of OECD countries.[1]

The last year I resided full-time in Korea was 2017. In Chapter Three, I observed that at the time, residential and non-residential construction was ongoing in Jeonju, the city where I lived. I also noted that it was common to see construction sites constantly in operation, even on Sundays and late evenings. In contrast, in the U.S., construction workers toiling on Sundays are uncommon. As I walked by these construction sites, I often wondered about the propensity for safety concerns when construction workers work long hours for seven days each week. As my stay in the country progressed, particularly after the *Sewol* ferry tragedy, I became more conscious of man-made accidents, besides those that occurred in and around construction sites.

Disasters

Natural disasters are caused by uncontrollable forces such as hurricanes, typhoons, floods, volcanic eruptions, earthquakes, landslides, and lightning. Because these disasters are not preventable, people can and should prepare for them. The preparation may include storing fresh potable water for drinking and food preparation, having sufficient canned food to last several days, and maintaining a well-supplied first aid kit.

With the advent of industry, man-made disasters began to occur more frequently. These incidents include freak accidents, train derailments, building and bridge collapses, oil spills, gas leaks, environmental pollution, nuclear meltdowns, and traffic accidents on land, water, or air. Because these tragedies are usually associated with human error, they are preventable but nearly impossible to predict. Their frequency should diminish, given the appropriate precautions and attentiveness to safety standards. Some incidents may be categorized as industrial accidents depending on the circumstances, the individuals involved, the people affected, and the magnitude. I will discuss those in Chapter Eight.

As I began researching man-made accidents in Korea before and after the *Sewol* ferry incident, the causes cited and the recurring themes that connected most of them intrigued me. The propensity for man-made accidents and unnecessary loss of innocent lives motivated me to continue my research and eventually write this book. I have lived long enough to recognize the basic premise of man-made accidents: Although preventable, they can occur anywhere, anytime. Korea has undoubtedly had more than its fair share of them. I sincerely hope that identifying the recurring themes can help prevent future man-made tragedies in Korea and across the globe by sensitizing people to take the necessary precautions to avoid them.

In the chapters about education, I illustrate how the emphasis on efficiency and overreliance on test preparation can lead to the acquisition of study habits detrimental to experiential learning, the most profound aspect of education, or a situation where the ends justify the means. In the chapters about man-made and industrial accidents, we examine how efficiency plays a central role as the conduit for greed and skirting public safety laws in pursuit of short-term financial gains or another instance where the ends justify the means.

From a humanistic perspective, one of the unfortunate outcomes of efficiency in man-made and industrial accidents is the loss of innocent lives. Humankind's existence on this planet has become extremely precarious. We need to minimize the risk factors by genuinely caring for one another and upholding public safety to avoid adding to the perils of natural disasters. These include those caused by extreme weather patterns attributable to global warming. Minimizing risk factors may mean that we need to reduce our emphasis on efficiency, ensure that our safety regulations are current and strictly enforced, and recognize that greed is self-serving and not in the best interest of humanity.

Rapid Urbanization

As expected, along with the remarkable macroeconomic success and the technological advancements after the Korean War, the country underwent an astounding urbanization and migration from rural to urban areas between 1960 and 1990. Based on World Bank data, the urban population experienced a remarkable 46-point increase from 28% to 74% of the total population in those 31 years. By comparison, in the following 32 years, from 1991 to 2022, the urban population increased at a more moderate pace of seven percentage points from 74% to 81%.[2]

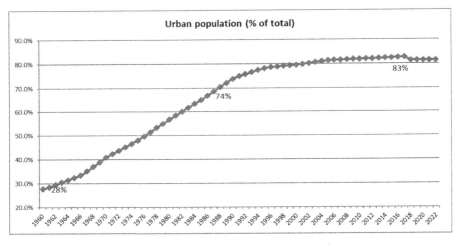

Figure 1: Urban Population (% of Total)[3]

The annual urban population growth in the 30 years from 1961 to 1990 was between 3.3% and 7.5%. This rapid urbanization rate reflects the economic expansion during the same period. By contrast, in the ensuing 32 years, from 1991 to 2022, the highest increment recorded was 2.5% in 1991. Furthermore, the growth rate has been decreasing ever since. It has remained less than 1% in each of the last 20 years, from 2003 to 2022. Finally, a negative urban population growth was registered in 2021 and 2022.

Because of the rapid and unprecedented migration from rural to urban areas, the construction industry experienced a windfall never seen before in Korea. This was particularly true in housing, as well as in general infrastructure development. As a result of the demand for housing in the latter half of the 1950s and in the 1960s, "many buildings and houses were constructed without

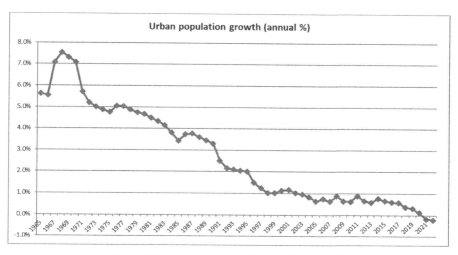

Figure 2: Urban Population Growth (Annual %)[4]

permits."[5] Furthermore, when Seoul was named host of the 1988 Summer Olympics, the required infrastructure development placed additional pressure on the already overstretched construction industry. Moreover, the country had protectionist policies in that period, requiring Korean companies to complete all construction. The development expansion provided unique opportunities for Korean entrepreneurs to generate profits of extraordinary proportions. Unfortunately, these conditions also opened the doors to greed, corruption, and disregard for public safety.

Man-Made Accidents

In this section, I analyze three man-made accidents. The selection criteria for the three incidents identified for discussion are as follows: They resemble other more recent events in context or regarding behavior patterns associated with the cause of the accidents. Also, I considered the intent and scope of this book in the selection process. I also reference several other incidents during this period of rapid urbanization and economic expansion from the 1960s to the 1990s.[6] In the same period, the Korean economy grew at an average annual rate of nearly nine percent, and per capita income increased more than a hundredfold. The purpose of this section is not to provide a complete inventory of incidents or even a thorough examination of the specifics surrounding each selected event. Doing so would be beyond the scope of this book. The goal of this section, as with the entire book, is to identify the behavioral patterns surrounding those three events and determine whether similar patterns resurfaced in accidents that happened more recently from 2014 to 2018. The second edition of this book includes accidents that occurred in 2019 and 2022.

Given the parameters of this book, I also purposely avoid discussing the specific disaster response for each event even though its effectiveness, or lack thereof, may have contributed to the number of unfortunate casualties. During the economic expansion, Korea, a developing country, lacked the technology, rescue equipment, and disaster response appropriate for responding to emergencies. The nation also lacked a systematic rescue system and seamless communication between governmental agencies, which are critical during emergencies.[7] Therefore, it would be inappropriate to draw conclusions about a technologically advanced Korea in the 21st century based on events that took place when the nation was still considered a developing country. For this reason, I limit the emphasis placed on incidents during this earlier period. However, I do not minimize the tragic loss of innocent lives. Recognizing the reappearance of similar behavioral patterns at a later stage of development provides a genuine reflection on society's level of advancement. By advancement, I specify that it is not economical or technological but define it in terms of ethics, consciousness, and values, such as compassion and equality, and the importance given to public safety.

The list of accidents from that period is plentiful, and the loss of innocent lives is tragic. In addition to the three incidents selected for analysis, the list includes the partial collapse of a bridge over the Han River, a gas explosion in Daegu, a fire in a subway station in Daegu, a train derailment near Gupo station in Busan, a gas explosion in a hotel in Seoul, a dynamite explosion in a train station, and the crash of a Korean Airlines plane in Guam, human error being the primary cause of the latter. The human toll of these accidents alone amounts to at least 865 innocent lives.[8]

Three Man-Made Accidents that Typify the Prevailing Conditions during the Period of Rapid Urbanization and Economic Expansion

During this period, the prevailing environment included the unprecedented infrastructure and housing build-up to accommodate the extensive urbanization, which caused many projects to be ongoing concurrently. "Together with other stimulants such as greed for fast money, [these projects] are believed to have led to compromises of several building codes both by the companies and authorities."[9] As a result, structures erected during this period, and those that remain, were and continue to be susceptible to structural failure.

April 8, 1970 – The Wawoo Apartment Building Collapse

From the late 1950s through the 1960s, the beginning of the rapid urbanization period, Seoul was forced to accommodate the unprecedented influx of citizens from rural areas living in illegal settlements.

> President Park Chung-Hee ordered the mayor of Seoul, Kim Hyun-Ok, to build citizens apartments and house the people from these illegal settlements in them. The mayor [...] had the nickname "Bulldozer" because during his time many areas in Seoul got erased and replaced by modern large-scale structures, such as apartments, wide roads and elevated freeways. Seoul [began] to [lose its] historic streetscape, a small labyrinth-like and organic road network.[10]

The five-story Wawoo apartment building collapsed on April 8, 1970, four months after completion. It is an example of a structure erected "more rapidly than usual" and whose history concluded in a tragic disaster.[11] Reports indicate that the building was constructed in six months, from June to December 1969.[12] The investigation conducted following the collapse shows that

> the foundation columns were not resistant to the self-weight of the apartments. An insufficient amount of rebar in the foundation constructed along the mountain slopes was the direct reason for the collapse.[13]

Other contributing factors cited include "poor and too quick construction, mistakes in the static calculations, bad quality of the concrete and mountain runoff water."[14] The *Wall Street Journal* reports that per the government's *Encyclopedia of Korean Culture*, the collapse of the Wawoo apartment building "was a man-made disaster caused by corruption of construction firms and supervision agencies."[15] This incident took the lives of 33 people and injured 39.[16]

Evidence of widespread construction deficiencies and disregard for safety standards during this rapid urbanization abounds. It is reflected in the results of "an inspection of the citizen apartment[s] [which] showed that 75% of the existing buildings [did not] fulfill safety standards."[17]

October 10, 1993 – The Sinking of the *Sohae* Ferry

The *Sohae* ferry sank in the waters of the West Sea near Wi-Do Island on October 10, 1993, with 355 passengers and seven crew members aboard. A total of 292 people drowned.[18] The ferry was carrying 141 people over its capacity, plus heavy freight.[19] Various sources point to the overloading of passengers and cargo, improper maintenance of the boat, reckless navigation in extreme weather conditions, and inadequate staffing as contributing factors to the ship's sinking.[20]

June 29, 1995 – The Sampoong Department Store Collapse

The fashionable Sampoong department store in the wealthy Seocho district of Seoul exemplifies the feverish urbanization pace and almost euphoric feeling of economic well-being that permeated the affluent. Construction of the nine-story building (five floors above ground and four underground) that housed the Sampoong department store "began in 1987, amid the development boom and competing interests from infrastructure for the 1988 Olympics."[21] The building was completed two years later and collapsed on June 29, 1995, six years after completion. In this case, the changes to the original blueprint design caused structural flaws. Furthermore, because the building was erected "on a landfill site that was poorly suited to such a large structure,"[22] the foundation made it susceptible to instability.

The blueprint design changes included the addition of a fifth floor above ground, conversion of the building's fundamental purpose from residential apartments to a department store with open space and a reduced number of columns, the addition of escalators, and a food court requiring heavy restaurant equipment. Also, a 45-metric ton air conditioning unit was installed on the roof, further adding to the weight and pressure placed on the columns:[23]

> The completed building was a flat-slab structure without crossbeams or a steel skeleton, which effectively meant there was no way to transfer the load across the floors. To maximize the floor space, Lee Joon [Sampoong chairperson and owner] ordered the floor columns to be reduced to [...] 24 inches (61 cm) thick instead of the minimum of 31 inches (79 cm) in the original blueprint that was required for the building to stand safely. In addition, each column was 36 feet (11 m) apart to maximize retail space, a decision that also meant that there was more load on each column than there would have been if the

columns were closer together [...] As a result of the fifth floor's presence, the columns held up four times the maximum weight that they were supposed to support.[24]

Actions taken in this case exemplify greed, corruption, poor judgment, and the *gap* and *eul* relationship discussed in Chapter Two. Having more authority, influence, and resources than Woosung, the firm initially hired to construct the building, Lee Joon, Sampoong's chairperson, ordered the construction company to make unreasonable structural blueprint changes. When Woosung refused to make the changes, Lee Joon fired the contractor and brought his own company to complete the project. The owner bribed government officials to approve these radical building design changes.[25]

Cracks in the building began to appear on the fifth floor months before the collapse: "The management all but ignored the warning and only moved merchandise that was stored [on] the fifth floor to the basement to relieve it of some weight."[26] Various sources also report that management ordered the air conditioning units turned off to minimize the vibration and prevent further widening of the structural cracks.

Engineers were called in on the day of the collapse to conduct a cursory inspection of the building after cracks that had started to appear in April of the same year began to widen. They declared the building unsafe. Subsequently, the board of directors met. They advised Lee Joon, the chairperson, to evacuate the building. Still, he refused, citing potential revenue losses. The superstore had become a hub for upper-middle-class families, primarily homemakers. It averaged 40,000 shoppers per day during the building's five-year history.[27] "By the mid-1990s, the store's sales amounted to more than half a million U.S. dollars a day."[28] Lee himself left the building before the collapse. Greed, irresponsibility, and disregard for human lives describe the corporation chairperson's actions on the morning of the collapse.

The Sampoong department store collapse killed 502 people and injured 937.[29] "Minutes after the collapse, footage showed bloodied people walking away from the debris in shock. Rescuers recalled finding the limbs and bodies of the dead, while survivors feebly called out for help, stuck under layers of cement and twisted iron."[30]

In the aftermath of the deadly collapse, Lee Joon and his son, Lee Han-Sang, "were convicted and sent to prison for 10 1/2- and 7-year terms, respectively. Twelve local building officials were found guilty of taking bribes of as much as $17,000 (U.S. equivalent) for approving changes and providing a provisional use certificate."[31]

Following the Sampoong department store collapse, "a government survey of high-rise structures found 14% were unsafe and needed to be rebuilt, 84% required repairs, and only 2% met standards."[32] These astounding findings indicate the alarming situation of building structures in Korea at the time.

The incidents discussed above are three of the many tragedies that occurred during rapid urbanization and economic expansion (1960s-1990s). The following section examines some man-made accidents that occurred from 2014 to 2018. The criteria for choosing these accidents include the timeframe and the profound societal impact. The intent and scope of this book are factors that played a crucial role in the selection process. The causes and circumstances surrounding the incidents selected represent cultural and behavioral patterns that reoccur. They were evident in the accidents that happened during the economic expansion and again in those that took place in the recent past.

RECENT MAN-MADE ACCIDENTS

April 16, 2014 – *Sewol* Ferry Disaster: Perfect Conditions for an Accident

The sinking of the *Sewol* ferry caused 304 deaths. Most of the casualties were high school students on a field trip to Jeju Island. As of this writing, five bodies have not been recovered. The Korean Coast Guard concluded that the primary cause of the *Sewol* ferry tragedy was an unreasonably sudden turn to starboard.

The *Sewol* ferry was retrofitted two years before the accident to increase its capacity by 239 tons. Thus, it could carry additional passengers and cargo. This redesign made it more prone to tip over because of the ship's imbalance between the port and starboard side. On the day of the tragedy, the ship was overloaded with freight. Based on the prosecutor's findings, it carried 2,142 tons of cargo, almost twice the maximum limit of 1,077 tons.[33] Also, per the prosecutor's findings, the freight was not safely secured. Reports indicate that the cargo was not securely tied to save time during unloading. This attitude demonstrates Korea's emphasis on efficiency, disregarding or minimizing safety concerns. Because the freight was not securely tied, the cargo underwent a shift, which made the tilt and imbalance more pronounced when the ferry made the sharp turn. As the ferry tipped over, some of the cargo fell and blocked the exits, making it more difficult for passengers to evacuate.

Moreover, the ship "was also possibly crewed by insufficiently trained personnel."[34] This assertion is supported by survivors' statements indicating that the crew had repeatedly directed the passengers to stay put while the ferry sank. The ineptitude, poor judgment, and irresponsibility of the ferry's captain and crew are poignantly described in an editorial piece published in the Korea Herald:

> The most unfortunate thing was that the Sewol and its passengers had an utterly incapable and irresponsible crew. Had they acted how any ordinary, average maritime officer, not a hero, would have in such a situation, many more passengers could have jumped off the ship in time and gotten picked up by boats that responded to the distress call.
>
> The captain and two other crew members were arrested [...] three days after they abandoned their own ship, leaving hundreds of young students and passengers behind. It still is a mystery why they kept advising the passengers to stay inside their cabins for about two hours even after the ship began listing.
>
> It is certain that the Sewol's crew lack not only the capability to operate a ferry that can carry up to 956 passengers and make proper judgment calls in an emergency but also the minimum level of professional ethics and sense of responsibility.[35]

On April 16, 2014, the day of the *Sewol* ferry accident, *Foreign Policy* published an article titled "Why Do So Many People Die in Ferry Accidents." It describes to the letter the circumstances surrounding the tragedy before the details that led to the ship's sinking were known:

> Ferries in the developing world are often overcrowded, which can throw off a boat's balance or make it top heavy and more prone to capsizing. And when crewmembers are inadequately trained, they are uncertain of how to respond in the event of a disaster, exacerbating these problems. Moreover, government safety regulations are far less stringent – or go unenforced – in developing nations.[36]

Remarkably, although the article cited above appeared on the day of the *Sewol* ferry tragedy, it could very well describe the conditions under which the *Sohae* ferry sank two decades earlier. Furthermore, the author's most striking point in this paragraph is that the circumstances he describes apply to "ferries in the developing world." Therefore, theoretically, the conditions should apply to Korea in 1993, when the *Sohae* ferry sank and 292 people drowned. These conditions should no longer apply to Korea circa 2014 when the *Sewol* ferry accident happened. In other words, despite the country's unprecedented economic and technological advancements, people lost their lives due to circumstances that did not have parity with the nation's progress.

As expected, given the ease of access to information in our day and age, details surrounding the *Sewol* ferry incident are much more readily available than about the sinking of the *Sohae*. Given Korea's economic and technological achievements in the two decades between the two tragedies and what we know about them, what can we surmise about progress in the less tangible areas—values and consciousness? The resurfacing of similar behavioral patterns and motives twenty years into an astronomical economic and technological advancement indicates that progress in the less tangible areas—values and consciousness—does not happen at the same pace as in the more concrete domains. Unlike financial and technological progress, cultural values and attitudes are deeply ingrained in the fabric of society. The public must work deliberately to ensure that values and consciousness keep pace with economic and technological progress. Unless parity is reached in all areas, innocent lives will continue to represent the price societies pay for the imbalance between them.

In the aftermath of the *Sewol* ferry accident:

- The Prime Minister, Chung Hong-won, resigned.
- The principal at Danwon High School, where many of the victims studied, committed suicide.
- The CEO of Cheonghaejin Marine, the company responsible for operating the Sewol, was accused of violating safety rules. The firm's CEO was sentenced to ten years in prison.
- Lee, Joon-seok, the captain, was convicted of murder and sentenced to 36 years in prison for professional negligence causing death.
- The *Sewol's* engineer was sentenced to 30 years in prison.
- Crew members received sentences between five and 20 years.

May 26, 2014 – Goyang Bus Terminal Fire in Gyeonggi

On May 26, 2014, as Koreans mourned the death of more than three hundred passengers in the *Sewol* ferry catastrophe, seven people were reported dead, and more than fifty others were injured in a fire. The blaze began on the first basement level of the Goyang Bus Terminal in Gyeonggi. Welding sparks generated by contractors hired to remodel the site to build a food court may have caused the fire. By law, companies wishing to complete a building renovation or expansion that would change the site's safety features must submit a construction plan. Before commencing work, they must also obtain permission from a city government agency and a district fire station. Allegedly, the contracting company, in this case, began the work before receiving approval from the local fire station.

Furthermore, reports indicate that the contracting company requested permission from the local fire station to alter the fire prevention shutters. The fire station did not approve this request. One such shutter apparently malfunctioned, which caused toxic smoke to leak into the second floor. This leak caused the bulk of the casualties resulting from smoke inhalation. It is unclear whether the fire shutter malfunctioned or construction workers deliberately tinkered with it to prevent it from working correctly. Experts believe fewer fatalities would have been registered if the fire shutter had worked.

January 10, 2015 – Apartment Fire in Uijeongbu, Gyeonggi Province

On January 10, 2015, a fire in the ten-story Daebong Green Apartment complex in Uijeongbu killed four people and left 124 others injured, 14 in critical condition. A total of 226 people lost their homes.[37] The criminal investigation conducted jointly by the police department and the National Forensic Service (NFS) found that the fire started on the first floor near the ignition of a four-wheel motorcycle belonging to a Mr. Kim. After reviewing CCTV security video footage, the investigating team determined that Mr. Kim had applied fire using a lighter to remove the key from the ignition. Apparently, it was frozen due to extreme cold weather conditions. Reportedly, the four-wheel motorcycle caught on fire. Subsequently, strong winds caused the blaze to spread to the cars parked on the ground floor and then moved quickly to the structure, including the upper floors. "[The investigating team] showed the [security video] footage to Mr. K. He acknowledged that he applied heat to the key box with a lighter, and the fire occurred due to his carelessness. The investigation team booked him on suspicion of negligence in a fire and negligence resulting in injury and death."[38]

The fire quickly spread to two adjacent residential buildings, one a 10-story and the other, a 15-story structure. In addition to the fatalities, estimates indicate that twenty vehicles in the above-ground parking lot of the apartment building were totaled.[39]

Figure 3: The Charred Remains of the Daebong Green Apartment Complex in Uijeongbu[40]

Figure 4: Firefighters attempt to put out the fire on the first floor of the Daebong Green Apartment complex in Uijeongbu.[41]

Fire officials reported that the Uijeongbu fire spread quickly from the first-floor parking lot to higher levels because of the highly flammable materials used to cover the outer building walls.[42] An article in the *Dong-A Ilbo* covering the apartment fire in Uijeongbu refers to the exterior cladding used in the buildings in question as the "Dryvit method." However, the generic designation for this process is exterior insulation finish system (EIFS) since "Dryvit" refers to the brand name of exterior cladding. According to the *Dong-A Ilbo*:

> The method is preferred by building owners because it is cheaper by more than 50 percent than the use of stone to finish the exterior wall, and the construction period can be cut nearly in half.[43]

The *Washington Post* substantiates the inexpensive qualities as well as the energy-efficient characteristics of this exterior insulation finishing method:

> Dryvit is a brand name for a type of exterior cladding known as EIFS — for exterior insulation and finish system[s]. It consists of [a] rigid foam insulation board attached to the wall, topped by a base coat of synthetic stucco reinforced with mesh and a textured finish coat of synthetic stucco. It's waterproof, highly energy-efficient, and relatively inexpensive.[44]

Benjamin Haag explains why EIFS has been so popular in building construction. He describes the popularity of the process as follows: "Exterior Insulation Finish System (EIFS) is a non-load bearing exterior wall treatment which, due to its excellent insulation properties and design flexibility, has been a popular choice for exterior building cladding for several decades."[45]

The flammability of EIFS, however, outweighs the energy-efficient and low-cost nature of this type of building cladding. Haag further explains that structures clad with EIFS present a real challenge for firefighters when they catch on fire. He describes the flammable features of EIFS and some of the challenges they present to firefighting personnel:

> Due to the polystyrene foam insulation component, EIFS is considered combustible. Polystyrene foam is a thermoplastic material which means it will melt and flow when heated. 'Polystyrene foam will produce combustible and toxic gases at approximately 570°F and will ignite in a range between 900°F and 1,000°F' (Spadafora, 2015). When ignited, a polystyrene fire will create high heat conditions, rapid flame spread, and dense black smoke. The heat release rate for

thermoplastics can be three to five times higher than [that] of ordinary combustibles such as wood or paper. The heat of combustion for ordinary combustibles generally ranges between 6,000 and 8,000 Btu/lb (13,960-18,600kj/kg). The heat of combustion for plastics generally ranges between 12,000 and 20,000 Btu/lb (27,900-46,520kj/kg). (FM Global, 2015).[46]

The technical figures cited above may leave readers wondering how flammable polystyrene foam really is. An experiment conducted in 2010 by the Korea Institute of Construction Technology and described by the *Dong-A Ilbo* gives the reader a more concrete and dramatic image of the combustibility of this material:

The Korea Institute of Construction Technology tried to set fire to [the] inside of [a] wall measuring three meters wide and six meters long after installing exterior material [...] using [the] dryvit method [...] [The] wall caught fire in a matter of just 90 seconds. The fire completely engulfed the exterior wall in four minutes, with intense flames reaching as high as six meters, generating black toxic gas. The situation was [like the apartment] fire in Uijeongbu.[47]

Based on reports regarding the speedy spread of the fires at the apartment building in Uijeongbu and the sports complex in Jecheon, discussed below, both billowed black smoke. Also, judging by the number of victims hospitalized in critical condition after inhaling toxic fumes, the fires behaved consistently with this cladding.

Also, two other factors contributed to the rapid spread of the fire. One was the absence of a sprinkler system. Only 11- and higher-story buildings were required to have a sprinkler system at the time of the fire.[48] The second factor was the building's pilotis-style structure. It is termed "pilotis" for the support columns or piles used to raise a building, usually to the second floor, to maximize the space for parking, storage, or both. However, this type of structure can create hazardous situations. This applies particularly to fires that begin on the first floor, as was the case with this incident, because of the possibility of the blaze spreading to cars in the parking area. This scenario has a high probability of destroying and blocking the first-floor exit, thus preventing residents from evacuating the building and blocking firefighting personnel accessibility. Additionally, the structure is susceptible to spreading heat, fire, and toxic gas to the stairwell and elevator pit.

All these challenges appear to be present in the Daebong Green Apartment complex inferno in Uijeongbu. A report in the *Korea JoongAng Daily* describes in detail what happened and how residents reacted to the emergency after being trapped in the building when the fire broke out:

> The flames obstructed the main doorways on the first floor, and smoke billowed up inside the buildings. Most of the trapped victims evacuated to the rooftops and waited for helicopters to rescue them. Others who lived on the lower floors jumped out of their windows or climbed down the outer walls before firefighters arrived at the scene.[49]

Finally, after the Uijeongbu fire and calls for stricter codes involving EIFS-clad buildings, "the Public Safety and Security Ministry vowed to start a campaign to **crack down** on the use of exterior materials that are susceptible to fire."[50] The *Dong-A Ilbo* states, "…the ministry [planned] to oblige building owners and builders to use fire retardant materials, **irrespective of the building's height or use** when installing insulation materials on the exterior wall."[51] Furthermore, the *Dong-A Ilbo* reported that under existing law at the time of the Uijeongbu fire, building contractors and owners were not required to use fire retardant materials, "except in high-rise buildings, [factories,] and facilities used by the public within commercial districts."[52]

In the end, the government passed regulations prohibiting flammable cladding in the construction of buildings six stories and higher.[53] These new regulations, however, only apply to new construction. Thus, the regulations leave existing buildings that contain flammable materials intact. These structures with flammable materials present formidable challenges for firefighters and a threat to the population at large.

After the police department investigated the cause of the Uijeongbu apartment fire, the review team announced that it had "charged 15 [people] including the person who, unintentionally, started the fire […] [The] team released a report on the findings through the press saying that it would send the case to the prosecutor with the intent to prosecute."[54]

December 21, 2017 – Sports Complex Fire in Jecheon, Chungcheong Province

Twenty-nine people were reported dead and 37 injured in a fire that started on the first-floor parking lot of a sports complex. The fire quickly engulfed the eight-story building and spread to approximately 12 cars parked in the parking lot. The building also housed a sauna, a gymnasium, and several restaurants.

On December 25, 2017, the *Korea Herald* reported that

> national forensic experts concluded Saturday [December 23, 2017] the fire
> started from the first-floor ceiling of the parking lot, quickly engulfing eight
> stories in just seven minutes. Among the dead, 20 suffocated from toxic smoke
> in the female sauna.[55]

Also, the media noted that experts pointed to the outer cladding material
used in building construction as the prime suspect for the rapid spread of the
fire. They named Dryvit cladding the culprit because they consider it a "cheap
but highly flammable finishing material."[56] They also pointed out that it emits
highly toxic gases into the atmosphere in fire situations, thus causing lung
problems for people who inhale them.[57]

Besides significantly lowering building costs and reducing construction
time, Korean contractors utilize energy-efficient materials like EIFS in building
construction for their energy-efficient properties. However, given the highly
flammable qualities of EIFS cladding, more substantially fire-resistant materials should be used.

Reports also disclosed that firefighters found that Electrical Piping Shaft
(EPS) walls were not fireproof, even though fireproof EPS walls are required
to obtain city approval. Fireproof EPS walls are supposed to delay a fire from
reaching the higher floors. The lack of fireproofing enabled the fire to reach
higher levels more quickly, thus potentially causing more casualties. Apparently, the city approved the use of the building regardless.

According to the *Korea Times*, "also problematic was the structure of the
building, which was raised above the ground on pillars."[58] As noted above, this
type of building structure is termed "pilotis":

> [A pilotis structure] is susceptible to fires that start on the ground floor as staircases act like smokestacks, causing flames to spread upwards [...] The incident
> is invoking comparisons with a fire [that] erupted three years ago [in January
> 2015] at an apartment in Uijeongbu, Gyeonggi Province. The building also contained the flammable material and was constructed in a similar style.[59]

Many buildings in Korea have comparable structures. Therefore, the potential for future similar incidents is significant.

Reportedly, in July 2017, the son of the building owner conducted a fire
safety inspection. Evidently, the fact that the second-floor emergency exit
was blocked because the space was being used for storage went unreported.

Figure 5: Firefighters and forensic investigators examining the first floor of the eight-story building that housed the sports complex in Jecheon.[60]

Supposedly, the fire department conducted a building inspection in October 2017. Reports are unclear whether the emergency exit issue went undeclared. Firefighting experts believe some fire victims might have been saved if the second-floor exit had been accessible.

On December 23, 2017, the *Yonhap News Agency* disclosed that the owner had purchased the building in August 2017 and had "remodeled it to house a gym, public sauna, and other facilities."[61] Two days later, on December 25, the agency reported that after raiding the homes of an owner and a manager of the fitness center

> to investigate if they were negligent in preventing [...] [the] disaster, [...] the police appeared set to press charges of manslaughter caused by professional negligence and violation of the fire law against the 53-year-old owner, while they will push for charges of manslaughter against the 50-year-old manager.[62]

Contributing Factors

Contributing to the casualties in the fire was a non-functioning sprinkler system, thus violating fire prevention laws. Other factors include insufficient emergency exits and illegally parked cars. The latter prevented the fire trucks from expeditiously accessing the site. News sources point out that it took authorities about 15 minutes to move some illegally parked cars to enable fire trucks to reach the building. Once the vehicles were removed, there was insufficient space for the firefighters to maneuver the water delivery to the raging inferno. Ironically, days after the fire, people reportedly continued to park illegally on the same street where the burnt sports complex was located.

One of the reasons why people continued to park illegally, still blocking access to emergency equipment, was the relatively low probability of receiving a parking citation. Even in the rare instance of getting a parking ticket, the fine would have been minimal. In this case, a potential penalty was not an effective deterrent. In Korea, before August 2018, violations for parking within fifteen feet of a fire hydrant used to run approximately the equivalent of $40 to $50. However, it is widespread practice for owners of these illegally parked cars to escape with a simple warning from the police or emergency personnel.

Because parking citations are seldom issued, the concept fails as a deterrent. Some Koreans recognize the low probability of being fined for breaking the law. Therefore, when faced with being fined for parking illegally near a fire hydrant or being inconvenienced by walking farther to their destination, they opt to break the law and risk incurring a warning or a fine. By contrast, in the United States, parking violations may cost as much as $150. The fee amount varies depending on the city. Additionally, drivers are responsible for late penalties. The car is issued a citation, and no second chances are given.

Korean law allows emergency departments to move illegally parked cars if necessary, but before August 2018, this was rarely done. It was unclear who was responsible for paying towing and storage or impound fees. By comparison, the car owner is responsible for paying these fees in the United States. They can be significant and may even surpass the amount of the parking citation fee by a considerable margin.

In Korea, before August 2018, if emergency personnel had to break the windows of a car to perform their duties, their department was responsible for the damage. This may explain the emergency personnel's hesitation to break the windows of vehicles that obstructed their work. However, recently amended pertinent laws give "firefighters on the field [...] more discretion and authority in emergency situations."[63]

In similar instances in the States, insurance companies would not cover the damages caused by emergency personnel to illegally parked vehicles obstructing their duties because of owner negligence. For example, Ameriprise Auto & Home Insurance Company defines negligence as failure "to demonstrate the appropriate amount of care or responsibility for the situation. The failure to take appropriate precautions can cause [the insured] to be liable for the damage."[64] Therefore, the car owner is the responsible party.

Drivers frequently tape their cell phone numbers on the dashboard to facilitate communication with car owners. They enable anyone who needs an illegally parked car moved to communicate with the owner. This is done for the convenience of drivers who may habitually park their vehicles illegally. Therefore, the burden is on the inconvenienced person rather than the inconsiderate driver. This practice also exemplifies the tendency toward efficiency in Korean culture.

Figure 6: Typical Image of Double-Parked Cars in Korea[65]

Recurring Patterns

The Seoul Fire Department has confirmed that factors contributing to the fire in Jecheon are also present in Seoul. Following the Jecheon fire, the department inspected 319 buildings that house public bathhouses and sauna businesses. One hundred-twenty, or 37%, of the buildings inspected failed safety

Figure 7: Typical Image of Illegally Parked Cars in a Residential Area in Korea.[66]

standards. Many buildings checked did not have accessible emergency exits, either because they were blocked or for other reasons. Some buildings had the fire sprinkler systems disabled to prevent their operation.[67] If the percentage of facilities that failed safety standards in Seoul holds for the entire country, the total number of affected buildings is staggering, even for a small country like Korea. However, Young Lee and I fear that the percentage of structures not meeting safety standards may be higher outside the capital.

January 19, 2018 – Sejong Hospital Fire in Miryang, South Gyeongsang Province

Almost a month after the sports complex fire in Jecheon, a fire erupted at Sejong Hospital in the city of Miryang. Forty-six people perished in this fire, including a doctor, a nurse, and a nurse assistant. Initially, the press announced 37 fatalities; however, the death toll rose after the preliminary estimates because some of the injured were in critical condition. The *Yonhap News Agency* reported a total of 146 injuries.[68] Toxic fumes inhalation caused most of the casualties. The media disclosed that faulty wiring started the fire in the ceiling of the pantry room, which doubled as a changing room. This facility was located on the first floor of the hospital's main building. At the time, the hospital complex included the six-story main building and an annex, which housed a nursing hospital for seniors and served as a nursing home.

On January 29, 2018, the *Korea Times* published a litany of suspected safety breaches and emergency guideline violations. The first indication of a possible safety guidelines violation was the firefighters' discovery of six victims who had perished in the elevator. Universal building safety guidelines specify that elevators are not to be used in case of fire or emergency evacuation. The elevator shaft could function as a conduit for toxic gases and fire moving upward if they are used. The discovery of these victims suggests that the staff may have failed to alert them against using the elevator.

Below is a series of additional safety violations that appear to reflect cost-cutting measures:

> On Friday [January 19, 2018], the 99 patients at the hospital with 95 beds were under the care of only one doctor and eight nursing staff, indicating one medical staff member was responsible for about 11 patients. The hospital had three doctors, only two of whom worked full-time, and 23 nursing staff, in violation of the law, which states that at least six doctors and 35 nursing staff members were required for a hospital of that size. Putting too many patients in one room was also a contributing factor that prevented swift evacuation. The hospital put 20 patients in one room, which according to some surviving patients, caused difficulties when entering, leaving, or moving around it. The amount of fee-for-medical services for admitting a patient a hospital can seek from the National Health Insurance Service is the same, regardless of the number of patients a room holds. This has been the primary reason for the hospital to put as many patients as possible in a limited space.[69]

The article also discloses that Sejong Hospital had illegally remodeled the building in 2006. Subsequently, the city government fined the hospital 30 million Korean won (~$28,000) for illegal building remodeling.

Hospital administrators came under fire from the public and the press for the lack of a sprinkler system, which might have helped reduce the number of casualties. However, at a press briefing, Song Byeong-cheol, Hospital Chairman, "argued that his hospital was not subject to the mandatory installation of sprinklers due to its small size."[70]

Government officials from the ruling and opposing parties offered the customary condolences to the victims' families and pledged to support them.

Various ministry representatives were deployed to the scene of the accident to assist with the aftermath of the tragedy. They also pledged to conduct a thorough investigation to identify the cause of the fire and the responsible parties. Moreover, government officials "pledged to carry out sweeping measures to enhance public safety."[71] As of this writing, no one has operationally defined the term "sweeping measures."

In March 2018, in the aftermath of the fire, 12 people deemed either directly or indirectly responsible were indicted. They included the hospital administrator as well as former and incumbent government officials: "The defendants include[d] the head of the hospital's board, who [was] accused of violating the Building Act, the Medical Service Act, and a number of other laws in the course of running the hospital…."[72]

Eventually, the chair of the hospital board and the general manager were imprisoned for illegally renovating the facility and not following safety rules.

Tougher Measures

After the last two deadly incidents that happened within a month of each other and given the public's complicity in the man-made accidents I researched, it became evident that a radical change was needed to modify people's attitudes toward fire prevention and public safety. Following these two deadly fires, the government announced it would conduct safety inspections nationwide on approximately 60,000 "high-risk" facilities. According to the *Korea Herald*, included in the "high-risk" category were "small- and medium-sized hospitals, nursing homes, flophouses, postnatal care centers, public bathhouses, and traditional marketplaces."[73] These businesses were classified as "high-risk" because many were in buildings exempt from meeting stricter safety regulations because of their size.

The latest two tragedies finally motivated legislators to amend the Framework Act on Fire-Fighting Services. The amendment served to minimize the impact of future fires. The intended effect of the revised law was to address some disconnects between the law and actual practice. One such disconnect was exemplified by drivers who failed to yield to firefighting vehicles in traffic, even though the trucks sounded their sirens. Another disconnect was the illegal random parking, which often obstructs access to fire hydrants, emergency equipment, and firefighters. If strictly enforced, the most invaluable contribution of the law will be to change the public's attitude toward fire prevention, firefighting, and upholding public safety.

The amendment, adopted by the Seoul metropolitan government on June 27, 2018, and implemented on August 10, 2018, authorizes local police departments to designate no-parking zones within five meters of fire hydrants. It also increases fines for drivers who obstruct firefighting trucks in traffic and park their vehicles within five meters of fire hydrants or in fire-truck-only zones. The penalty was set at one million Korean won (~$896). The substantial increase in the fine sends a clear message to drivers that the government is serious about enabling firefighters' work. The amendment establishes clear guidelines and stipulates the punishment of obstructionists to curtail future fire catastrophes.

Below are two of the amendment's key points in paragraphs four and five of Article 25 of the Framework Act of Fire Services. These paragraphs clarify prior uncertainties associated with the removal of vehicles that obstruct the effort of firefighters and related costs. The adoption of this amendment is well-intentioned. However, its success will be determined by the effectiveness of its enforcement and its impact on the general public's attitude toward communal safety, as the paragraphs explain:

(3) When making urgent mobilization for firefighting activities, the director general of a firefighting headquarters, the head of a fire station, or the fire brigade commander may remove or move any parked or stopped vehicles, objects, etc. that hinder the passage of fire engines or the firefighting activities.

(4) The director general of a firefighting headquarters, the head of a fire station, or the fire brigade commander may request the relevant agency, such as the competent local government, to provide assistance regarding tow trucks, human resources, etc. in order to remove or move any parked or stopped vehicles hindering firefighting activities under paragraph (3), and the relevant agency so requested shall provide the assistance except in extenuating circumstances. <Newly Inserted by Act No. 15532, Mar. 27, 2018>

(5) A Mayor/Do Governor may pay expenses to the persons providing tow trucks, human resources, etc., pursuant to paragraph (4), as prescribed by municipal ordinance of the City/Do. <Newly Inserted by Act No. 15532, Mar. 27, 2018>[74]

Actions Speak Louder Than Words

Public safety must be one of the core values of major corporations that provide services or make products that touch people's lives. These companies impact every business sector regardless of industry, from pharmaceuticals to airlines, power plants, and railroads. Adopting core values emphasizing public safety is not enough, especially if companies fail to back their statements with actions and sufficient funding. Corporations can quickly lose the public's trust if they place efficiency or financial profits over public safety. More importantly, it is unconscionable to put people's lives at risk, whether they be customers, patients, passengers, or workers, for the sake of efficiency or financial profits.

Korea has invested much effort, time, technology, and money to develop and expand the transportation system known as high-speed trains or bullet trains. The country ranks ninth among the elite nations with the most kilometers of high-speed rail, behind China, Japan, Spain, France, and Germany.[75] See Table 1.

Table 1: Countries with the Most High-Speed Rail[76]

Rank	Country	Operational High-Speed Rail (Km)
1	China	25,000
2	Spain	3,100
3	Germany	3,038
4	Japan	2,765
5	France	2,647
6	Sweden	1,706
7	United Kingdom	1,377
8	Italy	1,350
9	South Korea	1,048
10	Turkey	745

Korail, the state-owned national rail operator, has adopted safety as a component of one of its core values. At the time of this writing, these values are expressed on the official Korail website as follows: "Core Values: Safety First, Customer Satisfaction, Change, and Challenge [...] We prioritize safety over work performance."[77]

However, the public has questioned the company's commitment to safety. Despite this commitment, many train accidents, particularly high-speed KTX trains and subways, have happened. For three weeks in November and December of 2018, 10 accidents occurred, culminating with the derailment of the Seoul-bound KTX from Gangneung.[78] These accidents left 15 people injured. Reports indicate that the high-speed train was traveling at 103 kilometers (64 miles) per hour. Experts reported that the derailment could have "caused serious casualties," had the train been traveling faster or "moving through a curved section."[79] The *Korea Times* reported that "according to Korail records, there [were] more than 660 mechanical failures on its trains between 2013 and July [2018]."[80]

Train accidents represent more than mechanical failures. Reportedly, these accidents also reflect a reduction in Korail's maintenance budget. According to the *Korea Times*:

> Despite the increasing number of train failures each year, Korail cut its hiring budget for rail maintenance and repair workers by around 10 billion won ($8.9 million) from 2015 to 2017. Its records show it operated with 205 fewer repair personnel than recommended to keep almost 10,000 kilometers of railroad in working condition.
>
> The spending cuts, at the risk of passenger safety, are expected to continue. Korail recorded an operating loss of more than 500 billion won [~$445.1 million in 2017].[81]

Three observations are in order regarding the number of increasing mechanical failures and operating losses that have allegedly forced Korail to significantly reduce its maintenance budget: First, based on the number of mechanical failures, it appears that Korail has failed to live up to its public commitment to safety, which it claims on its website. Second, the public has questioned political appointments to key positions at Korail and other corporations. The media has cast doubt on the administration's resolve to deal with public safety concerns. They have also questioned whether the leadership appointed to run Korail has the necessary experience and expertise in rail safety. Specifically, an opinion article appearing in the *Korea Times* on December 14, 2018, explicitly questions non-expert appointments to susceptible positions dealing with public safety. The article cites as an example the resignation under fire of the former Korail CEO, Oh Young-sik, who "offered to resign after a strong backlash against his lack of expertise in trains and public transportation."[82] Furthermore, the piece goes on to strongly criticize other appointments to posts linked to public safety:

> It seems hardly a day goes by without a safety-related problem. President Moon Jae-in has often mentioned the Sewol ferry sinking to highlight his emphasis on public safety. But even after all the controversy over the appointment of the former Korail leader, Moon appointed another non-expert to lead the Korea Airport Corporation....

The latest series of accidents, coupled with incomprehensible appointments to public corporations that are closely linked to people's lives, lead many to believe that this administration is not very serious about doing things better than its predecessors to ensure public safety.[83]

Third, given the company's mechanical failure record and massive operating losses, is it time for the government to acknowledge that the current business model is not working? Is it time to try something different? Insanity, as per Einstein and others, is doing the same thing repeatedly and expecting a different outcome. Suppose government leaders genuinely want different results from Korail. In that case, they need the fortitude to do something different.

Concluding Thoughts about Man-Made Accidents

Reports indicate that the Sejong Hospital Fire in Miryang, one of the latest in a long string of man-made accidents and mishaps going back to the *Sewol* ferry catastrophe, eroded the people's confidence in the country's safety standards. In the wake of the most recent accidents, Koreans are beginning to recognize the repetitive patterns surrounding the constant breach of safety rules and regulations. However, imposing even the most stringent safety statutes alone will not prevent accidents. The public must adopt a mindset that accepts safety regulations and understands and internalizes the spirit and intent behind them. Most importantly, cultural values must inherently incorporate an intention to adhere to safety standards because doing so is in everyone's best interest.

Following the *Sewol* ferry catastrophe, the *Korea Herald* published an article titled "Culture Closely Tied to Korea's Vulnerability to Disasters." The author, Kim Hoo-ran, identifies two cultural factors contributing to man-made disasters. First, is failure to follow the rules, and second, is the *pali pali* culture. These are two characteristics permeating the Korean culture that I have also noted throughout my observations about everyday life, from work, eating, and driving habits to education. Below is an excerpt from the article:

Failure to stick to the rules has been a major contributing factor in most of Korea's man-made disasters.... Some of the accidents that could have been foreseen and prevented had the relevant rules and regulations been observed....

The culture of "ppalli ppalli," or "hurry hurry," is a byproduct of the era [that] saw economic development as the overarching goal. The whole country was in overdrive, disregarding rules and procedures if necessary, as it pursued accelerated economic development. Following decades of such circumvention of laws, Korean society became desensitized to the risks it was taking.[84]

Many of the catastrophes we discuss appear to have been caused by multiple factors involving safety code violations. Responsible parties and the general public violated these codes. The public's disregard for safety rules appears in long-established behavior patterns. They include utilizing facilities for unintended purposes, remodeling buildings and vessels without the proper permits or inspections, and pushing the limit of facilities, vessels, and equipment to a breaking point with the sole intent of maximizing efficiency and, thus, financial profits. In many instances, the public's behavior appears to be a contributing factor that exacerbates the challenges of an accident site. Blocking emergency vehicles in traffic en route to an accident site while sounding their sirens and parking illegally in front of hydrants or building entrances, thus blocking access to emergency vehicles, contribute to accident casualties in tangible ways.

The Power of Social Media

During my latest visit to Korea in 2023, I learned that law-abiding citizens, recognizing the considerable impact of inconsiderate and irresponsible people who indirectly contribute to accident casualties, are taking matters into their own hands. They are doing their part to change the long-standing paradigm of disregarding public safety. As an example of this deeply rooted mindset, people continued to behave irresponsibly even after stricter laws were adopted to facilitate the work of firefighting personnel. To curtail this conduct, responsible citizens have taken the initiative to use social media to shame individuals who engage in this behavior. They take pictures of drivers and their vehicles and post them on social media. As a result of this grassroots movement, emergency vehicles are beginning to weave their way through the congested streets of Seoul more quickly to arrive at their destinations more promptly. The result is limiting damage to structures and potentially saving innocent lives.

This approach positively impacts people's behavior because it is based on a Korean cultural attribute discussed earlier—social conformity—which is congruent with unity and harmony. Individuals whose behavior sets them apart from the rest of the crowd are disrupting social harmony. The act of posting pictures of these individuals on social media brings shame to the perpetrators and their families. Stricter regulations regarding public safety may not be effective deterrents in Korea; however, shaming through social media is helping to force violators to behave responsibly and raise awareness.

The subject of public or social shaming is a very complex and controversial topic that goes beyond the scope of this book. Therefore, we will not delve into it. However, suffice it to say that public or social shaming is an impulse deeply rooted in the human psyche that prompts us to promote the group's survival over the individual by utilizing policing tactics. Its premise aligns with Korean values that espouse the sacrifice of the individual for the good of the whole. Public or social shaming can effectively prevent individuals from following their worst instincts. Still, it can also get out of control and cause severe social and psychological harm to targeted individuals. Therefore, we recognize it as a human instinct and a tool used to apply social pressure but do not condone it when it crosses the line by violating human privacy rights and inflicting social or psychological harm to individuals.

Historical Perspective

Poor decisions, greed, corruption, and blatant disregard for public safety are symptomatic of developing nations. These are some trends that existed during the rapid economic expansion and urbanization. As a result of the prevailing conditions during Korea's transitional period from a developing nation to a technologically advanced society, the Korean people had to cope with some tragic and life-changing man-made accidents. Regrettably, some practices and attitudes vis-à-vis public safety evident during this transformational period have remained deeply ingrained in the culture and have resurfaced in more recent incidents. The fact that some of these practices and attitudes keep reappearing suggests that societies transitioning from a developing stage to a more advanced economic and technological level must work deliberately to ensure that ethics, values, and consciousness keep pace with other advancements. Therefore, societies in transition must consciously ensure that progress is congruent with the nation's fundamental principles.

University of Southern California History Department Professor Hwang Kyung Moon wrote a piece titled "Lessons from Disasters" following the *Sewol* ferry accident. He asserts that Korean people underwent a period of reflection and soul-searching after the tragic accidents during the economic expansion. He makes the following assertion:

> Koreans [...] came to understand that such behavior [The behavior associated with the collapse of the Sampoong Department Store.] was symptomatic of a

more expansive problem in their society and culture, and that, somehow, they all shared responsibility for it.

Societal elites and common people alike took a closer look at the mentalities and ethics of the period of rapid economic growth over the previous several decades. They wondered whether, in the rush to achieve industrialization, the country had lost its collective soul, willing to take too many shortcuts or failing to consider the broader, less tangible costs of chasing wealth.[85]

Given the incessant accidents in the more recent past and the recurring behavioral patterns associated with them, is it time for Koreans to undergo another reflection and soul-searching period? Do they need to determine whether the lessons from the past have fallen on deaf ears? Are they still chasing wealth at all costs? Is it time for Koreans to ask themselves: "What role do we, as a society, play in this accident-prone environment?"

The repeating patterns and similarities to prior accidents identified in this book should not surprise Koreans. News outlets have published opinion articles following significant events, comparing the conditions and identifying the commonalities between the latest incident and previous accidents. Given the repeat patterns, these articles understandably reflect emotions such as frustration, anger, despair, and a sense of impatience, and impotence. Yet, in the end, the authors and editors muster a ray of hope that things can change, provided that the general public's attitude shifts. Understandably, Korea's psyche was affected enormously after the sinking of the *Sewol* ferry because of the tragic loss of innocent lives and the string of deadly accidents that followed in the same year. The two quotes below from opinion articles illustrate my point.

The excerpt below is from an opinion article published following the Hyosarang Hospital fire on May 28, 2014, the latest in a string of accidents after the *Sewol* ferry tragedy.

We are dumbfounded that this litany of terrible events has come at a time when the nation is engaged in an intense debate over safety standards while people are soul-searching following Korea's worst ever maritime disaster which killed more than 300 people. What's most regrettable is that incompetence, irresponsibility and a lack of safety awareness are commonly behind all these disasters.[86]

The writer's words convey a feeling of frustration and a sober sense of reality and helplessness. He compares the tragedy at Hyosarang Hospital to another fire that occurred four years earlier. Additionally, the article acts as an omen of hospital accidents since its publication.

> The latest hospital fire is reminiscent of a fire that blazed through an elderly nursing center in Pohang, North Gyeongsang Province, four years ago, when 10 people were killed, mostly from smoke inhalation. It's pathetic that we learned nothing from that deadly incident....
>
> There is no denying a possible recurrence of similar calamities in them, given that hospitals and nursing homes for the elderly have mushroomed over the past decade in accordance with the country's rapid population aging.
>
> The recurring disasters are a reminder that there are no safe places in Korea, but that's why we should double [our] efforts to try to ensure safety in public facilities.[87]

In a separate opinion article titled "Old Habits Die Hard, the author briefly describes accidents that took place on May 2, May 26, and May 28, 2014, following the sinking of the *Sewol* ferry. He concludes:

> Those cases reveal that nothing has changed since the Sewol tragedy. Our society is business as usual, as if the shipwreck never happened. We still stick to our old habits.[88]

As I read this opinion piece, I sense the frustration of a writer in utter amazement at the public's apparent insensitive attitude after a tragic accident and the total disregard for its root causes in their eagerness to get back to business as usual.

The opinion piece writer further reports that Kim Geo-sung, Chairperson of Transparency International Korea, who was present at a roundtable discussion organized by the *Korea Times*, "stressed that the nation should focus on long-term remedies to rebuild society by restoring values that respect human lives."[89] I found this statement quite refreshing for a country that has paid dearly for efficiency and wealth at all costs.

The author concludes with a sober remark about the litany of accidents in the country and the need for societal change:

> I am extremely sorry to say that Korea still has a long way to go before becoming a safe place to live. We have to take a first step, however small it may be, to break out of our old habits and change ourselves to cure the ills of our society.[90]

These are all perfectly accurate assertions. However, the most critical point that Koreans today need to recognize is that the country has moved on from the period of rapid economic expansion to a more stable stage of development. This evolution has contributed to the country's prominent position among developed nations. The strategies that helped to propel Korea to its current position are misaligned with the current stage of development. At most, they are counterproductive. The time has come to recognize that the current stage of development in the evolutionary process calls for prioritization of intangibles, such as valuing human life and raising consciousness. At this level, the collective well-being, not individual convenience or materialistic wealth at all costs, dictates the course of action.

Update

Since the initial writing of this book, man-made accidents have persisted. The point is not that mishaps continue to occur since they happen even in the most advanced countries. What is significant, and at the same time sad, is that behavior patterns observed in previous incidents keep repeating. This recurring pattern seems to indicate that the lessons of earlier disasters have either been ignored or are not taken seriously.

July 27, 2019 – Nightclub Loft Collapse in Gwangju

Most notably, around 2:30 in the morning of July 27, 2019, two Korean nationals were killed and 17 injured when the loft of a nightclub in Gwangju collapsed.[91] Among the wounded were foreign athletes competing in the July 12-28 FINA (Fédération Internationale de Natation or International Swimming Federation) World Championships in Gwangju, located approximately 330 kilometers (~205 miles) south of Seoul.[92] According to reports, about 370 patrons were inside the nightclub when the accident happened. Approximately 100 were "on the loft area, which was 2.5 meters [~8.2 feet] above the lower floor."[93]

Initial reports by news sources, including *Yonhap News Agency*, the *Korea Herald*, and the *Korea Times*, indicate that at least a portion of the loft was "illegally" expanded "without the city's authorization."[94]

The *Chosun Media* disclosed the following information:

> According to the Gwangju Police Department, the nightclub operator expanded and fixed the illegal structure on the second floor three times. The report also

points out that the welding process was performed by an acquaintance of the club owner who did not have a welding license or qualified experience. Consequently, the police booked him on manslaughter charges.[95]

This latest accident presents another example of behavior patterns reflected in actions taken without regard to public safety by breaking the rules and making structural changes without the proper permits. As in other incidents, these actions have a similar motive: financial gains, which are actualized through efficiency and cutting corners.

Deadly accidents, such as the sports complex in Jecheon, the apartment fire in Uijeongbu, the hospital fire in Miryang, and the nightclub in Gwangju, provide the public with a reality check about the potential proliferation of construction issues. Usually, after these types of incidents, the government conducts inspections of similar facilities to determine the possible extent of the problems. After the loft collapse in the Gwangju nightclub, *Dong-A Media* reporters, not the government, investigated similar establishments in three cities:

> [They] reviewed the public records of Seoul, Busan, and Daegu nightclubs. The team randomly selected and visited 35 [of them]. They found 25 of the 35 clubs added illegal structures, such as a balcony. They also found that government officials cited 10 of those 25 clubs and ordered them to clear or detach the unlawful structures. However, they [nightclub operators] did not comply with the order and continued to operate the business.[96]

Furthermore, the article states bluntly why nightclub operators fail to comply with government orders to remove illegal expansions. The report asserts: "They are not following the demolition orders because the revenues from illegal expansions are much higher than the penalties they have to pay when caught in crackdowns."[97] This explicit statement supports an observation that Young Lee and I have made regarding the role of fines as deterrents. These penalties are in areas such as illegal parking, which prevents firefighters from performing their duties, and substandard construction that endangers people's lives. Fines must be high enough to deter illegal acts or actions that put public safety at risk.

However, the most important takeaway from the investigations by government officials after other deadly accidents in general and the research by

Dong-A Media reporters about unauthorized structural additions in night-clubs is the potential extent of problems with existing structures and the risk to the public. Given these findings, the potential for further loss of lives exists, even if all future construction and remodeling are done by licensed contractors following strict safety guidelines and with the required permits. However, sharing these findings with the public is a step in the right direction. It remains to be seen whether the government, building owners and the public will take the steps needed to implement an effective risk management program. Such a plan should include undoing years of misguided decisions.

October 29, 2022 – Itaewon Crowd Crush

On Friday, October 28, 2022, the first day of the Halloween weekend, large crowds of young men and women in their 20s and 30s landed in Itaewon, a popular nightlife district in Seoul, to start the celebration, the first since the COVID-19 pandemic without mask and distance restrictions. The exuberance was palpable. Available information indicates the district's narrow streets and alleys lined with restaurants and bars were packed. The previous year, the event was not nearly as well attended. However, in 2022, people felt liberated from the pandemic and were anxious to celebrate Halloween. The large crowd on Friday should have warned the authorities about what would come the following night.

Based on news sources, merchants in the area had requested the city to require Seoul metro trains to bypass the Itaewon station during the Halloween celebration for crowd control purposes. However, the Seoul Transportation Corporation claimed it did not receive a formal request.[98] Sources report that approximately 130,000 people passed through the Itaewon subway station on Saturday, October 29, far exceeding the number of riders for previous Saturdays of Halloween weekend as far back as pre-pandemic year 2018.[99] See Figure 8.

On Saturday night, the crowd was much larger than the night before. Estimates indicate that more than 100,000 people descended upon Itaewon before the night was over. According to news sources, the call log to the police department shows that at least 13 emergency calls started roughly around 6:34 p.m., warning of the chaos and perceived danger caused by the excessively large crowd and pleading for help. However, "no significant reinforcements

Figure 8: Crowds exit Itaewon Station on October 29, 2022.[100]

were sent for hours."[101] In addition, only four emergency calls resulted in mobilized police officers. The revelers packed into World Food Street and the sloped 16-foot-wide alleyway "where most of 158 lives would be lost in a gruesome crush."[102] The inclined alley is lined with bars and restaurants, and it connects World Food Street and Itaewon Road just a few feet from the Itaewon subway exit. See Figure 9. One of the attractions was a DJ party scheduled to start at 10:00 p.m. at the 108 Hip Hop Lounge located in the alley. See Figure 10.

Figure 9: Site of the Halloween Crowd Crush in Seoul's Itaewon District[103]

Surprisingly, only 137 police officers were assigned to the area, or one police officer for every 730 people. Their mandate was to focus on "traffic duty and crime prevention."[104] Since the police department did not anticipate the Halloween crowd to be larger than in previous years, they focused their effort on a demonstration in another part of the city. This is yet another example of efficiency serving as the driving force for taking action.

By 10:00 p.m., the celebration had reached a crescendo with thousands of costumed young men and women walking up and down World Food Street and packing into the sloped and narrow alleyway. At 10:15, people started falling over on top of each other like dominoes at the most crowded part of the alley. See Figure 10. The few police officers that were on the scene at the time tried but had a difficult time pulling the unconscious victims, given the weight of the crowd. At the same time, revelers were still pushing their way into the alley from World Food Street. Experts estimate that the "crowd density shot up to 10.74 people per square meter at 10:25 p.m. on the barely 4-meter-wide (13.1 feet) bottleneck path."[105] See Figure 11. They also note that closing access to both sides of World Food Street before the crush occurred would have helped to mitigate the number of victims.

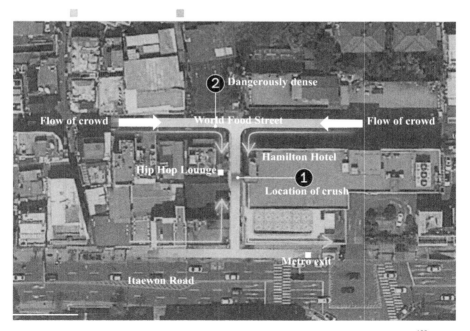

Figure 10: Flow of Crowd, Dangerously Dense Area, and Location of Crush[106]

Figure 11: Crowds pack inclined alley from World Food Street.[107]

News sources disclosed that

at least 16 more emergency calls came in between 10:08 p.m. and 10:22 p.m. when video shows five officers trying to pull out unconscious victims.

Yet it wasn't until 10:39 p.m. that emergency personnel closed both ends of the alley – a lag of roughly half an hour that allowed foot traffic to continue into the area, hampered rescue efforts, and undoubtedly increased the fatalities, according to the experts' review of the materials. Another 11 minutes elapsed before police mounted a broad response, according to department records.[108]

The first four ambulances were dispatched at 10:27 p.m., followed by six more minutes later. Witnesses reported that around 11:00 p.m., police officers were directing people to make way for ambulances to enter the alley. There were so many victims that ordinary people volunteered to administer CPR. Twenty-six of the 158 casualties were foreign nationals.[109] Later, a teenager who lost his best friend and his girlfriend in the tragedy committed suicide. The government, under pressure, decided to add the young man to the official death toll.

On January 13, 2023, Son Je-han, chief of the special police investigation team looking into the crowd crush, held a press conference in Seoul to announce the inquiry's findings: "The special police investigation team concluded the crowd crush was a 'man-made' disaster caused by authorities' failure to come up with disaster prevention measures and respond promptly to an emergency situation."[110] In short, it was a preventable tragedy. Additionally, the investigating team referred 23 government officials for prosecution for fatal professional negligence and other charges.[111]

- One of the traits that struck me about Koreans is their work ethic.
- Efficiency is a way of life for Koreans, as evidenced by the *pali pali* culture.
- The advent of industry brought about more man-made disasters.
- Without a doubt, Korea has had more than its fair share of catastrophes.
- From the human perspective, one of the unfortunate byproducts of efficiency, as evidenced by industrial and man-made accidents, is the loss of innocent lives.
- The unfortunate loss of innocent lives motivated me to conduct research and write this work.

Industrial Accidents: The Result of the Imbalance between Efficiency, Financial Gains, and Public Safety

The reasons for including a separate chapter on recent industrial accidents are threefold. First, the environment and circumstances associated with these incidents differ from those examined in Chapter Seven in that they occur while performing work-related duties, in most instances for industrial companies. Also, industrial accidents happen because of unsafe conditions, unsafe acts, or both. Furthermore, they can affect many people or a large area. However, not all accidents that involve many people are industrial accidents. For example, the sinking of the *Sewol* ferry and the Sampoong Department Store collapse were not industrial accidents even though they affected many people, and unsafe conditions and acts were present. Second, recent industrial accidents are producing profound repercussions in Korean society. Third, the potential to raise the consciousness of an entire nation to the necessity of improving working conditions and upholding public safety has begun to materialize. Before delving into the specifics surrounding the events selected for discussion, the following two definitions will help to clarify the parameters used to identify the incidents discussed in this chapter.

Industrial Accidents Defined

The *Collins English Dictionary* provides two definitions of an industrial accident:

1. An accident that happens to an employee of an industrial company during the course of their work.
2. A large-scale accident that is caused by an industrial company and affects a lot of people or a large area.[1]

This chapter will focus exclusively on accidents that happen to "employees of an industrial company during the course of their work."

The second definition comes from *Career Trend*:

> Industrial accidents are severe mishaps that result in injuries to people and damage to property or the environment. For example, an explosion or fire at a pyrotechnics manufacturing facility is an industrial accident, as is the accidental release of toxic chemicals to the environment when a storage tank fails. Types of industrial accidents vary from one place to the next, but **most are a result of unsafe conditions and unsafe acts**.[2]

The "unsafe conditions and unsafe acts" portion of this definition is critical because the predisposition to accidents is significantly reduced without these unique conditions and acts.

As with man-made accidents in the previous chapter, the number of incidents within the definition of industrial accidents remains sizable. However, as mentioned earlier, this book focuses primarily on behavioral patterns within the Korean cultural context, not exclusively on accidents. Therefore, as we considered the potential incidents for inclusion and their related circumstances, we looked for patterns that epitomize the cultural norms to select the specific events discussed below.

Seoul Metro Accidents

We will begin the discussion of recent industrial accidents with those that took place from 2013 to 2016 at Seoul Metro, which oversees the day-to-day operations of lines 1-4 of the Seoul subway.[3] Seoul Metro experienced four deadly industrial accidents from 2013 to 2016: 1) January 20, 2013, at Seongsu Station; 2) August 29, 2015, at Gangnam Station; 3) May 28, 2016, at Guui Station; and 4) September 3, 2016, near Seongsu Station. All these incidents resulted in fatal tragedies, and they meet the criteria specified in the Career Trend definition of industrial accidents: They were the **result of unsafe conditions or unsafe acts**. They also meet the Collins English Dictionary definition of an industrial accident in that they happened **to an employee of an industrial company during the course of their work**.[4] In all four cases, the individuals killed while performing job-related duties were members of subcontracting firms contracted by Seoul Metro, which is part of the Seoul Metropolitan Government (SMG).[5]

January 20, 2013 – Seoul Metro Accident at Seongsu Station

Information about this accident is rather sketchy because of the time elapsed since the event. However, reports indicate that on January 20, 2013, an inspector was killed at Seongsu Station while performing an inspection alone on subway screen door sensors.

According to the *Korea JoongAng Daily*, after this tragedy, Seoul Metro implemented new guidelines to prevent future "accidents involving screen doors."[6] Therefore, this accident marked the before-and-after era requiring maintenance workers to perform their duties in pairs "at all times when repairing screen doors."[7] In other words, "working alone on screen doors became a violation of safety guidelines."[8] Also, "workers are supposed to only work on the outside of doors during subway operation hours and report to the station before working inside the doors."[9] However, because mishaps under similar conditions kept occurring, it was evident that workers were not following the new guidelines consistently. As a result of the persistent accidents at Seoul Metro, the public has questioned the effectiveness of the safety training and oversight of the company's subcontractors.

August 29, 2015 – Seoul Metro Accident at Gangnam Station

Soompi reported that according to *KBS* (Korean Broadcasting System) *News*, Mr. Cho, a 28-year-old maintenance worker, was killed by a subway train while performing repair work on a screen door at Gangnam Station on August 29, 2015. This report shows Mr. Cho was working alone even though subway safety regulations require that "at least two workers [be] present at all repair sites."[10] The report mentions other regulations related to operations, including the stipulation that

> No repairs are ongoing while the subway is in operation, and [...] in the case of a repair that must be done during hours of operation, a report is made, and appropriate measures are taken.[11]

However, the article also underscores that there are no consequences for breaching the regulations.

> A Seoul Metro representative stated, 'There is no penalty for not following the rules. There is simply a clause that states that in the case of an accident, the service company is to take full responsibility.'[12]

The paragraph cited provides insightful comments about an environment prone to accidents. First, safety rules exist, but they are not enforced. Second, as noted by the company representative, there are no penalties for not following the rules. The first two points are patterns of behavior in Korean society that were observed and extensively discussed in previous chapters. These patterns concern such activities as driving and illegal parking, which are also related to public safety. Third, the Seoul Metro representative alludes to the liability associated with the contractor-subcontractor relationship. He stipulates that the subcontractor bears full responsibility in case of an accident. As stated earlier, this practice appears to be in place to protect large companies, particularly the *chaebols*. By its very nature, it is analogous to the *gap* and *eul* relationship. In such a dualistic situation, the entity with the most influence, power, and resources receives better treatment or the most concessions. Fourth, an article published by the *Korea Times* covering this accident confirms that Mr. Cho was "an employee of the operator's subcontractor."[13] The operator was Seoul Metro.

Additionally, the article reported that Mr. Cho "opened the door manually at around 7:30 p.m. to run a check on it, although it was during subway operation hours."[14] A train arrived while he was working on the track side of the platform. Consequently, he was jammed between the door and the train. As a result, Mr. Cho sustained fatal injuries.

In the *Korea Times*' article cited above, the writer quotes a Seoul Metro official as saying:

> Repair workers can open the door, but during subway operation hours, they are supposed to only work on the platform side, not on the track side.[15]

This statement underscores the lax supervision of subcontracting workers by both Seoul Metro and the subcontracting company. It also suggests that the training may be inadequate. It is unclear whether Mr. Cho was aware of the regulation or not. The news source also reported that according to the Seoul Metro official, no one contacted the operations control center requesting a temporary halt to the operations. Furthermore, he is quoted as saying:

> According to safety requirements, two or three workers should conduct repairs [...] during subway operation hours, but Cho undertook the job alone.[16]

However, the article based on *KBS News* presents a very different picture. It includes Mr. Cho's fiancée's statements, which appear to confirm the pressure

applied by the subcontracting company and the unsafe conditions maintenance workers face. She is quoted as saying:

> He [Mr. Cho] used to complain that he was instructed to work alone during
> subway hours of operation. Since he was the youngest employee, he often took
> care of simple repairs and inspections by himself.[17]

Given the discrepancy between the statements attributed to the Seoul Metro
officer and Mr. Cho's alleged actions, one must question Seoul Metro's supervision over the operations of the subcontracting company and its employees.

May 28, 2016 – Seoul Metro Accident at Guui Station

A 19-year-old mechanic named Kim was killed by an arriving train while repairing a platform safety door at Guui Station on Seoul Metro's line two. As in
the previous two fatalities, Mr. Kim was reportedly working alone. However,
safety guidelines call for this work to be performed by two individuals so they
can look out for one another and thus avoid oncoming trains. Mr. Kim, along
with 124 other employees of Eunseong PSD, a subcontractor of Seoul Metro,
was "assigned to fix 7,700 platform safety doors at 97 stations."[18] According to
an article in the *Korea Times*:

> In 2014 alone, platform doors on the four lines [lines 1-4] had some 12,000
> malfunction reports, an average of more than 30 a day. Upon receiving a report,
> mechanics should arrive at the station in less than an hour or face penalties, ac-
> cording to the contract.[19]

This information indicates that the pressure placed on the maintenance
workers caused by a human resources shortage and time constraints was substantial and impactful. The article reveals, "The subcontractor [Eunseong PSD]
refused to increase manpower to save costs."[20] The *Korea JoongAng Daily* reported that after Mr. Kim's death at Guui Station, Seoul Metro eliminated the
requirement to complete the repairs within one hour of a reported malfunc-
tion.[21] Eliminating this requirement would relieve some of the pressure on the
mechanics.

According to the *Korea Herald*, in June, following the deadly accident at
Guui Station, the third in three-and-a-half years under similar circumstances,
"Seoul Metro admitted that [the accident] was due to lax safety standards and

[a] flawed management system."[22] Also, after this incident, Seoul Metro strictly enforced the requirement that all mechanics work in pairs.[23] In other words, three and a half years passed, three subcontracting workers died, and public pressure rose to a boiling point before Seoul Metro finally enforced a basic safety rule.

After the fatality at Guui Station, the topic of outsourcing safety and maintenance-related work received a great deal of national attention. Public leaders kept the pressure on Seoul Metro and other companies engaged in this practice by calling for a "halt [to] outsourcing practices."[24] For example, Justice Party Chairwoman Sim Sang-jeong was quoted as saying, "Seoul Metro's irresponsible, indiscriminate corner-cutting practices caused the death [at Guui Station]. Furthermore, Seoul Metro is not the only company with such dangerous practices."[25] This statement amounts to a public chastising of Seoul Metro and an acknowledgment of the pervasive nature of outsourcing in Korea. The Chairwoman took the argument further by calling on Koreans to instigate profound societal change to prevent future tragedies. She said, "We must fundamentally change our society that keeps producing preventable tragedies."[26]

Working Conditions Update – One Year after the Guui Station Accident

One year after the incident at Guui Station, the *Korea Times* published an update on the working conditions at Seoul Metro. It described actions taken by the company to avert recurrences of similar mishaps and a report on the legal consequences of the Guui Station event. According to the update, "the team-of-two rule [was] being strictly followed."[27] However, irregular workers were still "overworked and underpaid."

> Regular workers are guaranteed a rest after a nine-hour shift, but irregular workers often have to work 15-hour shifts, which entails frequent night duties.[28]

If accurate, these working conditions border on the inhumane. Not only are they ethically unsound, but they also place workers and the public at risk since the duties assigned to the mechanics impact public safety. Common sense suggests that the more hours employees work without taking a break, the more prone they are to make mistakes. In industries dealing with public safety, an error might be fatal for the workers and the public.

Compensation

As far as pay is concerned, regular workers' monthly salary reportedly increases based on seniority. In contrast, "that of irregular workers remains stagnant."[29] The victim's monthly salary was 1.44 million Korean won ($1,286) or 17.28 million won (~$14,532) per year.[30] This amount is dwarfed by the average annual salary of Seoul Metro permanent employees, who earn "nearly 70 million won ($61,865)."[31] After 20 years on the job, the yearly salary gap between a regular and an irregular employee is 24 million won (~$20,402).[32]

Not surprisingly, a high attrition rate prevails among subcontracting workers at Seoul Metro. In 2017, the *Korea Times* reported that the company was "allowed to hire 206 irregular workers;" however, "the number [...] rarely exceeds 190, as many quit because of the excessive workload."[33]

Legal Ramifications

After the Guui Station accident, the government held both Seoul Metro and Eunseong PSD liable. The prosecution charged officials from both contracting and subcontracting companies with serious professional crimes:

> The prosecution has indicted nine officials at Seoul Metro and Kim's employer, subcontractor Eunseong PSD. The two companies have also been indicted.
>
> The Seoul Eastern Prosecutors' Office said the nine are charged with professional negligence resulting in death for failing to follow safety guidelines and [to send] officials for regular on-site safety inspections.[34]

Public Outcry

Because of this and prior incidents at Seoul Metro, the public began to call for the company to stop high-risk outsourcing duties and "hire all of its safety and maintenance workers as full-time employees."[35] Pressure on Seoul Metro mounted even further when the media reported irregularities involving Seoul Metro and Eunseong PSD. News sources revealed that Eunseong PSD "was forced to hire retired officials from Seoul Metro, many without real mechanic skills, [thus] forcing the regular mechanics to cover more shifts and put their lives at risk."[36]

Reportedly, at the time of this accident, Seoul Metro subcontracted with four other companies besides Eunseong PSD. Reports indicate that Seoul

Metro required all five subcontractors to hire former company officials. According to an article published by the *Korea JoongAng Daily* on June 17, 2016,

> There are 136 former officials of Seoul Metro currently employed at its five subcontractors, including Eunsung PSD. Of them, 106 are aged 60 or older, and most of the remaining 30 are in their 50s....
>
> All of the 136 were rehired [by] subcontractors under conditions that their mechanic skills and expertise were not to be tested; that they receive at least twice the salary of regular employees of the subcontractors; and that should the subcontractor go bankrupt, or if their contract with them ends, they can be rehired at Seoul Metro.[37]

Reportedly, Seoul Metro's practice of requiring subcontractors to hire former company officials was not new in 2016. The *Korea JoongAng Daily* informed that this practice dates back to 2008 when the company began outsourcing maintenance work. In that year, the number of retired Seoul Metro officials working at subcontracting companies was as high as 407.[38] The question here is, what is the impact of Seoul Metro's unorthodox practice on public safety? The positions taken up at subcontracting companies by retired Seoul Metro officials with unspecified qualifications forced subcontracting personnel to perform the same amount of work with fewer qualified employees.

Requiring subcontractors to hire former Seoul Metro officials is not standard business practice. It may even be considered unethical at best and corrupt at worst. Even if this is an isolated incident, higher government orders have struggled with ethical issues.[39 and 40] Although no causal link exists between the potentially unethical or corrupt issues at Seoul Metro and those at higher societal levels, it seems likely that the cultural structure is prone to these types of abuses. The unfortunate consequence of this unethical practice is the stasis that results. The country cannot move forward and shake off the "developing country" image that Korea held in the decades following the Korean War.

September 3, 2016 – Seoul Metro Accident near Seongsu Station

On September 3, 2016, only three months after the fatal accident at Guui Station, another industrial incident within the jurisdiction of Seoul Metro claimed the life of a 28-year-old irregular worker. The news article only shares the last name of the deceased, Park. Mr. Park fell to his death from a bridge near

Seongsu Station. At the time of the accident, Mr. Park and four other workers from 3s Engineering, one of Seoul Metro's subcontracting companies, were performing bridge reinforcement-related work. They were reportedly "removing the supporting fixtures" from the bridge when the accident happened.[41]

Other Recent Industrial Accidents

The following stories about recent industrial accidents are related to employers other than Seoul Metro. The reason for including them is to demonstrate that specific behavioral patterns surrounding industrial accidents are observed in various contexts and involve different players. In other words, they are not exclusive to Seoul Metro. Including these stories is particularly important since the observations made in this book about Korean culture and society are based on behavior patterns that tend to recur.

June 1, 2016 – A Subway Construction Site Collapses at a Station in Namyangju, Gyeonggi Province

A preliminary report indicates that a gas tank explosion in the city of Namyangju may have caused the collapse of an underground construction site. This incident killed at least four and injured ten people. Every victim was employed by Maeil ENC, a POSCO Engineering & Construction subcontractor hired to erect subway rails.[42]

As to the cause of the blast, the *Korea Times* reports that

> According to police, the explosion occurred because of the overnight leakage of propane gas from a tank, and it was the fault of the workers who failed to move the tank to a separate place the previous day as required by law.[43]

This statement lends credibility to the outsourcing critics' claim that emphasizing profit margins over public safety is the primary motivator behind subcontracting. The critical assumption is that this practice engenders inadequate or nonexistent safety training, lax safety standards, and flawed management.[44]

The collapse of the subway construction site in Namyangju is another example of an industrial accident stemming from the outsourcing business practice between large corporations and subcontractors. This and other recent industrial accidents aroused the public's concern about "lax safety standards."[45] Increasingly, the public seems to acknowledge that these inadequate standards result in "dangerous working conditions," leading to frequent fatal accidents involving subcontracting workers and the practice of outsourcing dangerous work by major corporations.[46]

Given the frequent fatal industrial accidents, the countrywide accepted practice of subcontracting received widespread criticism from diverse Korean and international community segments. For example, Catholic Kwandong University Professor Park Chang-geun commented explicitly about the collapse of the subway construction site in Namyangju. The *Korea Times* quoted him: "The workers at the subway construction site would not have been aware of the safety manual."[47] Professor Park teaches in the Civil Engineering Department at Catholic Kwandong University. He is also a member of the Safety Evaluation Committee of the Korean Infrastructure Safety Corporation, a government entity.

In the article cited above, the writer reacts to the same incident and searches for solutions to stop the rash of fatal industrial accidents. He credits the following statement to Hyun Jae-soon, director of planning at the Wonjin Institute for Occupational and Environmental Health:

> The government should prevent big companies from entrusting safety work to a subcontractor. Also, the punishment for those responsible should be tougher so that an accident like this could bankrupt the company.[48]

The seemingly constant deadly accidents involving prime contractors and subcontractors did not go unnoticed by the international community or the United Nations. The *Korea Times* reports:

> The issue of subcontracting was also raised by the United Nations delegates who were visiting Korea to study business and human rights. Michael Addo, a member of the United Nations Human Rights Office, indicated Wednesday [June 1, 2016, the same day as the subway construction site collapse in the city of Namyangju] that prime contractors should bear more responsibility for things that happen down the chain of contracts.[49]

Each of these statements by individuals from very different backgrounds addresses disconnects in the existing paradigm of outsourcing dangerous work. This relationship exhibits the following conditions: 1) inadequate or nonexistent safety training of subcontracting workers, 2) the critical role of government in permitting the outsourcing of safety work by prime contractors, 3) the relatively mild consequences for violators, and 4) the abrogation of responsibility on the part of prime contractors in accident cases. These four areas should serve as the impetus for more effective outsourcing and adopting a paradigm that values public safety as much as profit margins.

In an article in the *International Business Times* (*IB Times*) regarding the subway construction site collapse in Namyangju, analysts note: "Many safety problems in South Korea are due to poor regulation of the existing laws, and also wide ignorance that persists regarding safety in general."[50] This assertion confirms Young Lee's and my observations about the litany of man-made and industrial accidents that have plagued Korea for years, especially recently. The country's technological advancements sharply contrast with the lax enforcement of existing regulations and the apparent disregard for public safety. These practices appear to be a byproduct of an inclination toward efficiency and short-term financial gains.

Clearly, in a capitalist economy, such as Korea's, financial gains and profit margins attained through efficiency are vital in ensuring the viability of a company. At the macroeconomic level, they are the lifeblood of a nation's economy. When appropriately managed and reinvested, they enable a company and a country to generate economic growth. Young Lee and I know the essential role financial gains have played in Korea's economic and technological advancements. What we are suggesting is a paradigm that balances financial gains with public safety.

June 25, 2016 – Air Conditioner Technician Falls to his Death

Per a June 25, 2016, news report on the "MBC News Desk" program, a 42-year-old air conditioner technician fell to his death from the third floor of an apartment building in Seoul. He was employed by a company that subcontracted for Samsung Electronics. According to the news story, the technician was required to make 60 monthly repairs for a base monthly salary of 1.3 million Korean won (~$1,217).[51] He also received additional incentive bonuses of $5-$35 for jobs over the 60 base repairs.[52]

The pressure to complete a fixed number of repairs and a chance to earn extra money to support his two children resulted in a distinct rush to complete the assigned jobs, plus more. He used a good portion of his salary to pay for his children's private education costs at *hagwons* or possibly university tuition. To earn the most money possible, the technician allegedly disregarded the use of required safety equipment, such as a helmet and safety ropes. Reportedly, he also performed the work alone rather than with a partner. Because the technician was working for a subcontracting company, Samsung Electronics was not responsible for the accident.

Sadly, this is not an isolated incident whereby an air conditioning technician loses his life while performing his job to earn a living.

July 9, 2017 – Air Conditioner Technician Dies

On July 9, 2017, another air conditioning technician, Kim, who worked for a subcontractor under contract with Samsung Electronics, collapsed while performing a work-related assignment under similar circumstances.[53] He eventually died in the emergency room. According to his wife, Kim had not had a day off in four months.[54] Notably, this and the previous air conditioner technician incident happened during peak season when temperatures and humidity in Korea are high, and the demand for air conditioning repairs spikes.

These incidents demonstrate the pervasive aspect and negative impact of the subcontracting practice in Korea. They also provide a window to the human side of these tragedies, the pressure these workers are under, and the sacrifices they must make to support themselves and their families. Ultimately, some make the ultimate sacrifice in this subcontracting arrangement that seems to value short-term financial gains over working conditions and human lives.

December 11, 2018 – A Subcontractor is Killed in a Thermal Power Plant in Taean

Kim Yong-kyun was a 24-year-old maintenance worker with Korea Engineering and Power Service (KEPS). KEPS was a subcontractor to the state-run Korea Western Power (KOWEPO). Mr. Kim died at a thermal power plant in Taean, South Chungcheong Province, approximately 130 kilometers or 81 miles southwest of Seoul, after being trapped by a coal conveyor belt. The young worker, who was in the fourth month of his temporary job, suffered a gruesome death when the conveyor belt, which was running at a speed of 16 feet per second, decapitated him.[55] Since he was working alone, no one was available to shut down the equipment when Kim was trapped.

The *Korea Times* reported, "According to police, [Mr.] Kim was inspecting the conveyor belt alone, although guidelines state at least two workers must do on-site work together for safety reasons."[56] The news outlet also indicated that "[Mr. Kim] lost contact with the office around [10:00] p.m." on Monday, December 10, and his body was found at 3:20 a.m. of the following day.[57] This indicates that the body may have been lying on the ground for five hours before being discovered.

Reports disclose that Mr. Kim received only "three hours of safety education before being deployed on the conveyor belt."[58] A similar statement from Mr. Kim's co-workers reported in the *Korea Times* corroborates the claim of insufficient safety training at the site. Furthermore, his co-workers allegedly filed "28 complaints asking for improvements in the hazardous working environment, but they were all rejected as they could cause 'facility damage.'"[59]

Large corporations save money by circumventing the safety training for a particular project, which would be required for their employees. As such, they capitalize on the savings generated by hiring subcontractors instead of training their own workers. This arrangement enables subcontractors to hire irregular workers for lower wages and avoid paying benefits, thus cutting costs and increasing profits for them and large corporations. *Labor Notes* reports:

> [Mr. Kim] had to pay out of pocket for a safety helmet and a flashlight while taking home less than $1,500 a month without benefits. This was less than half the wage[s] of regular workers, not even factoring in [the] benefits they can earn.
>
> At the time of his death, [Mr.] Kim's backpack contained a broken flashlight and three cups of noodles, the only meals he could afford.[60]

These statements encapsulate the low wages and harsh working conditions associated with contingent, short-term labor. Furthermore, they underscore the desperate situation young people in Korea find themselves in when they fail to land a permanent position in a major corporation.

In the broader context, these conditions partially explain Korean families' emphasis on education. When children fail in education, they cannot land a high-paying corporate job and often put their lives at risk when forced to work for a subcontractor.

Industrial accidents involving subcontractors happen frequently, and they take place at various sites. As per the *Korea Times*, 97% of accidents in the five years before this incident involved subcontract workers. Furthermore, 12 subcontracted workers lost their lives at the power plant in Taean in the previous eight years.[61] Despite these statistics, the government issued the power plant a clean bill of health by designating it as a "zero accident workplace" for the previous three years. This designation is assigned when a company avoids serious accidents or deaths.

Moreover, "the government had also exempted KOWEPO from paying the premium for industrial accident insurance worth 220 million won ($1.9 million) for five years until 2017"[62] because of the "workplace-without-accidents" certification. The *Korea Herald* corroborated this information in an article titled "Original contractors should be responsible for subcontractor accidents." The report confirms the savings amassed by KOWEPO resulting from the company's "safety" record and the government's practice of disregarding industrial accidents against the primary contractor when a subcontractor is involved. The article states that

> Korea Western Power, the company that operates the power plant, was given tax reduction benefits based on its safety record because accidents involving subcontract workers are not recorded against the original contractor.[63]

The certification system only counts the accidents of workers hired by the contracting company. Consequently, the government incentivizes large companies to expand their money-saving subcontracting practices by waving industrial accident insurance premiums when no company employees are involved in mishaps, regardless of the number of subcontractor incidents. Critics point to this disconnect as an incentive for major corporations to underreport industrial accidents. Another incentive "is the government's practice of giving higher [priority] to companies with lower industrial accident rates during the 'prequalification' assessment of companies that mean to make a bid for large construction projects."[64]

The unfortunate outcome of this "inaccurate" reporting process is perpetuating an unsafe environment for workers and the public. Instead of working toward promoting public safety, the traditional and current system works against it.

Following Mr. Kim's incident, newspaper outlets revealed that the Korean public began questioning the rigor of safety inspections at the plant. According to the *Korea Times*, the Korea Safety Technology Association conducted a safety inspection two months before the accident. This inspection included the conveyor belt involved in the deadly incident. As expected, the plant passed such a review. Consequently, the publication surmised that "the inspection was carried out superficially."[65]

This incident received considerable attention from the public because Mr. Kim's death was the latest in a series of fatal industrial accidents. The frequency and persistence of these tragedies underscore the country's emphasis on efficiency and quick financial returns at the expense of safety standards. Reports indicate that Mr. Kim's death is far from being an aberration. Instead, it appears to reflect the norm.

> [Mr.] Kim was collateral damage as the country has turned into a predatory economy that feeds on its temporary workforce. In South Korea, in an average

year, more than 1,000 workers are killed in accidents at their workplaces, the highest fatality rate among the 36 OECD member countries. **About 76 percent of these deaths are of temporary workers.**

The alarming official figures likely understate the actual fatalities of temporary workers, as their accidents often go unreported.[66]

On June 27, 2016, *Hankyoreh* published an article that exposed the reasons for the paradox between the relatively low industrial accident rate and the high work-related fatality rate. The disparity in these rates is reflected in the data submitted for Korea when compared to the OECD average. In 2013, Korea had an industrial accident rate of 0.59%, while the average for OECD countries was 2.7%, which implies that Korea's work environment was significantly safer than the rest of the OECD countries. The accident rate is calculated from the reported accidents per 100 workers. Conversely, Korea had a work-related fatality rate of 6.8 out of 100,000, the highest among OECD countries.[67]

The discrepancy between Korea's remarkably low industrial accident rate and its significantly higher work-related fatality rate reflects the state of safety in the workplace. According to *Hankyoreh*,

> The explanation of this paradox is that South Korean industrial accidents are being covered up. That is to say, industrial accidents are not being called industrial accidents until death makes them impossible to conceal.[68]

An article titled "S. Korea industry's deadly conditions built on culture of cover-up," written by Bryan Harris, Song Jung-a, and Kang Buseong, published on December 5, 2017, by the *Financial Times*, corroborates the concern over the discrepancy between Korea's low industrial accidents rate and its high death rate compared to other OECD nations. The article states that "labour experts, activists and even official government reports [...] allege that companies cover up the incidents" for the reasons already discussed.[69] Another reason behind the alleged accident cover-up is to avoid "damage to their brand."[70] The latter makes sense since Korea depends so much on its conglomerates for national economic viability.

The critical question is, how extensive is the cover-up of industrial accidents and illnesses? Although the *Financial Times* article quoted above focuses on acknowledged hidden industrial accidents and diseases at Hankook Tire, the authors indicate that allegations of a "failure to protect workers" extend to other major companies.[71] This group includes the semiconductor division of Samsung Electronics. The company has been snarled in a dispute with approximately 240 workers "who say exposure to chemicals triggered a host of diseases, including leukemia, lymphoma and brain tumors."[72]

To identify the root of the issues associated with industrial accidents in Korea, the authors of the *Financial Times* article quote Paek Do-myung, an academic. Mr. Paek works as a public health expert at Seoul National University. He explains the situation in the following manner:

> South Korea's industrial accidents problem is much more serious than other manufacturing powerhouses… because individual safety and workers' rights have traditionally taken a back seat to the country's economic development and corporate competitiveness.[73]

This statement alludes to a contributing factor behind the Miracle on the Han River—the national enthusiasm for the country's economic development since the end of the Korean War—an unwavering commitment to a national cause despite the high toll paid in innocent lives. The national fervor is evident through the cultural element embedded in the statement. As stated, Koreans are expected and willing to make personal sacrifices for the country's advancement.

Outsourcing: Definition and Worldwide Usage

Outsourcing, or subcontracting, is a business strategy that generates financial gains in Korea and other capitalist countries worldwide.

> In 2018, the global outsourcing market amounted to $85.6 billion. However, it's been estimated that as many as 50 percent of outsourcing deals end badly. This isn't a reason to reject outsourcing. It simply proves how important it is to carefully choose an outsourcing partner and manage your supplier relationship.[74]

This is a sobering statement when applied to the relationship between Seoul Metro and its subcontractors. It is particularly fitting in the incident at Guui Station since the company was reported as admitting that the accident was a result of "lax safety standards and [a] flawed management system."[75] Thus, underscoring the importance of managing the relationship with the supplier.

Several business sources, including *MicroSourcing* and *Customer Think*, cite the Deloitte 2016 and 2020 Global Outsourcing Survey results to show why businesses outsource worldwide. According to the results of the 2016 survey, the top four reasons and their respective percentages are as follows:

- Serves as a Cost-Cutting Tool – 59%
- Enables Focus on Core Business – 57%
- Solves Capacity Issues – 47%
- Enhances Service Quality – 31%[76]

Deloitte's 2020 survey conducted during the pandemic still identified that "cost reduction remains the primary objective [of] outsourcing. Approximately 70% of survey respondents indicated that they used outsourcing as a cost-cutting tool."[77] Based on the industrial accidents presented in this chapter, Korean companies that engage in outsourcing are in line, at least with the top reason provided by the 2016 and 2020 Deloitte survey respondents.

The Relationship between Major Corporations, Subcontractors, and the Public

Major Corporations

Major corporations are all-powerful, primarily government- or family-owned *chaebols*. They need subcontractors to:

- avoid the monopoly syndrome;
- maintain good public relations to avoid accusations of destroying the competition, including mom-and-pop enterprises;
- circumvent or minimize work that may not be profitable for them or within their scope;
- reduce or eliminate training and supervision costs in the subcontracted areas;
- avoid insurance costs;
- avert financial responsibility when accidents occur;
- sidestep moral responsibility.

Subcontractors

In many instances, subcontractors are small to mid-sized companies, or even mom-and-pop owned businesses, which cannot compete with large corporations financially or in the scope of projects. They benefit from the relationship with major corporations by:

- generating business and maintaining a steady revenue to stay afloat;
- keeping their staff working or adding employees to their payroll who would otherwise be unemployed or hired by major corporations;
- providing a service that major corporations would prefer not to be involved in;
- keeping prices low for the public.

The Public

In this relationship, the public primarily benefits, most importantly, by paying lower prices for goods and services that major corporations provide in partnership with subcontractors.

The *Gap* and *Eul* Concept in the Relationship between Large Corporations and Subcontractors

Corporations outsource jobs they prefer not to oversee to reduce costs. They utilize the bidding process to award contracts. Subcontractors submit bids to corporations, which usually assign the deal to the lowest bidder for efficiency and financial gain.

In the case of construction and other industrial accidents, select individuals, such as safety managers from the contracting and subcontracting company, are usually identified as responsible parties and prosecuted. If contracting and subcontracting companies are involved in the accident, the latter has traditionally absorbed the financial liability for the accident. This liability designation has been practiced for years, primarily providing legal and financial protection for large corporations or *chaebols*. The government and the public view these corporations as the engine of the Korean economy because of their enormous job creation power. Consequently, in this relationship, individual subcontracting companies have been essentially sacrificed. The government and the public view them as less powerful, less influential, and less able to create jobs independently, making them less likely to impact the economy than conglomerates.

This dynamic exemplifies the *gap* and *eul* relationship and the generational gap between baby boomers and millennials. Recognizing the invaluable contributions of the conglomerates to the unparalleled rise of the Korean economy after the war, the public historically condoned the government's special treatment of *chaebols*. For years, this unconditional support derived primarily from baby boomers who lived through the difficult times before, during, and after the Korean War. Baby boomers witnessed the critical role played by the *chaebols* in the Miracle on the Han River.

However, given the recent fatal industrial accidents involving partnerships between contracting and subcontracting companies, an increasing number of critics of the status quo, particularly millennials, have raised their voices.[78] They demand a halt to the "outsourcing of dangers" by enacting and enforcing laws that prevent shifting responsibility from contracting to subcontracting companies.[79]

Under the traditional arrangement, large corporations outsource projects to subcontractors that submit low bids in a competitive process. Once a contract is secured, these subcontractors often cut corners on safety measures to make a profit and remain afloat. Cost reduction may include hiring low-cost, irregular, contingent laborers to avoid paying benefits and providing appropriate safety training. It may also involve performing tasks with fewer employees, even when safety measures call for workers to perform their jobs in pairs. Each of these cost-cutting measures results in unsafe conditions.

Some sources point to the disproportionate number of accidents in Korea associated with irregular or temporary workers. The *Korea Herald*, for example, reported that

> In 2014, irregular workers, who accounted for 20 percent of the workers at conglomerates with more than 300 staff members, made up nearly 40 percent of those who died of fatal work accidents, according to the Labor Ministry.[80]

In 2016, the *Korea Times* reported a similar statistic for 2015. The article makes the following assertion:

> Deaths of workers from subcontractors are not new. According to the Ministry of Labor and Employment, such deaths accounted for 40.2 percent of the total worksite deaths from industrial accidents last year [2015], up from 37.7 percent in 2012.
>
> Out of seven workers who died at construction sites of Hyundai Heavy Industries this year [2016], five were subcontractor workers.
>
> In Korea, [it is] legal and common for prime contractors, mostly big builders or transportation operators, to hire subcontractors because it is cost-efficient and the subcontractors take charge of worker management instead of them.[81]

The statistics evidence a commonality between the percentage of irregular workers in large companies and the percentage of those who die in fatal industrial accidents. This link gives credence to subcontracting critics who maintain that conglomerates are outsourcing dangerous work.

Based on a survey of 791 temporary workers conducted by the National Human Rights Commission of Korea in 2014, "irregular workers are more vulnerable to work [- related] accidents because they tend to be assigned heavier workload[s] and more dangerous jobs."[82]

The Role of Government, Corporations, and the Public as Major Economic Players

The three primary players in the Korean economy are the government, large corporations or *chaebols*, and the public. With their diverging interests, these three entities have a robust interdependent relationship. Figure 1 below depicts this strong interdependence.

As depicted by the above flowchart, major corporations have an enhanced capability to conduct business efficiently partly because of government and public concessions. For example, government-adopted regulations favor large corporations. As a result, companies like Samsung Electronics, Seoul Metro, and POSCO can deliver lower-priced goods and services to the public. Under this arrangement, the conglomerates can contribute to the 2%-3% annual economic growth sought by the government and expected by the public. In return, the public accepts government-adopted regulations that favor corporations and the inherent vulnerability and substantial risk of an accident-prone environment.

The robust interdependence between these three entities makes the status quo difficult to change despite the number of fatal accidents. Given that the desires and objectives of each entity are met consistently through this arrangement, it would require a conscious effort by each of the players to adopt a climate in which all parties win, and no one loses. The existing relationship sacrifices public safety for short-term financial gains and lower prices.

How difficult is it to make substantial changes to the current structure?

As we have seen, accidents have occurred while subcontractors perform jobs for major corporations. Safety violations are not unusual to surface as the primary cause of incidents. However, the irony here is that within this structure,

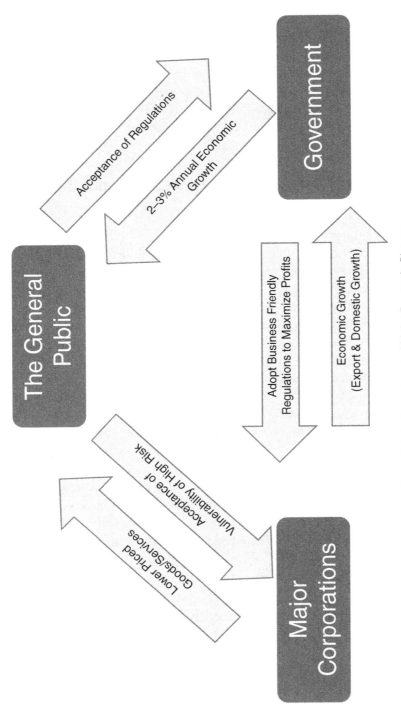

Figure 1: Interdependence of Major Economic Players

subcontractors are often not required to provide safety training for their employees, especially temporary workers, as was the case in the April 16, 2014, *Sewol* ferry accident.

As we saw earlier, corporations avoid liability for accidents by outsourcing. In this structure, subcontractors employ temporary workers for financial efficiency. However, when subcontractor employees perform the work, the subcontracting company is held legally and financially accountable for accidents. By contrast, only *some* key officials of the contracting corporation (e.g., on-site safety managers) are held responsible.

The public's typical reaction when tragedies occur involving outsourcing companies and subcontractors is outrage and a desire to identify the head of the subcontracting company and key officials of the primary contractor who oversee the project (e.g., on-site safety managers), fire them, prosecute them, and move on. However, focusing on individuals alone does not go far enough to avoid similar future accidents. The government, major corporations, subcontractors, and the public must also recognize their role in this interdependent relationship and live up to their responsibility.

Suppose the public is genuinely interested in minimizing the number of accidents. In that case, they must pressure the government to adopt regulations requiring major corporations to absorb their fair share of the financial responsibility and subcontractors to balance the emphasis between safety and profits. If these two conditions were to materialize, the public would have to be willing to endure the cost increases associated with these added expenses. For example, if subcontractors placed more emphasis on safety and were required to uphold safety regulations, their costs would increase. These costs would be passed on to major corporations, and they, in turn, would pass them on to the public, which would be poorly received given the current paradigm. This reaction exemplifies the rigidity of the existing interdependence of the three major economic players and why it is difficult to make substantial changes.

Moving from a Separation to a Unity Consciousness

The interdependent relationship between the government, major corporations, and the public points to what appears to be a separation consciousness, which calls for each entity to have different motivations, goals, and objectives. With only a few exceptions, each body works toward its own goals and objectives, which may not align with those of the other two players. What is needed for all three entities to work effectively in concert for the benefit of all is the adoption of a unity consciousness. This would create an environment where success is not only measured by corporate profits but also by a significant reduction in safety-related accidents because of strict adherence to safety regulations that generate stiff penalties for those who choose to disregard them.

Adhering to these standards may also mean that short-term profits will be impacted. Thus, the government and the public may have to accept a temporary adjustment to the expected 2%-3% GDP increase per annum. Furthermore, the public may have to endure higher prices of goods and services. Despite the short-term economic impact, this new environment would engender a collaborative attitude toward common goals, objectives, and problem-solving. In the long run, if the three entities collaborate harmoniously for the benefit of all instead of allowing profits, lower prices, and greed to dictate their actions, the needs of all three will be met. Adopting a genuine unity consciousness would take Korea back to its roots as a nation united for the good of all.

At Long Last, a Step in the Right Direction

In 2018, thanks to mounting public pressure, Korea finally adopted an integrated system that requires contractors and subcontractors to share responsibility for industrial accidents. However, the policy only applies to "limited industries, including production, railroads, subways, and those with more than 1,000 full-time workers. Other industries such as energy production, mining, and shipping have been exempted."[83] Although the new system is a step in the right direction, it cannot completely address the fundamental cultural issues underlying the safety problem.

The "Kim Yong-kyun Bill"

Subsequently, "on December 27, [2018], after a week of public outcries and protests following Kim's death,"[84] the Parliamentary Environment and Labor Committee passed an amendment to the Occupational Safety and Health Act (OSHA) (a.k.a. Industrial Safety Act). The media and the public also refer to this law as the "Kim Yong-kyun Bill."[85] The nickname honors the 24-year-old maintenance worker who lost his life in the KOWEPO thermal power plant in Taean. The purpose of this bill is to prevent future industrial accidents by

> "...expanding the duties of the company hiring subcontractors [...] by holding it responsible for the safety management of the subcontractor employees and strengthening the punishment of the employer and company when a worker dies in a work-related accident."[86]

In addition, "the amendment bans corporations from subcontracting 22 types of high-risk job[s] such as metal plating."[87]

Adopting the "Kim Yong-kyun Bill" is crucial in preventing future industrial accidents involving contractors and subcontractors. The question remains: does the new law go far enough? Even though the punishment for violators of safety regulations, in the form of imprisonment and fines, has increased in the recently approved amendment, the bill falls short of its initial intent. The *Kyunghyang Shinmun* reports that it remains a watered-down version of the original draft.[88]

Nevertheless, adopting this amendment signals that Korea is making progress toward decreasing the number of industrial accidents. However, as with any new law, particularly in Korea, it is yet to be determined how strictly it is enforced and whether it achieves the desired purpose. In the broader context, the Korean legislature has passed the "Kim Yong-kyun Bill" and other recently approved regulations to protect workers and reinforce public safety. These new laws signal that Korean society is undergoing a subtle, long overdue, but profound transformation. In the long run, this shift should benefit the entire country.

- The country's technological advancements sharply contrast with the apparent disregard for public safety caused by an inclination toward efficiency and short-term financial gains.
- We are cognizant of the vital role that financial gains have played in Korea's economic and technological advancements. What we are suggesting is a paradigm that balances financial gains with public safety.
- "[The] country has turned into a predatory economy that feeds on its temporary workforce. In South Korea, in an average year, more than 1,000 workers are killed in accidents at their workplaces, the highest fatality rate among the 36 OECD member countries. **About 76 percent of these deaths are of temporary workers.**"[66]
- "South Korea's industrial accidents problem is [...] more serious than other manufacturing powerhouses [...] individual safety and workers' rights have traditionally taken a back seat to the country's economic development and corporate competitiveness."[73]

CHAPTER NINE

National Reaction to Catastrophes

When accidents occur frequently, one must consider to what extent they are true "accidents" and not the result of cultural imperatives. Clearly, Korea has no monopoly on accidents since they happen even in the most advanced countries. The point here is not that mishaps occur in Korea but that recurring behavioral patterns, including those of the general public, have contributed enormously to some of these incidents. These behavioral patterns appear to be deeply rooted in societal attitudes.

To their credit, when tragedies occur, Koreans demonstrate their resiliency and ability to rally behind national emergencies. They steadfastly face national difficulties, such as the Asian financial crisis, the *Sewol* ferry catastrophe, and the Jecheon hospital fire. In the last two examples, the government mobilized resources to assist the victims and their families.

Some plaintiffs who filed lawsuits seeking damages from the government and Cheonghaejin Marine related to the *Sewol* ferry disaster, as well as some newspaper reporters and editors, underscore the rescue operation's missteps.[1] Even so, the fact remains that the rescue operation for the *Sewol* appears to be significantly more tangible than for the *Sohae* two decades earlier. It is an indication that some progress is being made in terms of rescue-and-recovery operations. Understandably, however, this progress is of little consolation to the families of the 304 victims of the *Sewol* ferry tragedy.

National Reaction to Catastrophes

Typically, the Korean public has a three-pronged reaction to catastrophes. First, after the initial shock and mourning, the citizenry's response evinces outrage. They strongly demand to identify and punish the culprits and parties in charge. These include individuals associated with a company or corporation involved in the accident and the political party currently in office. Second, they demand a heartfelt public apology from responsible individuals, including the company's CEO and the country's president. Third, they call for the government to intervene and "fix the problem."

Outrage and a Desire to Identify and Punish the Culprits and Parties in Charge

Experiencing outrage and a desire to identify and punish the perpetrators and individuals in charge are natural emotional reactions to avoidable accidents. However, in the Korean context, analyzing this desire gives us a glimpse of Korean cultural traits that may not be evident to the casual observer. After a tragedy, a large portion of the population yearns for the next stage of the healing process so the country and the populace can resume a "business-as-usual" environment.

The desire to identify and punish the wrongdoers and responsible parties represents a cultural trait. It reflects the inclination toward group conformity and the belief that individuals should sacrifice for the group, both essential for achieving unity and harmony, two fundamental aspects of Korean culture. In the case of wrongdoers, their unlawful behavior makes them stand out from the crowd, thus disrupting social harmony.

Even though perpetrators and responsible parties are identified and punished, accidents caused by disregarding public safety continue to reoccur. An examination of accident triggers indicates that behavioral patterns associated with disdain for safety regulations also repeat. This suggests something is amiss with the conventional national reaction after a catastrophe.

Demand for a Heartfelt Public Apology from Responsible Individuals

The absence or delay of a sincere public apology from responsible individuals after a national catastrophe or incident that receives nationwide attention causes public outrage. However, demanding and receiving the customary public apology does not go far enough. These apologies merely smooth over the latest incident while avoiding examining the fundamental issues. Young Lee and I understand that CEOs and the nation's president should be held responsible for public safety. Still, one person cannot change the public's attitude toward public safety, especially when the public's contribution to accidents is glossed over. The citizenry must recognize that public safety is everyone's responsibility. They must give this concern the attention it deserves. One person, or one leader, alone cannot achieve this.

Demand for the Government to "Fix the Problem"

A sense of helplessness after a tragedy combined with a desire for expediency prompts the public to call the government to step in and "fix the problem." The truth is that legislators can adopt strict safety regulations. Still, suppose the public disregards them and continues to emphasize efficiency for financial profits. In that case, safety regulations will only be effective if enforced and carry severe economic consequences for lawbreakers. However, some Koreans are concerned that legislators will not pass legislation that negatively impacts *chaebols* out of fear of hindering the nation's economic momentum. Baby boomers and some conservative young people who recognize the *chaebols'* contributions to the country's economic vitality tend not to want the government to adopt laws impeding the conglomerates' viability. The widespread perception that the country's economic well-being depends on the financial profitability of the *chaebols* is due to the notion that they are the engine and job creators of the economy. As such, they are perceived as "untouchable" in the eyes of many Koreans.

Aside from the historical economic reality of the *chaebols*, the cultural aspect of this mentality may be deeply rooted in Korean culture, where the group, in this case, the larger society, is more important than the individual. The mindset appears to have been promoted in the 1960s and 1970s under President Park Chung Hee (1963-1979) when the country underwent significant reconstruction. The nation was recovering from the ravages of the Korean War and had undertaken an unprecedented infrastructure build-up. His motto 새마을운동 [*Sae ma eul eun dong*], or "Let's rebuild the country," provided a cry for unity and sacrifice for the good of the whole. However, Young Lee and I again reiterate that the country is at a different stage now than in the '60s, '70s, '80s, and '90s. Today's economy is much larger; societies both in Korea and abroad are more complex, and globalization and interdependence are here to stay. We also recognize that conflicting interests result in a more difficult decision-making environment for government leaders.

An Overarching View of the National Reaction to Catastrophes

While examining the public's conventional reaction to catastrophes, we recognize several questions are in order. In preparation for the following discussion, we present some of these questions as food for thought. One fundamental question is, does society support the reduction of catastrophes caused by disregard for safety regulations? If the answer is no, then the discussion and debate end there. If yes, how effective and practical is the national reaction to catastrophes? Is the public's response to tragedies a knee-jerk response based on emotions or political agendas? Or is it an efficient way of dealing with unfortunate and painful situations? Does the response pattern address the reasons these types of accidents keep recurring? Or does the entire nation need to be more self-reflective and critical and ask, what are we as a society doing wrong? What is the general public's attitude toward safety standards, regulations, and penalties? How can we as a nation prevent the unnecessary loss of innocent lives? Should the country continue to focus on identifying the key culprits and parties in charge, demand their punishment, and go on with a business-as-usual attitude? Should the identification and punishment of key lawbreaking individuals and responsible parties be sufficient to exonerate the public so people can keep approaching safety standards, regulations, and penalties in the same disdainful manner?

Young Lee and I recognize that deciding what to do about public safety issues generates controversy among people on both sides of the aisle, particularly following a national catastrophe. After an event of this magnitude, it is expected to hear calls for the president's resignation or impeachment. This is particularly true for individuals whose political affiliation differs from the party in power. Some demand reform and strict adherence to safety regulations. Others say, "Once the perpetrators are brought to justice, let's move on with our lives." The driving force behind the public's attitude toward safety standards, regulations, and penalties appears to be a craving for efficiency. This impulse has pain avoidance, personal convenience, self-interest, greed, and a desire for economic prosperity at its root. Repeatedly, the result is the loss of innocent lives.

What is the takeaway here? Is it that innocent lives lost in accidents represent the price the nation must pay for progress at all costs? Is this the sacrifice expected of individuals for the good of the whole? Is it that efficiency for the sake of profits must be the guiding principle for the nation? Or is disregard for safety standards and regulations acceptable as long as you do not get caught? Or is it something else?

The efficiency strategies learned for problem-solving in a test preparation environment seem to carry over to everyday life. For example, just like students can pick the correct answer from the options given in a multiple-choice test but cannot show the steps for solving the problem, a heightened emphasis on efficiency reveals the inability of various entities to identify and rectify the systemic and recurring root causes of accidents.

Similarly, just as students prefer multiple-choice tests over essay, short-answer, and fill-in-the-blank tests, society opts for the quick solution of identifying wrongdoers and prosecuting them over conducting a thorough study to determine the systemic causes of accidents. As a result, man-made and industrial accidents are usually resolved efficiently. To expediently return to business as usual, corporations and government entities fail to acknowledge and address contributing fundamental factors behind these recurring incidents when they first surface. Eventually, they address these vital systemic concerns after a pattern develops and officials are under pressure from the public. In the meantime, innocent lives are lost unnecessarily.

From an outsider's perspective, the unfortunate, sad, and frustrating nature of these "accidents" is that the cultural appetite for efficiency takes precedence over human safety. The urge for personal convenience and intense striving for material wealth outweighs the discomfort of an occasional tragedy. In other words, a segment of the population believes that sacrifices by a few are inevitable for the country to maintain its financial viability and vitality. Therefore, some innocent lives will be lost in the process.

Viewed from this perspective, these lives are a sad but unavoidable price to pay for the benefit of all. This mentality may derive from the cultural inclination to expect individual and collective sacrifices for the good of the whole, which helped Korea rise from the rubble after the war, thus achieving the Miracle on the Han River. To a Western observer subscribing to a moral human imperative of individual safety, which promotes life under any circumstance and rejects unnecessary death for any reason, including the good of the country, the Korean public must more closely examine and eradicate the root causes of these accidents.

Suppose the end goal is to avoid repeating those incidents. In that case, the public's post-accident reaction lacks a demand for an analysis of the role of societal attitudes, an acknowledgment of the people's complicity, and a concrete plan to avoid similar future mishaps. Absent this reflection, the focus remains on the main perpetrators but ignores the public's role in the event. Put another way, some people in Korean society emphasize quick and easy fixes to return to business as usual. These fixes only underscore society's perennial emphasis on pursuing efficiency instead of undergoing a systemic analysis of the contributing factors behind these incidents, which an appreciation of individual human life requires. It is no wonder some Koreans are asking publicly, haven't we learned from all these accidents?

This national nearsightedness denies the public's complicity in these incidents. A more explicit message must be conveyed, which clarifies that the temptation to "cut corners" and the *gap* and *eul* relationship contribute to catastrophes and abuses. Unfortunately, these concepts are ingrained in the culture. Until this mentality is eradicated, accidents will continue to punish the country's psyche. A crucial step in the purge process is the public's acceptance that safety regulations have a purpose, and it is in everyone's best interest to abide by them.

We are not saying that the prosecution of wrongdoers and a heartfelt public apology to society, particularly the victims' families, are unnecessary. They are essential for a healthy healing process. We suggest profound fundamental attitudinal changes are required if Koreans decide that individual human lives are more valuable than efficiency and economic gains.

Systemically analyzing disasters and implementing preventive measures are integral to learning from our mistakes and play a critical role in creating a safe environment. By viewing incidents from a broad-based outlook, one may determine where the system failed and is vulnerable to compliance violations. Once the investigation is complete, what seems to be lacking is the implementation of fundamental and sustainable attitudinal changes.

The Korean economy is now well past the developmental stage. Today, the country finds itself among the elite economies of the world. Even though efficiency is one of the principles of capitalism, has the time come for Korea to de-emphasize the "cut-throat" competitiveness and efficiency-at-all-costs approach and accentuate actions that benefit humanity? When viewed from an objective and humanistic perspective, catastrophes could be more consistently avoided if the nation adopted a more balanced mentality that values both financial benefits and universal safety. In this manner, the tendency to "cut corners" and disregard safety standards and regulations could be diminished if not eradicated.

Is the Country Ready for Profound Change?

The country can implement lasting changes if review systems emphasize prosecutions of wrongdoers and remediation of the system. Thus, these corrections will ensure that appropriate and current safety rules are strictly enforced and stiff fines are in place to discourage future violations. These measures would send a clear message to the public about the primordial importance of public safety and zero tolerance for violators. Adherence to strict safety standards will require a shift in the nation's mindset. Shifting attitudes to emphasize safety and careful planning rather than efficiency will inconvenience many people and most likely reduce profits and increase costs associated with such areas as construction, entertainment, food, health care, hospitality, housing, and transportation.

In addition, if the public is interested in reducing or eliminating abuses and catastrophes caused by disregard for safety standards in the construction industry, the government needs to undertake a national campaign to undo a myriad of cost-cutting measures in areas such as construction. Practices that took place in pursuit of efficiency and saving money on building costs must be eradicated. They must

- engage in careful planning;
- inspect existing buildings for questionable construction practices;
- ensure that safety inspections are timely and conducted thoroughly by adequately trained individuals;
- reinforce, retrofit structures, or address safety concerns by demolishing and rebuilding them when issues cannot be resolved any other way.

Such a "clean-up" campaign would be costly and most likely increase the price of goods and services. The public would have to bear this additional cost, but the investment could create jobs and, most importantly, save innocent lives.

One fundamental question is, what does the public want? Do they prefer to maintain the *status quo* to avoid increasing costs, or do they wish to move Korea to a more balanced developmental level whereby ethics, values, and consciousness align with the economy's strength and technological progress? The government cannot legislate attitudinal change. The desire for change must come from the public. Only the people can instigate meaningful strides toward adopting a culture that values public safety, recognizes the intent of, and supports the strict enforcement of safety regulations.

Implementing a cultural shift of this magnitude will not come quickly, easily, or without financial repercussions. However, eventually, the country will be better off. Korea will assume its place among the world's elite nations, and more importantly, innocent lives will be spared.

We are optimistic that Koreans will eventually take the necessary steps to raise the nation's consciousness regarding public safety to a level equal to, or higher than, the desire for financial returns. It is part of human evolution. Adopting the "Kim Yong-kyun Bill" is a small step in the right direction. However, it is up to the Korean people to decide whether to honor "*Hong-ik In-gan*" [홍익인간], the unofficial motto of Korea and a founding principle of the nation, meaning "to broadly benefit humanity/devotion to human welfare"[2] or "to strive for the well-being of humankind."[3]

Consciousness Raising

Some Koreans, particularly academics, are beginning to point to the absence of a systemic approach to deal effectively with public safety. They also ask about strategies to confront the public's attitude toward this subject and the need to change. As an example of this nascent consciousness-raising, an article titled "Safety Before Money – People Have to Change in Order for the Country/Government to Change," appearing in the *Seoul Times* on April 16, 2018, quotes Gangwon University Public Administration Science Professor Kim Dae Gun:

> Accident awareness and response have improved. However, the regulatory and systemic aspects have yet to keep pace with said progress. Legislators are very deliberate [in] passing new, stricter safety regulations. For Korea to evolve as a safe country, Koreans' awareness and attitude toward public safety need to evolve. Such a change among Koreans can influence legislators to pass the necessary safety and enforcement regulations. Safety enforcement through regulation will help to change the Korean people's behavior.[4]

It is encouraging to see this emerging consciousness-raising. I agree wholeheartedly with Professor Kim Dae Gun's opinion that legislators should adopt stricter safety and enforcement regulations and that the people's mindset regarding public safety must change. These changes are needed for Korea to evolve and claim its rightful place among the world's highly developed countries economically, technologically, and in public safety.

Following the fire in Jecheon, an opinion article written by Lee Jae-min, Professor of Law at Seoul National University, underscores the need for people to change their attitude vis-à-vis yet another issue related to public safety—"random parking" or "liberal parking." It has been identified as a significant obstacle for firefighting personnel responding to fire emergencies. In some cases, drivers who park illegally have contributed to fatalities in large structure fires. Therefore, although random or liberal parking may appear mundane to people from other developed countries, its impact on Korea's psyche cannot be underestimated.[5]

In this opinion article, Professor Lee identifies the relationship between the Korean love affair with personal convenience, short-term financial gains, and the propensity for breaking the rules and inconveniencing their fellow Koreans to achieve their goals. Professor Lee's urgent call for social change provides a breath of fresh air in a country that has endured innumerable human tragedies.

Articles such as the one cited show that elements are beginning to contribute to the consciousness-raising of the masses. According to a code of ethics that values human lives, it behooves Korea to have individuals with the courage to sensitize the public about upholding safety standards and adhering to regulations. This is true even in areas as mundane as parking.

Positive Signs

Despite the litany of recent man-made and industrial accidents, some encouraging signs indicate that progress toward establishing a higher awareness of individual and collective suffering is occurring. Government officials and legislators appear to be taking significant steps toward adopting procedures that reduce death tolls in accidents of any origin. Specifically, because of public pressure, government officials and legislators are taking stricter measures and adopting legislation to protect contingent workers' rights and uphold public safety.

For example, the Seoul metropolitan government amended the Framework Act on Firefighting Services. The amendment, which went into effect on June 27, 2018, gives Seoul's local police and fire departments the authority to deal more proactively and decisively with violators. It also increases fines and enables fire departments to act more forcefully in firefighting situations. The December 27, 2018, passage of the Occupational Safety and Health Act amendment, also known as the "Kim Yong-kyun Bill," is another example of the forward movement in legislating the protection of contingent laborers and upholding public safety.

Furthermore, government officials appear to be taking public safety more seriously. Unlike the actions driven by corruption and greed surrounding the June 1995 Sampoong Department Store building collapse, on December 12, 2018, the Gangnam District Office dared to order the evacuation and closure of the 15-story Daejong Building. This action was taken due to reports that the building had shown signs of "structural defects."[6]

Goal Setting with Measurable Achievables

In January 2018, the former Deputy Prime Minister for Economic Affairs, Kim Dong Yeon, announced his economic and technological development plan. It contained concrete goals with measurable achievables. These goals included a 3% GDP annual growth and $32,000 GNI per capita. Additionally, he proposed the implementation of an autonomous bus system in Seoul by 2020 and the utilization of 3,700 drones in public services, including mail delivery, police services, and firefighting, by 2021.[7] Although these goals may have ceased to be applicable because the deputy prime minister for economic affairs was replaced, by making these targets public, the government made them official and enlisted the support of the people.

By contrast, safety-related government pronouncements are general and lack concrete metrics. The language includes the following statements: "We want to make Korea safe." "We want to ensure that these accidents do not happen again." or "We will ensure that safety regulations are obeyed." It is unclear what the Korean government's definition of "safe" is. Does it mean 5%, 10%, 15%, or 20% fewer accidents annually? Or is a different metric being used? How are government officials going to ensure that the public obeys safety regulations? Is the government going to impose strict and stiff fines for violators? Are existing penalties going to be enforced? Are current sanctions going to be increased so they genuinely become a deterrent for would-be violators?

In summary, it is unclear how these lofty, general goals will be achieved or what steps will be taken to ensure they are met. Contrary to Kim Dong Yeon's economic goals, specific, concrete metrics for public safety goals have yet to be presented. Doing so would ensure that the success and failure of public safety goals are quantifiable. When objective criteria or concrete metrics are stated, government officials, prominent corporation executives, and small company owners can be held accountable for the stated goals.

However, it is challenging to hold anyone accountable when vague goals are stated without presenting concrete metrics and stipulating the responsible parties. In this case, the vague goals become empty promises. These pledges might either save face, appease a nation, or both. In the case of shoddy construction prone to accidents, highly flammable buildings, and structures that do not meet safety regulations, it makes sense to be transparent by informing the public how many facilities are inspected each year. Moreover, once those inspections are done, would it make sense to be transparent and share with the public what percentage of the buildings fail to meet safety standards? How many buildings must be demolished and rebuilt following strict safety regulations? It would make sense to be transparent and publish how many building owners are fined for violating safety regulations and for how much. These violations may include remodeling a building without the proper permits, failing to undergo the appropriate inspections, blocking emergency exits, allowing illegal parking to block emergency equipment access, and deactivating fire sprinkler systems.

A New Paradigm

Some Koreans would support being faithful to the formula that brought the country from the poverty level at the end of the Korean War to have a guaranteed seat among the G-20 nations. That formula, they will argue, includes an emphasis on efficiency and short-term financial gains. However, the country's economic and technological advancements have placed the nation at a vastly different level based on a rock-solid foundation. This position enables the citizenry to forge the country's future and take advantage of forward economic and technological momentum. This privileged position has gained Korea the respect and admiration of friends and foes. The time has come for policymakers, business leaders, and, most importantly, the public to establish a new paradigm. Such a model should include the following:

- a focus on long-range goals with measurable objectives at designated intervals;
- a citizenry with a mindset that understands the rationale behind safety regulations and balances short-term financial gains with public safety;
- government leaders with the stamina to pass stringent safety regulations and the fortitude to enforce them rigorously;
- business leaders and policymakers willing to play a proactive role in public safety. They should also be willing to work with academicians and others to analyze public safety matters using a systemic approach.

Changing social paradigms rooted deeply in a nation's fabric and undoing years of building construction that fails to meet safety standards will take time and money. However, the effort and financial investment will demonstrate a serious commitment to public safety. It will signal a new era for Korea.

- When accidents occur frequently, one must consider to what extent they are true "accidents" and not the result of cultural imperatives.
- A segment of the population believes that sacrifices by a few are inevitable for the country to maintain its economic viability and vitality. Therefore, some innocent lives will be lost in achieving financial prosperity.
- "For Korea to evolve as a safe country, Koreans' awareness and attitude toward public safety need to evolve."[4]
- The government cannot legislate attitudinal change. The desire for change must come from the public.

CHAPTER TEN

How Current Conditions and Changing Values Impact Korea's Economy and Population

The Food-Sharing Concept

Two notable humanistic values historically held by Koreans include generosity and food sharing. Food sharing with friends, neighbors, and even strangers is widely practiced. It remains true even in modern-day Korea, with its impressive skyscrapers, technology and infrastructure, competitive society, extensive use of makeup, plastic surgery, Botox, and the omnipresent K-pop. The concept of food sharing, which I introduce in Chapter Three, is a touching and charming quality. It is a value I admire profoundly and will remain engraved in my heart for as long as I live. The times I was invited to enjoy a meal in someone's home are too numerous to describe in this book. Suffice it to say that I felt honored to be asked to share a meal with various people. Also, I have fond memories of total strangers offering me food while walking toward Buddhist temples in small towns and traveling from one city to another using public transportation.

It is common practice for bus drivers to provide passengers on intercity trips with 15-minute comfort breaks at rest stops. Unlike those in the U.S. and elsewhere, these rest stops are truly vibrant malls. They include coffee shops, music stores, and full-service restaurants or food courts. Because of time constraints during these breaks, most passengers gravitate toward items they can enjoy on the bus, such as roasted chestnuts if they purchase any food. If I was traveling alone, it was common for the person sitting next to me to offer me some of the food they bought.

On one occasion, under different circumstances, I recall walking toward a Buddhist temple in a small town where I stopped to rest. Sitting on some rocks was a father and his two children. They were enjoying tangerines. After I sat down, the father half-peeled and offered me a tangerine. This gesture was so moving that I could not imagine refusing the stranger's kindness. I observed a similar food-sharing behavior among the students enrolled at the American school where I taught.

Living so far away from home, I stayed in contact with my Korean friends who taught at the university level. They became an essential part of my experience, not only in terms of becoming intimately familiar with the fabric of the culture but, more importantly, as a support network. In a sense, they became members of my extended family. We met regularly to share a meal even though we lived in different cities. We took turns visiting each other, usually on one-day trips. On one occasion, when they traveled to Jeonju, they suggested that we have dinner in a restaurant on what they commonly referred to as *makgeolli* (also spelled *makkoli*) street. The purpose was so I could experience the food and accompanying rice wine by the same name. The food is served in small portions to let customers taste as many dishes as possible. In the Spanish food vernacular, these dishes would be labeled *tapas*.

"Koreans have been brewing *makgeolli* [막걸리] since the Shilla Dynasty (57 BC to 935 AD)."[1] It was the alcoholic beverage of choice in Korea in the 1960s and 1970s. However, in the 1970s, it began losing appeal as younger generations turned to imported beverages such as beer. *Makgeolli* regained popularity among young people in the 21st century because of its health benefits and low alcohol content.[2] It contains six to eight percent alcohol by volume.[3] The vitamin and probiotic-rich beverage is fermented, unfiltered, milky-white, semi-sweet, and lightly effervescent. It is served in bowls like soup.

As my friends and I were having dinner, I could not help but notice that I was the only non-Korean in a packed restaurant. This fact did not go unnoticed by other patrons, I am sure. The people sitting beside us were curious about my preferred dishes. As we continued to enjoy our meal, they became friendly. They started to order dishes for us that they noticed I particularly enjoyed. I attempted to reciprocate their kindness, but they would not hear of it. I could sense that their effort to be friendly and kind was genuine. I asked my friends whether this behavior was common. They explained that it was more typical in non-metropolitan areas than in big cities like Seoul, where the proliferation of Westerners is more prevalent. They further clarified that it probably used to happen in Seoul a couple of decades earlier.

When I inquired about other food-sharing traditions, my friends shared one that seemed particularly interesting. When people move into a new neighborhood, they prepare or purchase sweet rice cakes, known as *tteok* (떡), to share with their new neighbors. This tradition is prevalent in rural areas. *Tteok* is a celebratory food often shared on New Year's Day, weddings, and birthdays.

It "can range from rather elaborate versions with nuts and fruits down to the plain-flavored *tteok* used in home cooking."[4]

I was fortunate to experience many more food-sharing moments, too numerous to recount in this book. However, the one that stands out as an expression of kindness occurred while I was bedridden for about five days with the flu. One late afternoon, someone knocked on my door. Since my apartment was located in a secure dorm area accessible only to residents, I was particularly puzzled by the knocking. As I opened the door, I was surprised to see one of the school administrators. She inquired about my condition and handed me specially prepared, homemade chicken soup and side dishes in re-sealable containers. I enjoyed two servings of the delicious meal, which helped me regain my strength.

In all my travels to other parts of the world, I have never experienced such genuine generosity in food sharing as I encountered in Korea. This tradition is alive and well, especially in rural areas. However, other long-standing traditions seem to be declining.

The Impact of Globalization

As we analyze the changes in values, traditions, customs, and behavioral patterns in Korea today, we must recognize globalization and social media's impact on cultures across continents. As a result, some of these elements are shifting or disappearing, others are being questioned, and still, others are being imported and exported. Eventually, they are adopted by people in other parts of the world. Because of the pronounced cultural differences, this trend is particularly palpable in the exchange between East and West.

For example, food seems to be at the forefront of this cultural exchange. The American fast-food concept, namely hamburgers and pizza, entered Eastern countries during the last twenty to forty-five years. McDonald's invasion of Eastern countries is a prime example of this exchange. Table 1 below shows the year McDonald's opened its first restaurant in each Asian country listed and the number of locations as of 2014 and 2022.

Conversely, Asian foods have become popular worldwide. For example, Paris Baguette, a Korean-based chain of bakeries and coffee shops, was set to open its 150th store in North America in September 2023.[5]

These two examples reflect the power of globalization. They illustrate the proliferation of not only commerce but also traditions, practices, fads, customs, rituals, beliefs, and, most importantly, values from one country or region of the globe to another. Television, movies, social media, the Internet, and

Table 1: McDonald's First and Total Locations in Asian Countries[6 and 7]

Country	First Location[a]	Total Locations as of 2014[b]	Total Locations as of 2022[c]
China	1990	N/A	4,978
Japan	1971	3,300+	2,968
Philippines	1981	400+	705
India	1996	300	512
Taiwan	1984	~397	409
South Korea	1988	~300	399
Malaysia	1982	N/A	341
Indonesia	1991	~150	279
Hong Kong	1975	N/A	250
Thailand	1986	~195	227
Singapore	1979	120+	143
Vietnam	2014	N/A	29

Note. Data are from *Getchee* (2014)[a and b] and *Statista* (2023)[c]

access to unrestricted travel have contributed enormously to this phenomenon. Globalization is making us more alike rather than different from one another.

In the United States, Chinese food had a head start over others because of the long history of Chinese immigration, which began between 1848 and 1865. It coincided with the discovery of gold in California, also known as the Gold Rush, and the start of the transcontinental railroad. In the recent past, however, Thai, Indian, and Korean food has gained popularity in many parts of the country.

Similarly, in the West, more people than ever before are involved in Eastern-inspired meditation and yoga. The arts and the media have had a role in the cultural exchange we are witnessing. For example, it is easy to see the influence of hip-hop and Michael Jackson on K-pop. Now, K-pop has become a global phenomenon.

Internal cultural changes instigated by country-specific conditions have motivated a portion of the evolution in values. External influences, such as exchanges between East and West, initiate another portion of the evolution. The influence of Western values on Eastern societies may be more evident than vice versa because of the radical cultural shift that this evolution represents. Some of the adopted values often conflict with traditional local principles. Globalization, social media, and the Internet have accelerated the evolution of values worldwide at a more profound level, particularly in Asia and, more specifically, in Korea. Two emerging value changes underway in Korea are a shift from unity and conformity to an individualistic model and from respect to disrespect for senior citizens. Other shifting values include the adoption of a materialistic attitude as reflected in the emphasis on physical appearance and the universal appreciation for luxurious or expensive items to distinguish oneself from the masses. The pervasive competitive mentality is partially responsible for this change. Other change agents include Western cultural influence and the adoption of the efficiency concept, a classic capitalist trait. The discussion below will focus on changing values rather than those already deeply embedded in Korean culture, which we discuss in more detail in Chapters One through Four.

Family Values and Respect for Elders

Nowadays, family values are emphasized much less, and respect for elders is disappearing rapidly. Instead, youth and physical appearance are revered, as witnessed by the prominence of young people in the media and the extensive use of cosmetics, plastic surgery, and Botox. Baby boomers hold a respectable societal position thanks to their accumulated wealth. However, the generational gap between the elderly and young people in their 20s and 30s is widening.

Young Lee and I recognize that the challenges a generational gap represents are universal. However, in Korea, the concept of respect for older adults is undergoing a radical 180-degree shift to disrespect for seniors. Instead of referencing the traditional Korean phrase "respect seniors" (경로), the expression with the opposite meaning, "disrespect seniors" (혐로), is more often mentioned. The power struggle between the older generation, i.e., baby boomers, and the younger generation is reflected in popular Korean dramas. The growing gulf between the two appears to have three definite sources:

- a sense that senior citizens represent an economic burden to younger people, e.g., the higher cost of social services associated with a growing aging population;
- political discord between the zeal of the older generation to support traditional values and the younger generation's rejection of the same;

- youth's perception of seniors as owning most of the individual wealth, which was amassed by heavy investments in real estate in somewhat of a speculative frenzy and produced skyrocketing housing prices, particularly in metropolitan areas like Seoul and Busan. Data published by the *Korea Times* reveals this real estate speculative craze and indicates the gap between the haves and have-nots. The Ministry of Land, Infrastructure and Transport data show that "nearly 8,000 homes were purchased by just 30 people"[8] from 2018 to June 2023. Additionally, the news article informs that "the aggregate value of the [...] homes was worth 1.19 trillion won ($897.37 million)."[9] The report further specifies that 24 of the 30 purchasers concentrated their acquisitions in "Seoul, Incheon and Gyeonggi Province, where the housing demand is the highest in the country."[10]

Consequently, young people justifiably see themselves as financially challenged by the older generation's aggressive investing, which has made real estate unaffordable for them, given their salaries. Consequently, it is becoming more difficult for them to experience total financial independence without their parents' support. Many remain in their parents' homes even after securing a job because of the exorbitant housing prices.

The other side of the coin concerning the perceived reasons for the gap between the older and younger generations is that the baby boomers helped rebuild the country after the Korean War. Through individual and collective sacrifices, they helped transition the nation out of poverty in the 1950s and 1960s. In essence, they helped build Korea into the model economy it is today.

In this tug-of-war between the two generations, it is also crucial to recognize the younger generation's contribution to the transformation of Korean culture, which is being exported worldwide through K-pop, K-drama, K-beauty, plastic surgery, food, and technology. The technology coming out of Korea can compete in today's consumer-oriented society against all comers, including Apple, Ford, GE, GM, Google, Honda, Intel, Kenmore, Toyota, and Whirlpool. For better or worse, Korean culture will never be the same. This cultural transformation is making significant contributions to the Korean economy as well.

I experienced a certain reverence for older adults when I first began traveling around Korea in my mid-40s in the late 1990s. This respect for elders was evident in subtle ways. For example, it was common for young people to offer me their seats on the Seoul subway if I happened to board at a time when there were no seats available. It is true, however, that I was one of a handful of Westerners visiting Korea in those days, not counting those in the armed services. Nowadays, Westerners are more plentiful as the number of tourists has increased significantly, and so has the number of Western residents mainly working as educators in *hagwons* and international schools. However, I believe age was a more critical factor than race in the young people's behavior toward me.

In comparison, as I traveled on the Seoul subway during my latest stay as a gray-haired Westerner, only another senior citizen offered me his seat, which I politely declined. It is true, however, that now the Seoul metro, and perhaps others, have designated seats for seniors, which I believe is different from 20-30 years ago. As a result, younger people may not feel compelled to give up their seats to older adults for this reason.

Although the above example of the shift in the treatment of seniors may appear mundane to the casual observer, evidence has been published recently supporting this observation. The National Human Rights Commission of Korea conducted a survey. It published its findings in the 2018 "Report on Senior Human Rights."[11] Through the survey, the Commission found that 56% of the young people surveyed believed that senior citizens take jobs away from them. Another key finding indicates that young people consider that any increase in social services for seniors represents an additional burden on them. The report also showed that 81.9% of people in their 20s and 30s who participated in the survey responded "yes" to the statement: "The conflict between the younger generation and senior citizens is very serious."[12]

Undoubtedly, the root of the conflict is complex and multifaceted. Still, it is natural for younger people to feel the economic pinch associated with the increasing costs of social benefits for a growing aging population. Relatively fewer actively working young people are available to pay for these services. Unfortunately, the situation may be exacerbated in the future, given the prevailing low fertility rate registered in Korea, which we discuss later in this chapter.

The difference in political views between senior citizens and millennials may be a case of the older generations retaining traditional, age-old values and questioning those of younger generations. Albeit subtle in many respects, the divide between these two entities may have become more pronounced and palpable recently as different population segments declared stances on the impeachment of the first female president, Park Geun-hye. It was evident in various demonstrations throughout the country that, for the most part, senior citizens showed support for the former leader. By doing so, they showed reverence toward her father, former President Park Chung-hee. He ruled Korea from 1963 until his assassination in 1979. Thus, her supporters identified with traditional values. Young people generally stood on the opposite side of the scale: They supported impeachment. Also, young people's adoption of the term *Hell Joseon* about present-day Korea underscores the generational gap between the younger and older generations.

Because of these differences, young people increasingly perceive seniors as conservative, inflexible, unwilling to, or incapable of adapting to a new era with new ideas. For example, young people view the older generation as technologically inept and unable to utilize computers and social media. Consequently, seniors realize they are being left behind in some areas and fear further isolation and ostracization. Thus, many are trying to adjust to present-day technology gradually or, at the very least, partially acquiesce to the demands of a new era. They are realistic enough to recognize that they cannot stop the wave of change by resisting it. Instead, some are trying to ride the wave. Senior citizens generally acknowledge the benefits and sacrifices associated with the drive to become more efficient. They know that efficiency has moved the country forward relatively quickly. Also, they have embraced the notion of maintaining an attractive physical appearance. Most senior citizens dye their hair black and use makeup. Those with the means to do so wear stylish, youthful clothing.

Regarding the use of technology, some senior citizens make a concerted effort to update their skills by attending workshops or classes that teach them how to use computers and social media. Many choose to stay socially active. They enroll in music, singing, drawing, and traditional Korean dance courses to acquire new knowledge, fine-tune their skills, or remain in shape. Many attend church, participate in church-related activities, and share meals with friends in their favorite restaurants. Some go hiking with friends on weekends, a favorite Korean activity.

Despite these efforts by senior citizens, the divide between millennials and older generations remains vast, particularly regarding family values, individual sacrifice for the good of the whole, and respect for the elderly. Consequently, older adults find themselves in a quandary. Should they adhere to traditional values? They realize that by keeping to conventional principles, they will likely grow the generational gap and become even more isolated and disrespected. Alternatively, should they accept the new values espoused by the younger generation and provide support for them? Should they try to move with the times, close the generational gap, integrate into the country-wide decision-making processes, and attempt to regain some of the lost respect? A third option may be to compromise. Perhaps older adults could accept some of the changes but not others. Reversing the trend of changing from respecting to disrespecting elders is the responsibility of both parties. Both sides need to find a middle ground through understanding one another and respectful communication.

Emphasis on Materialism

Although television dramas still present historical perspectives and storylines involving *chaebols* and *gap* and *eul* relationships, the focus on materialism—youth, physical appearance, and wealth—is evident in Korean soap operas. Indeed, these concepts are also prevalent in some American dramas; however, the difference lies in the pervasiveness and degree of intensity exhibited in Korean television dramas.

Some of the most popular dramas that focus on materialism and have enjoyed success outside of Korea include *Boys over Flowers* (2009), *Secret Garden* (2010), and *The Heirs* (2013). *Boys over Flowers* is a story about an average girl who finds herself attending a prestigious prep academy after saving a student's life.[13] *Secret Garden* is a Cinderella story between a stuntwoman and a high-end department store CEO.[14] *The Heirs* is another Cinderella story about a handsome conglomerate heir and his family's housekeeper's daughter, an ordinary poor girl.[15]

More recently, *Squid Game* (2021), a series produced by Netflix, depicts a competition through which infinite wealth is made available to the survivor of a series of fatal events.[16] The series theme is economic inequality, and the participants' need for money motivates them to join the deadly game. "The show, which Netflix chief Ted Sarandos has said is on track to become Netflix's most-watched series ever, has dominated charts the world over."[17]

The role models in these dramas are good-looking young women and men in excellent physical condition with shaped eyebrows, wear makeup, and have undergone plastic surgery for a chiseled look. Soap operas and K-pop have contributed enormously to the increase in the use of cosmetics in general. Korea has the distinction of being the eighth-largest cosmetics market in the world.[18] Estimates indicate that the market size in 2016 was approximately $7.1 billion. Furthermore, the market expanded at an annual growth rate of 8.2% for the prior five years.

The surge in cosmetics use by men has been fueled by K-pop idols who popularized an "effeminately masculine" or "beautiful male" aesthetic. Nowadays, Korean men, particularly millennials, commonly use cosmetics, and not just body and aftershave lotion and toner, but BB (blemish balm) cream and other products:

> South Korea accounts for about 20% of the world market for men's cosmetics. This means annual sales of more than $1 million come courtesy of a mere 25 million men, and this figure will inflate by 50% over the next five years.[19]

The competitive nature of society, in general, and the job market, in particular, have influenced the surge in the use of cosmetics. Koreans widely believe that skin appearance gives individuals an advantage in job applications. Employers may have contributed indirectly to the emphasis on physical appearance, as most require job applicants to include a headshot on their résumé.

A cultural side note is in order here. In the United States, with a few exceptions, requiring job seekers to include a photograph with their job application is illegal. Two exceptions would be acting and modeling jobs for which the applicant's appearance is relevant to the position. Several laws make requiring a photograph illegal, including "the Civil Rights Act of 1964 (Title VII), Age Discrimination in Employment Act of 1967 [...] the Civil Service Reform Act of 1978, [and] the Americans with Disabilities Act of 1990 (Title I and V)."[20] It is important to note that these regulations were adopted in the latter part of the 20th century. The rationale behind these laws is to prevent hiring and employment discrimination based on age, sex (including gender, gender identity, sexual orientation, and pregnancy), national origin, and disability. This difference between Korea and some Western countries, particularly the U.S., is striking. I referenced the ethnic and racial homogeneity of Korea versus the diversity of the United States in Chapter Two. This factor and the historical context of the U.S. have undoubtedly contributed to the adoption of laws protecting individuals' civil rights. The U.S. laws above underscore the pursuit of equity and the belief that job applicants' skills, preparation, and experience are more directly related to their job performance than physical appearance.

In Korea, cosmetic surgery and Botox parallel the extensive use of cosmetics. Cosmetic surgery is quite commonplace nowadays in Korea, as it is throughout the world. Two of the most popular body parts undergoing cosmetic surgery are the eyes and the nose.

The country's mentality around cosmetic surgery has changed in recent years. As discussed in Chapter Two, some Korean societal values today are rooted in Confucianism, especially as it was practiced during the Joseon era (1392-1897). Korean Confucianism espoused values and ethical practices, including benevolence, politeness, diligence, obedience to superiors, wisdom, and goodness. The latter includes trustworthiness and honesty.

Someone who adheres to these values and ethical practices would not alter their looks for practical reasons. Furthermore, cosmetic surgery was historically considered shameful because those who had it done were essentially trying to change the body their ancestors gave them. Under Confucianism, even cutting one's hair was considered disrespectful or disobedient because hair was considered a part of the body people inherited from their ancestors.

In the infancy days of plastic surgery (mid-1950s-1960s), the older generations, baby boomers and older, considered the procedure dishonest or immoral because it enabled individuals to change their appearance. People also viewed it as a sign of insincerity. Individuals who underwent plastic surgery were thought to be deceiving others. This deception consisted of misleading others into believing that their looks were better than they were. In addition, individuals undergoing the procedure experienced feelings of guilt for disobeying or disrespecting their ancestors.

Consequently, in the past, Koreans considered plastic surgery taboo. Individuals who underwent the procedure did not want it to become public knowledge. It was deemed shameful because it showed they were pretentious and highly concerned about their physical appearance.

Those beliefs are now considered passé. Nowadays, some Koreans have compelling reasons to undergo cosmetic surgery. It provides them with yet another opportunity to differentiate themselves from the masses and gain an edge in a highly competitive environment. Koreans undergo the procedure to heighten their prospects in the job application process, a potential marriage or matchmaking, to underscore their higher socioeconomic status, or to enhance their appearance. Essentially, plastic surgery has become a status symbol. Those wealthy enough to afford it send a message consciously or unconsciously to the rest of their fellow countrywomen and men that they have money. Therefore, many are very open with friends, family members, and acquaintances about undergoing the procedure. Some even upload videos of their recovery progress on social media.

Korea also exports its culture. Through television dramas and K-pop, Korea presents its version of Hollywood to the rest of the world, particularly Southeast Asian countries and China. As a result of the remarkable success of K-pop and K-drama, the nation has become a mecca for plastic surgery. Cosmetic surgery clinics and medical tourism companies actively promote themselves abroad. Consequently, organized trips by medical tourism companies for people seeking plastic surgery are becoming increasingly popular. One reason for this popularity is that cosmetic surgery in Korea, specifically in Gangnam of "Gangnam Style" fame, has the distinction of high quality. This image is due to the surgeons' reputation as some of Asia's most accomplished.

As a result of this outstanding reputation, and with the help of the popularity of K-pop and K-drama, people from Southeast Asia and China are flocking to Gangnam to have these procedures done. One reason Koreans and foreigners go to Gangnam for plastic surgery is that it is where movie and television celebrities and K-pop idols undergo their procedure.

Furthermore, Seoul's fashionable Gangnam district houses medical tourism companies. They appear to have the government's support, and their promotional campaigns are well organized. Visit Medical Korea's website offers medical tour packages in various areas, including traditional Korean medicine, stem cell treatment, artificial hip joint replacement, plastic surgery, and aesthetics. The website lists 2,084 hospitals and 1,682 facilitators throughout the country. Facilitator companies promote medical tourism through services, including consultation and hotel bookings. A spot check of the translation services available at these hospitals and facilitators' offices indicates that they include the following languages: Arabic, English, Chinese, Japanese, Mongolian, and Russian. The website shows that the Korea Tourism Organization, a government entity, provides its services.[21]

An example of the emphasis on materialism, as it relates to the competitive nature of Korean culture, is found in my personal experience with a parent's interest in her child's future success. This parent believed that taller people usually have greater success in life and their careers. Therefore, she arranged for her child to receive growth hormones. While I taught this student, he endured growing pains and grew to be quite tall. By the time he was in the 10th grade, he was about six feet tall.

The Concept of Automation

The widespread use of automation in everyday life is taken for granted by Koreans who profit from and enjoy the benefits of efficiency, convenience, and consumer savings it generates. Although automation is commonplace in Korea, it may be subtle and unnoticeable for the average tourist. However, the effects of everyday lifestyle are striking for foreigners who can immerse themselves in various aspects of society and the economy. We provide some examples of technologies that support efficiency in the introduction and the first three chapters. Those examples and others are reviewed here from an economic perspective. In today's Korean economy, automation relates to efficiencies associated with unemployment and other pervasive national challenges.

Practical Benefits of Automation

At a practical level, automation generates several benefits. Below are examples of Korean automation strategies that improve efficiency and generate operational cost savings while enhancing convenience and customer service.

Traffic control dummies: My extensive travels throughout the country enabled me to drive by various construction sites where traffic control dummies are used 24 hours a day, alerting drivers to be extra cautious. Their use enables construction companies to save money on personnel costs. Assuming those savings are passed on to the project owners, they, too, benefit financially.

Call buttons on restaurant tables: Besides providing efficient customer service, universally used call buttons enable restaurant owners to save money on personnel. Restauranteurs pass the savings to customers through lower food costs, thus making restaurants more competitive. As a result, customers are the ultimate beneficiaries of this practice. Restauranteurs must utilize cost savings strategies to remain competitive and generate profits. Based on my experience, restaurant food prices in Korea are relatively lower than in the United States when comparing similar dishes.

Centralized food-ordering kiosks: These self-service systems are available in food courts, department stores, bus terminals, supermarkets, and rest stops, where various fast-food restaurants are nearby. The purpose of these self-service kiosks is to make food ordering from multiple restaurants more efficient. These systems enable customers to view the menu and food prices, place an order, and pay the bill for any participating restaurants. Once customers place their orders, they proceed to the restaurant to pick up their food. By providing these self-service kiosks, restaurant owners save money on cashier personnel. Once again, the ultimate beneficiary is the customer who enjoys convenience and lower food prices.

CCTV (closed-circuit television) cameras: CCTV cameras are ubiquitous in Korea. They are readily seen on the streets and in and around buildings. CCTV is used for surveillance, grounds security, crime prevention and investigation, and parking enforcement. Consequently, police and security personnel costs are significantly reduced, if not eliminated.

Speed monitoring system: Speed monitoring cameras strategically located on city streets and highways enable traffic control agencies to reduce street surveillance and highway patrol costs. Agencies also save money on traffic enforcement and clerical personnel since the system can generate citations.

Navigation systems: The Korean navigation system's capability to alert drivers about the location of traffic and speed monitoring cameras enables drivers to avoid speeding citations and possibly other moving violations.

Dashcam recorders: Drivers use the videos produced by the pervasive dashcam recorders installed on windshields as evidence in accident cases. Similarly, insurance claims adjusters utilize the recordings to manage accident-related claims efficiently. Readily available evidence saves time on accident investigations, and customers enjoy a more convenient and efficient claims-filing process. Furthermore, litigation costs are significantly reduced, thanks to the evidence these cameras provide. Therefore, insurance companies save money on personnel by hiring fewer claims adjusters and customer service employees. As a result, insurance companies may pass the savings on to customers.

Client service machines in banks: Most bank branches utilize service machines that issue sequential ticket numbers and direct clients to the appropriate teller based on the individual's transaction needs and arrival time. This customer-service efficiency benefits clients directly and indirectly: Customers receive quality customer service, and banks generate cost savings on staff salaries, which they may pass on to their clients.

Self-service machines in government offices: Customers who need essential services, such as obtaining proof of residency, utilize self-service machines to complete their transactions. By automating their services, government entities provide enhanced customer service and generate savings on personnel costs by hiring fewer office clerks.

A comparable efficient use of technology in the United States is the self-checkout service available at some major chain supermarkets. This service allows customers to avoid standing in long check-out lines and process their transactions by scanning each item in their shopping carts, bagging their groceries, and paying their bills with a debit or credit card.

Automation in hospitals and clinics: Based on my observations, there are many hospitals and clinics nationwide. Therefore, patients have many options. Consequently, the fierce competition generated by healthcare providers compels them to utilize technology to enhance efficiency and cut administrative costs by reducing the number of employees, such as receptionists. The efficiency in healthcare translates into savings for patients in the form of lower medical costs. Based on my experience, medical services in Korea are significantly less expensive than in the U.S.

Intended and Unintended Consequences of Automation

The purpose of including these automation examples is not to condemn Korea's efforts to integrate efficiency into routine service activities and processes. On the contrary, we applaud it. Young Lee and I recognize that automation is embedded into everyday life as societies advance technologically. Similarly, technological advancements facilitate efficiency in all sectors of the economy, which can enhance customer service and generate cost savings. However, it behooves policymakers to recognize the economic effects of maximizing efficiency's intended and unintended consequences and consider these outcomes when making long-term projections and adopting economic policies.

One of the most direct links between automation and the economy is unemployment. The public has voiced complaints about job elimination caused by automation. However, it is impossible to take a step backward once technological advancements are successfully implemented for automation purposes. Therefore, we pose a hypothetical question regarding the complaints about job elimination associated with automation. Suppose it could revert to a prior condition where automation and job losses did not exist. Would the public relinquish the efficiency and monetary savings that automation generates? From personal experience, the public enjoys automation's direct and indirect benefits, including efficiency, convenience, faster service, self-reliance, and lower prices, and eventually accepts the inevitability of job elimination.

However, automation is not the sole factor contributing to unemployment. Cultural elements embedded in Korean society contribute indirectly as well. The preconception that Koreans have of education as the path to financial security, economic prosperity, and prestige, along with the democratization of higher education and the quasi-compulsive eagerness for universal baccalaureate degrees or higher, has severe ramifications at various levels. As discussed in Chapter Four, one impacted area is employment due to the pervasive degree inflation and the oversaturation of overqualified individuals for the available jobs.

Forced Exit from the Labor Force

We have established that one of the unintended consequences of the democratization of higher education is a high degree inflation. More students are graduating from university every year than the economy can absorb. Therefore, the overabundant labor supply of overqualified, overeducated individuals makes it exceptionally advantageous for employers to be financially efficient by refreshing their staff regularly to keep costs down. Therefore, it is common for people in their 40s and 50s to be ousted from the labor force to make room for a younger, less costly, albeit less experienced staff. Once again, economic efficiency is a factor.

As a result, job-related age discrimination is alive and well in Korea. However, given the practical nature of Koreans, they do not view it as discrimination. Instead, they consider this labor force renewal to be a direct result of the country's economic condition and, thus, a fact of life. Koreans know their time in the labor force is limited, so they prepare for this transition. They understand they need to save money during their 20s and 30s. Often, individuals forced out of the labor force do not have sufficient savings for their retirement because of the costs associated with their children's private education. In some cases, after forced retirement in the prime of their lives, they still face educational expenses (e.g., the cost of *hagwons* or university tuition for their children). When individuals find themselves jobless and have insufficient savings, they rely on the older generation to provide them with a place to live and sometimes even enough money to start a small business.

Oversaturation of Small Businesses

Those with financial resources, theirs or their parents', or who can borrow money often opt to launch a small business, albeit without specialized skills or prior entrepreneurial experience. The most popular choices are coffee shops, convenience stores, pizza parlors, and other food preparation and delivery businesses. However, the most common option is to open a fast-food restaurant or convenience store subject to franchising. The oversaturation of these businesses is evident, particularly in coffee shops, convenience stores, and restaurants. It is not unusual to find similar establishments competing for the same clientele in the same block.

Consequently, the competition is brutal, and working conditions are incredibly demanding. In many cases, the income is less than minimum wage, given the long hours required to operate a small business successfully. Also, the bankruptcy rate is relatively high when owners lack small business management and entrepreneurship training. The Korean Federation of Small and Medium-Sized Businesses surveyed 700 small-business owners with less than five employees. They found that, on average, small business owners work 10.9 hours per day, as the ability to hire part-time workers is limited.[22] On average, they take only three days off from work per month.[23] This reality underscores how hard self-employed small business owners must work to make a living. As harsh as this situation is, it may resemble the life of small business owners in other parts of the world since running a small business is a 24/7, 365-days-per-year proposition. Even though the situation of small business owners is less than ideal in Korea, their options are limited.

Unsurprisingly, OECD data support the assertion that the self-employment rate in Korea is exceptionally high. According to 2018 OECD statistics, the country's self-employment rate is 25.1% of total employment. By contrast, the United States' rate is 6.3%, and Japan's is 10.3%.[24] In October 2018, the number of small business owners in Korea was estimated to be 6.7 million, or approximately 26% of the economically active population.[25] The consistently high percentage of the financially active self-employed population is a testimony to the Korean people's entrepreneurial spirit and the limited options available to individuals being nudged out of the labor force. These statistics may also be remnants of the days when Korea was still considered a developing country. Professor Ha-Joon Chang, who teaches economics at the University of Cambridge, asserts that "people are far more entrepreneurial in the developing countries than in the developed countries."[26] His assertion is based on data from an OECD study which shows that

> In most developing countries, 30-50 percent of the non-agricultural workforce is self-employed [....] In some of the poorest countries, the ratio of people working as one-person entrepreneurs can be way above that [....] In contrast, only 12.8 percent of the non-agricultural workforce in developed countries is self-employed.[27]

Degree inflation seems to contribute to Korea's high unemployment rate. As previously mentioned, the oversupply of overqualified candidates in the job market opens the door for financially efficient managers to replace middle-aged workers with younger, less costly, albeit less experienced employees. This practice leaves many individuals with family responsibilities in their mid-40s to mid-50s unemployed. These people are desperate to make a living and possibly pay off loans. Consequently, opening a small business is viewed as a quick and efficient solution for an individual's unemployment dilemma. However, the macroeconomic challenge remains unresolved, and the high bankruptcy rate of small businesses is exacerbated.

Franchise companies enable individuals with little or no small business management training to try entrepreneurship by providing the necessary services, products, ingredients, and merchandise. Therefore, opening a small business by franchising is a simple, efficient, albeit risky way of becoming a business owner. Ultimately, if the venture fails, it is the individual's financial burden, not the franchise corporation's. This tension results in fierce competition among small business owners and a high bankruptcy rate. Many small business owners are forced to borrow money to support themselves and their families while trying to get the business off the ground. Understandably, this predicament aggravates the family's financial situation.

Another reason individuals may choose to generate some income by becoming small business owners after retirement is insufficient retirement savings caused by the high cost of their children's private education. Ultimately, what appears to be a sure bet becomes a long-term struggle for economic survival.

Traditional Expectations Versus New Attitudes

In the past, young men were expected to be married by age 30 after graduating from university, completing their military service, and working for a few years. Young women were expected to be wedded by their late 20s. However, nowadays, young men and women increasingly opt to remain single for an extended period. In many cases, they choose to give up marriage altogether because of the financial commitment of having a family and raising children and the fear of being unable to meet these expectations. Some men extend their single life to work and save enough money to successfully undertake the socially acceptable path. This path includes having enough money to support their family and provide a quality private education for their children.

Hell Joseon

By using the satirical and critical term *Hell Joseon*, young people are voicing their rejection of the country's values. They are symbolically repudiating the characteristics of Korean society that make it difficult for them to find opportunities and happiness. These traits include some of the attributes discussed in this book: competition, personal sacrifice, high youth unemployment, and the unfulfilled promise of education as a panacea for financial success. They are notably rejecting the traditional formula for getting ahead socially and economically. The younger generation's rejection of this concept stems from their perception that the conventional path is no longer viable and the playing field favors the affluent. Therefore, they are forced to give up the things that make human beings happy.

Young people are convinced that the country's economic miracle does not apply to them. They feel misguided, let down, and disenfranchised, but most importantly, their crushed self-esteem renders them incapable of meeting expectations in the prevailing competitive environment. Consequently, they feel helpless vis-à-vis the prospect of giving up the precious things in life that most humans cherish.

Young Koreans go by different names depending on the number of things they must give up in life. The *Sampo* generation comprises those forced to give up relationships, marriage, and children.[28] Exorbitant private education expenses cause some of these life-changing decisions. The private education cost that depleted their parents' life savings is one they cannot afford for their offspring if they dare to have any.

When they are required to abandon homeownership and social life, they become the *Opo* generation.[29] Young people's perception that homeownership in Korea is practically impossible for working individuals without financial assistance from parents or relatives is understandable. According to *Numbeo*, the property price index for Seoul in 2015 was 16.8 years.[30] In other words, given the median salary in Seoul, an individual would have to save their full salary for 16.8 years to afford an average-priced home. That figure is trending upward. *Numbeo* reported that the property price index for Seoul went up to 18.1 and 29.6 years based on the median salary in 2018 and 2023, respectively.[31] Once dreams and hopes are added to the list of sacrifices, they become the *Chilpo* generation.[32] When the list of things the young must give up is all-encompassing, they call themselves the *N-Po* generation or those who must give up everything in life.[33]

The plight of this disenfranchised crop of young people has become so hopeless that they use self-deprecating language to mock their condition. They depict their lives as hellish and use the satirical term *Hell Joseon*, which alludes to the Joseon era (1392-1897), to refer to Korea.[34] They hierarchize themselves as "clay spoon," those who have nothing, as opposed to "golden spoon," those who are privileged or born with everything they need, and "silver spoon," those who are born with some privileges but not quite everything. To them, Korea represents a society where an individual's status is predetermined by their family's wealth or lack thereof. Therefore, if individuals are born into families with limited resources, any sacrifices they or their families make to improve their lives are of little or no consequence.

Gross Domestic Product, Annual Growth, and Gross National Income Per Capita

In Chapter 1, we discussed GDP annual growth and GNI per capita in general terms to show Korea's economic trajectory from the war's end to the present. In this section, we present specific GDP and GNI data in preparation for the next segment on youth unemployment to show that not everyone benefits from the Miracle on the Han River.

According to the World Bank, Korea has achieved remarkable success in the last several decades, combining rapid economic growth with significant poverty reduction. From 1988 to 2022, the country has maintained a phenomenal GDP annual growth average of 4.9%. In the last ten years (2013-2022),

GDP annual growth normalized between 2.2% and 3.2%, except for 2020 and 2021. These two years were atypical because they were the first two full years of the COVID-19 pandemic.[35] Similarly, GNI per capita experienced steady increases during the same period, except for 2020, the first full year of the pandemic. However, it rebounded nicely in 2021. See Table 2.

Table 2: GDP Growth and GNI per Capita (Atlas Method, Current US$)[36]

Year	GDP Growth	GNI Per Capita
2013	3.2%	$26,980
2014	3.2%	$28,160
2015	2.8%	$28,720
2016	2.9%	$29,330
2017	3.2%	$30,300
2018	2.9%	$32,750
2019	2.2%	$33,830
2020	-0.7%	$33,040
2021	4.1%	$35,110
2022	2.6%	$35,990

Youth Unemployment

Even though GDP growth has been remarkable, youth unemployment is considered high. "Youth unemployment in South Korea hit a record 9.8 percent in 2017, almost three times the national rate of 3.7 percent and worse than the 4 percent youth unemployment rate in Japan and 8.1 percent in the United States."[37] That inauspicious mark was surpassed the following year when youth unemployment reached 10.1% and equaled in 2019. The new record of 10.1% was equaled again in 2020 during the first full year of the COVID-19 pandemic.[38] See Table 3.

Many young people with a bachelor's degree hold odd jobs that can barely pay the cost of a matchbox-style apartment, some groceries, and street fast food with highly questionable nutritional value. They have irregular jobs, often associated with minimum wages or full-time jobs at part-time pay with no fringe benefits.

Table 3: Youth Unemployment Rate[39]
(% of Total Labor Force Ages 15-24, Modeled ILO Estimate)

Year	Youth Unemployment Rate
2013	7.9%
2014	8.6%
2015	9.9%
2016	10.2%
2017	9.8%
2018	10.1%
2019	9.8%
2020	10.1%
2021	8.1%
2022	6.9%

The Moon government expressed concern about the high youth unemployment. His administration planned to propose a supplementary budget to boost business subsidies. Per the *Segye Times*, March 21, 2018, the subsidy's purpose was to close the gap temporarily between the entry-level salary at large corporations (~$35,000 or 38 million Korean won) and small to mid-sized companies (~$23,000 or 25 million Korean won).[40] The emphasis here is on "temporary" for three to five years. The *Segye Times* also reported that many believed this subsidy would not help solve the fundamental problems associated with high youth unemployment.[41] A similar, previously implemented unemployment subsidy program also failed. People expressed concerns on social media about the proposed subsidies. Many predicted the program would fail for the reasons listed below.

Several factors indicate that working conditions are better in large firms than in small to mid-sized companies. Workers have expressed the following concerns:

- Work hours are longer in small to mid-sized companies than in large corporations.

- Smaller firms occasionally cannot pay employee salaries on time.
- Smaller companies tend to hire temporary workers or contract workers, usually for a maximum of two years. These individuals have reason to be severely anxious about their future after the initial two years.
- Many young people would not settle for a salary-matching situation.
- Workers expressed concern that the three- to five-year subsidy was a stop-gap measure with an eventual potentially negative impact. They worried that the salary and working conditions gap between small to mid-sized companies and large corporations would widen after the subsidy expired. Consequently, their purchasing power and quality of life would be negatively impacted. Young people were particularly apprehensive about placing their future at risk for a small temporary subsidy.

In Search of a Fresh Start Abroad

Many of these discouraged and desperate but adventurous individuals have started a trend of creating a savings plan to emigrate to or obtain a working visa from another country, such as Australia, to start a new life. They hope to begin a life with a higher prospect of succeeding and maintaining at least some of their life dreams intact. Following is a case study from my personal experience that illustrates this situation.

A university student saved money to leave Korea for Australia to train as a chef. Before making his final decision to leave Korea, we gathered on a couple of occasions along with some of his closest friends. At these gatherings, we could sense his depression to the point where we were concerned about his safety. Fortunately, he was a mature young man and did not act impulsively. Eventually, he made peace with his decision to leave Korea for a brighter future and regained his sense of humor and thirst for life. Once he made his decision, he invited us to attend a farewell gathering, where we all contributed financially according to our means to help make his daring journey come true. He left Korea to pursue his dream of becoming a chef, finding a more stable financial situation, and leading a life with less competition and stress. Subsequently, his girlfriend joined him in Australia, where they still live after almost ten years. He is working as a cook, learning to become a chef, and enjoying life more than he would have had he stayed in his native Korea. He is now in the process of applying for Australian residency.

I was fortunate enough to stay connected with him via text messaging. I told him I was writing this book and asked if he would be willing to answer a few questions regarding his decision to uproot himself to Australia. He agreed. Below are some of the thoughts he shared about his choice to leave Korea:

> I feel very lucky to work in the kitchen where [I am] support[ed] [by a] good staff and [we] work as a team. I already achieved more than I expected. [Being] a good chef is what I want for now.
>
> [If I had stayed in Korea,] I think I might [be] work[ing] as an office worker. In korea... My body would be comfy and relax[ed], but mentally I don't think I [would have] stop[ped] searching for something that makes me happy.
>
> I decided [to keep] working [in Australia] ... no need to keep searching for something related to my future.[42]

The feeling I perceive from reading his comments is a sense of relief. Being away from the pressures in Korea enabled him to pursue his dream of becoming a chef without the social stigma of working in the service industry. It also relieved him of the stress caused by future employment concerns.

Based on my experience, this is not an isolated case. Other young Koreans are looking to pursue their dreams elsewhere. What will happen to Korea as a result of this exodus of energetic, entrepreneurial young people who are emigrating to other countries in search of a better life?

Young people leaving for a better future elsewhere presents a significant challenge and an opportunity for the country. This phenomenon is not new to Korea. In the 1960s and 1970s, the exodus of middle-class families and young people to the United States and other Western countries became a brain-drain concern. Later, this apprehension dissipated. Eventually, some well-educated, English-fluent, second-and-third generation Koreans born in the West, primarily scientists and engineers, returned to Korea and contributed to the country's globalization efforts.

Despite the nation's unprecedented economic success since the war's end, it is evident that its economy has experienced challenges in recent years. Part of the problem, especially during and after the 2008 U.S. financial crisis, was caused by the economic slowdown. Decreasing exports, a slowdown in the Chinese economy, and the decline in the oil price contributed to this challenge. Since Korea must import its oil, one would think that the low oil price would benefit the economy. However, oil-producing countries had less money to import goods. Since Korea is an exporting nation of high-tech machines, automobiles, and such, its economy ails when other countries cannot purchase its exports.

Fertility Rate

Korea's fertility rate has declined steadily for approximately 40 years. World Bank data indicate that the fertility rate from 2010 to 2021 was as follows:

Table 4: Fertility Rate 2010-2021[43]

Year	Fertility Rate
2010	1.23
2011	1.24
2012	1.30
2013	1.19
2014	1.21
2015	1.24
2016	1.17
2017	1.05
2018	0.98
2019	0.92
2020	0.84
2021	0.81

Even though we are presenting the available data for the last 12 years as of this writing, the decline pattern is similar as far back as 1999. In fact, the rate has been less than 2.0 since 1984.[44] Interestingly, this coincides with the start of the democratization of higher education and the development of Gangnam. The persistently low fertility rate cannot replace the current population. Therefore, the trend is bound to have long-lasting economic and security repercussions. Although other industrialized countries are experiencing a similar phenomenon, cultural and economic factors make Korea's low fertility rate uniquely challenging.

Cultural and Economic Factors Contributing to the Low Fertility Rate

In Korea, private education expenses are indeed associated with the cost of raising children and remain a source of consternation for prospective parents. This factor is significant in a country like Korea, where the perception that private education is essential for students to stand a chance in the nation's competitive academic environment is universally accepted. The exorbitant real estate prices are another factor associated with the low fertility rate.

As a result of these primary factors, an increasing number of young men perceive themselves as unable to provide the standard of living women expect for themselves and their children. Similarly, many young women feel incapable of meeting the social expectations placed on them. Traditionally, women were expected to stay home to raise children and care for their husbands. Nowadays, Korean women play a more active role in the workplace; however, social expectations are difficult to ignore, let alone eradicate.

Consequently, career women find it challenging to maintain their careers and meet traditional expectations of married women, e.g., doing housework, caring for their husbands and children, and grocery shopping. Therefore, increasingly, they are opting to remain single, or if they choose to marry, they may elect not to have children. Although these trends are pervasive in other industrialized countries, Korea's cultural fascination with efficiency exacerbates these trends to a problematic extent.

Cultural, social, and economic factors are pivotal in deciding whether to remain single, marry, and have children. According to the Korean mentality, the ideal parent should be able to provide financial assistance to their children. Moon Moo-gyeong, head of international research and cooperation for the Korea Institute of Childcare and Education, conducted research and confirmed this belief. He presented the survey results at the Childrearing Advancement Forum on December 13, 2016. According to the survey findings, "parents believe that financial ability is the most crucial requirement for being an ideal parent."[45]

Furthermore, respondents deem themselves "inadequate as parents because of their perception that they are not providing enough financial assistance."[46] Therefore, some Korean couples consider themselves incapable of measuring up to these sociocultural expectations and opt not to have children rather than become parents and run the risk of being unable to provide the necessary financial support for their children. Specifically, the above survey found that parents spend "an average of 24.8% of their household income on raising their children."[47] Furthermore, "59.7% of parents feel pressured by these expenditures."[48]

Household Projections

For years, demographic projections about decreasing household size have anticipated what is happening in Korea. Forecasts about households with children versus those without and one-person households signal that the trend will continue past 2030. In 2010, Statistics Korea projected that households with children would undergo a significant reduction in the 20 years from 2010 to 2030. Households with children were projected to decrease from 54.7% to 45.5% of total households.[49] In the meantime, households without children (including one-person households) were projected to increase from 36.7% to 45.9% of total households.[50] These trends will have a decided impact on the Korean economy and society. Because more than half the time has elapsed since these projections were made, Korean leaders must determine the accuracy of these forecasts and how prepared the country is for this eventuality.

Statistics Korea published the result of a similar demographic study in 2017. The two main differences between the 2010 and the 2017 studies are as follows: The 2010 study compares 2010 and 2030 demographic projections, whereas the 2017 study matches 2015 demographic data with 2045 projections. The 2017 study also extracts the one-person household figures from the households-without-children numbers. In other words, all three demographic cohorts are presented separately, i.e., households of couples with children, couple-only households, and one-person households.

The decided advantage of the 2017 study represents a double-edged sword. On the one hand, it provides projections further into the future than the 2010 study. This advantage is significant for government leaders and others because it allows for additional time to make the necessary plans to prepare for the future. On the other hand, human nature being what it is, key players may fall into the complacency trap. They may think 2045 is far away, and the urgency to engage in serious planning and action may not be as critical.

Not surprisingly, the 2017 study confirms the trends anticipated back in 2010.[51] Specifically, households of couples with children are projected to decrease between 2015 and 2045. Conversely, couple-only and one-person households are forecast to increase in the same period.[52]

These projections have profound implications for the Korean economy and, specifically, for families. Projecting what will happen in the future with a high degree of certainty is difficult. However, there is no denying that the demographic projections are beginning to materialize on university campuses. Therefore, it behooves government, business and academic leaders, policy-makers, economists, and demographers to work collectively. This resource group can generate and analyze computer models that yield possible scenarios. Based on these assumptions, leaders should implement policies and set goals to produce desirable outcomes that address the challenges anticipated by the demographic projections. Such outcomes should aim to create enough jobs, promote innovation, automation, productivity, and economic growth, strengthen public safety, and maintain social stability. Automation, as it relates to productivity, is paramount given the projected reduction in the labor force.

One likely scenario is that fewer working adults will contribute to support quality social services for a growing aging population. If these household projections materialize, and, as of the publication of this book, all signs indicate that they will, unemployment might well level off. One factor that impacts unemployment is automation, which Koreans seem to embrace wholeheartedly. It is difficult to imagine a scenario whereby unemployment is not affected if innovation in technology and industry continues to expand. What will happen if businesses and industries continue incorporating technology and automation into day-to-day operations in pursuit of enhanced customer service, greater efficiency, and higher productivity and profit margins? Korea's track record points to a continuation of similar practices. Will these practices exacerbate the existing high youth unemployment rate? Will they instigate social unrest or perhaps another wave of brain drain brought about by young people leaving the country in search of better job opportunities elsewhere? For the Korean economy to thrive, large corporations must continue to innovate, generate enough jobs, and maintain or possibly increase export levels.

The efficiency generated through automation, as well as technical and industrial innovation, is already having an impact, not only in Korea but in other advanced societies as well. Clearly, Korea does not have a monopoly on efficiency in all its forms since efficiency is one of the foundations of capitalism. Those living in capitalist countries benefit from efficiency and enjoy leisure time. However, statistics show that Koreans have less leisure time than people in other capitalist countries. The question is, what is the cost for Koreans? Korean-style capitalism seems to have a more concentrated flavor like K-pop and *kimchi*, possibly because of the cultural values and idiosyncrasies, among them unity and harmony, conformity, consensus building, willingness to make individual and collective sacrifices for the greater good, the emphasis on efficiency, and the *pali pali* culture.

The Economic Squeeze

The Korean economy is being squeezed on both ends of the demographic spectrum with a low fertility rate and a fast-aging population. According to

Statistics Korea, the past and projected percentage of senior citizens aged 65 or over through 2050 are as follows:

Table 5: Past and Projected Senior Citizens Aged 65 or Over[53]

Year	% of the Population 65+
2017	13.8%
2018	14.3%
2020	15.6%
2030	24.5%
2040	32.8%
2050	38.1%

Quartz Media describes the aging side of the double whammy situation (i.e., low fertility rate and an aging population) as follows:

> With seniors on the verge of making up 14% of the population, Korea is on the cusp of becoming an "aged society"—a threshold that it reached much quicker than other developed countries. According to the National Statistics Office (pdf, p5), it took Japan 24 years to go from an "aging society" (defined as seniors making up 7% of the population) to an aged one—the number of over 65's stood at 34.6 million in Japan, or more than 27% of its population, according to figures released in 2016. It took Germany 40 years and France 115 years to make the same transition. Korea became an aging society just 17 years ago.[54]

The last two administrations have been cognizant of the economic impact of this precarious situation. The article goes on to quote a statement by former President Moon:

> President Moon Jae-in said the country is facing a "national crisis," and that if the country doesn't do more in the next few years to encourage women to have more children, including child care, housing, and employment reforms, there would be "no way to repair the damage."[55]

During his campaign, current President Yoon Suk Yeol, who assumed his post in May of 2022, committed to addressing Korea's low fertility rate. He has referred to the nation's demographic projections as a national "calamity"[56]

Short- vs. Long-Term Solutions

The question remains, what are policy leaders and the country willing to do to confront this "national crisis"? Are they ready to approach these complex issues from a systemic or holistic perspective, or will they settle for short-term solutions? Will the nationalistic impetus resurface, as it did when the country faced difficult situations?

So far, quick fixes are the order of the day to stem the impact of the low fertility rate and possibly reverse it. Some cities, for example, have implemented childbirth grants or one-time benefits to incentivize married couples to have children and thus increase the fertility rate. Because cities award these grants, their dispersal varies depending on where couples reside. For example, the Seoul government allocated the equivalent of $300 grants for the first child and $1,000 for the second. The Busan government made no awards for the first child, the equivalent of $500 for the second and $1,500 for the third. These were all one-time grants that most couples rightly did not consider incentive enough to have children, given the money needed to raise them.

Following these limited city-specific attempts at providing one-time incentives for married couples to have children, the Moon government implemented more generous grants. "Each newborn child was provided with 300,000 won a month over their first year."[57] Subsequently, in a budget proposal, his successor, President Yoon, recommended a plan that would

> provide every family with a newborn child a monthly allowance of 1 million won ($740), in its latest move to encourage more births and try to address the world's lowest fertility rate.
>
> The handout will begin next year [2023] at a level of 700,000 won a month and then rise to the full amount in 2024 [....] Once the child turns one, the stipend will be reduced by half and run for a further year.[58]

The Outlook for Elementary through High School in the Context of a Low Fertility Rate

Communities large and small throughout Korea are feeling the impact of the low fertility rate through the closure of elementary, middle, and high schools. Between 1976 and 2022, "a total of 3,896 schools closed nationwide."[59] An additional 2,173 schools are slated for closure in the near future due to a lack of students.[60] The rapid urbanization of the 1970s and dwindling birthrates have hit rural areas the hardest. Based on 2022 census data, more than 50 percent of the nation's population is concentrated in the greater Seoul area.[61] Despite this concentration of the citizenry around the nation's capital, "three elementary schools and one middle school"[62] had closed as of 2021. In addition, four high schools were being considered for closure by the Seoul Metropolitan Office of Education (I).[63] According to the *JoongAng Daily*, about "193 schools closed between 2017 and 2022, 88.6 percent of which were located outside of the greater Seoul area."[64]

Population fluctuations are like tidal waves that hit the coastline the hardest initially. Then, as the beaches become saturated, areas farther inland feel the ripple effect. Unsurprisingly, elementary schools are feeling the brunt of the rapid decline in student population. Middle and high schools and, finally, higher education institutions will feel the ripple effect. The latest government research shows that "1 out of 6 elementary schools in Seoul will have fewer than 40 students per grade level...."[65] Forty becomes significant because it yields 240 students overall per school or two classes per grade level. These low enrollment numbers present enormous challenges for teachers and administrators to maintain the quality of the academic program as well as co-curricular and extra-curricular activities. According to the Seoul Metropolitan Office of Education,

> The number of "small-scale schools" that have fewer than 240 students will increase by 101, an almost 50 percent increase from this year [2024] with 69 schools.... This means 16.5 percent of elementary schools in the capital city will lack students in just four years.[66]

Given these grim projections, we realize the following questions become pertinent: At what point can a school no longer provide a meaningful, relevant, and valuable quality education? And, at what point does it stop being sustainable? The closure of a community school can be a traumatic experience for students and the community. Therefore, it makes sense for the various stakeholders to discuss the pros and cons of school closure and have their voices heard to make the best decision for all concerned. Once the decision is made, the stakeholders can become a support network to ensure the community can thrive after this traumatic experience.

Some schools are avoiding closure by merging. When merging is impossible, local communities repurpose former schools as service facilities for seniors, the largest demographic group in rural areas. For example, one former school in Chungcheong province was turned into a local college for the elderly.[67] Abandoned schools have turned into ghost structures. Some of these abandoned facilities are visible on the horizon from the nation's highways. During my last visit to Korea in 2023, I noted that a former school in downtown Busan had been turned into a community center. Given the persistent low fertility rate, local communities will continue to face school closures and the question of what to do with these facilities. Similarly, the affected students will continue to brave the adjustment process when reassigned to different schools.

The Outlook for Higher Education in the Context of Demographic Projections

Available population data provides valuable evidence for the future of higher education. The decrease in the 18-year-old cohorts since 2000 and the high youth unemployment rate may indicate an increase in Korea's efficiency, given that Korea's GDP has remained stable for the last few years. An article in the *Maeil Economy* published on June 18, 2018, cites some sobering statistics from the Korean National Statistics Office.[68] The 18-year-old cohorts have decreased since 2000 and are projected to continue the pattern at least through 2040. The 18-year-old population is projected to decline by a staggering 48% from 2000 to 2040.[69] This drop is the product of the steady decrease in the fertility rate.

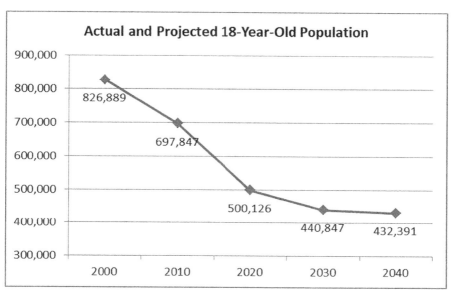

Figure 1: Actual and Projected 18-Year-Old Population[70]

According to *Forbes*, the projected decrease in first-year college students will cause financial hardship to the universities that cannot meet their quota. However, the impact will reach beyond these academic institutions. This situation may set in motion a domino effect with far-reaching implications. A reduction in funding for affected universities will follow the drop in first-year college students, negatively impacting the programmatic quality of higher-learning institutions. Eventually, local economies may feel the effect as well.

The challenges caused by the persistent low fertility rate require Koreans at all levels, including policymakers, university professors, government, education and business leaders, economists, researchers, and demographers, to put on their thinking caps and strategize how best to face these challenges and develop a long-term plan to address them. Quick-fix solutions do not work in the long run. They only prolong the pain and exacerbate the situation while giving the appearance that an effective solution is being implemented. As individuals with different backgrounds and expertise come together to face this difficult task, they must be mindful that a nation is like an organism. Challenges of this magnitude cannot be solved if viewed in isolation. They require an integrated approach.

Short-Term Solution to a Long-Term Challenge

A couple's decision to opt for one child is the rule rather than the exception. The long-standing low fertility rates evidence this choice. Eventually, the reduced number of people in the workforce makes the cost of social services for an aging population more difficult to sustain. The result is a negative impact on the economy.

The effect of the low fertility rate is already being felt at the university level, where declining enrollments are prevalent. To address this challenge, some academic institutions actively recruit students from other Asian countries, primarily China, where university-aged students abound. Korean university faculties are concerned about these international recruits' educational preparation or the lack thereof. They are troubled by the idea that these students are linguistically challenged because, in most cases, they must learn Korean before they can function effectively in an academic setting. Without Korean language mastery, the academic achievement of these students is highly questionable.

The overall concern for administrators is that the influx of academically unprepared international students may force faculty to water down the curriculum. International students also represent a challenge to universities because academic institutions must provide the necessary infrastructure for second-language acquisition. Specifically, Korean language classes should be offered so these students can participate, compete, and benefit from an academic environment. Also, universities must deliver the appropriate support services to expedite the adjustment of these students to their new environment.

On August 16, 2023, Education Minister Lee Ju-ho unveiled the "Study Korea 300K Project," which aims to recruit 300,000 foreign students to Korea by 2027.[71] The program will target science, technology, and engineering students with the ultimate goal of supporting the country's high-tech industries.[72] The government intends to eliminate obstacles that have discouraged international students from choosing Korea to make the program more attractive. For example, "under the new scheme, [the Education] Ministry will team up with the Ministry of Justice to establish a fast-track visa system to woo foreign science and technology talent so that foreign-born applicants will no longer face red tape and excessive visa delays."[73] Another concern of international students in the past has been the restriction on the number of hours they could work. Under the new plan, they can perform up to 40 hours per week.[74] In addition, participants who receive a master's or doctoral degree in crucial science and technology areas will be eligible to obtain permanent residency or Korean citizen status in three years instead of the usual six.[75 and 76]

It is no coincidence that the "Study Korea 300K Project" targets science, technology, and engineering students, given the nation's emphasis and accomplishments since the end of the war. The program also reflects the focus on efficiency and the effort to maintain Korea's homogeneity. It opens the door slightly to foreigners as long as the country can reap some benefits.

Admitting significant numbers of international students to Korean universities is a relatively new concept. It is another efficiency-driven, quick-fix solution to a long-term challenge. Its impact and unintended consequences on the country's higher learning institutions may be felt for a long time. Less highly ranked Korean universities have no choice. They either grow their student population or they may face possible closure. Some institutions, especially those in the lower tier, could diversify their curriculum to ensure their graduates acquire the skills necessary to support business and industry rather than emphasize general education. The question is, are they willing to do that?

Assuming the projected leveling-off of university-bound Korean students will occur, institutions must approach declining enrollments as a long-term challenge and thus generate long-term solutions. Universities that recruit international students as a possible long-term solution must recognize their moral obligation to develop or enhance the necessary infrastructure. It includes student services that support the institution's academic integrity. Suppose they wish to utilize this option to keep their doors open. In that case, they must ensure international student success and avoid negatively impacting academic programs. Running two parallel but academically unequal programs would be impractical, costly, and immoral. It would also be a disservice to all concerned—domestic and international students, professors, and the institution's reputation. Building the necessary infrastructure may prove to be a costly proposition. Therefore, financial gains may not materialize for a while.

Back to the Roots

Because of the rapid urbanization experienced from the 1960s to the early 1990s, as discussed in Chapter Seven, the farm population decreased between the late 1960s and the early 21ˢᵗ century. Per a *Yonhap News Agency* article, "The combined number of South Koreans [living] on farms plunged to 2.84 million in 2013 from 14.4 million in 1970."[77]

However, a small but significant trend has emerged in recent years. Because of the impressive urbanization since the 1960s and the resulting lifestyle challenges, such as overburdened infrastructures, traffic congestion, housing shortages, exorbitant housing prices, air pollution, and a fast life pace, some families are moving from big cities to rural areas. These families are searching for a slower life pace, close contact with nature, and a much less competitive environment. The article cited above states that in 2015, "a total of 11,959 households living in the countryside came from big cities[....]"[78] This figure represents an 11.2% increase over the 10,758 households the prior year.

Albeit small, this migration trend toward rural life, along with the exodus of young people to other countries and the *Hell Joseon* sentiment, represents an indictment of some of Korea's adopted values instrumental in achieving the Miracle on the Han River. Since Koreans have tasted economic and technological success, these contrarian waves are likely not sufficiently powerful enough to change the country's path. However, could they be warning signs to the rest of the country that something is amiss? Could they be a wake-up call to remind everyone that the pendulum has swung too far in one direction? Could they be a call to the citizenry that it is time to become more humanistic and take better care of each other, be less materialistic, be less competitive, and be less driven to efficiency and success at all costs? The collective effort may contribute toward reducing the widening gap between the haves and have-nots and preventing future catastrophes.

- The concept of food sharing is a touching and charming quality. It is a value I admire profoundly. It will remain engraved in my heart for as long as I live.
- Cosmetic surgery provides Koreans yet another opportunity to distinguish themselves from the masses and gain an edge in a highly competitive environment.
- The divide between millennials and older generations remains vast, particularly regarding family values, individual and collective sacrifice for the greater good, and respect for the elderly.
- In essence, young people who refer to Korea as *Hell Joseon* are symbolically rejecting the societal characteristics that make it difficult for them to find opportunities and happiness. Furthermore, they are repudiating the traditional formula for advancing socially and economically because they perceive the conventional path as no longer viable, and the playing field as skewed in favor of the affluent.
- The Korean economy is being squeezed on both ends of the demographic spectrum by a low fertility rate and a fast-aging population.

CHAPTER ELEVEN

Behind the Public Façade, the Perfect Storm

Korea's Public Image

The transformation of Korea's public face to the world began in 1988 when Seoul hosted the Summer Olympics. To this day, the country continues to polish its image. Anyone who watched the opening ceremony of the PyeongChang 2018 Winter Olympics witnessed a carefully choreographed and technologically saturated event. It included using over 1,200 drones and lots of beautiful faces, some artificially chiseled, except for the children who are naturally beautiful. The games showcased a polished image of Korea with historical and cultural overtones.

Undoubtedly, all countries that host these events do their utmost to present a polished image. Therefore, Korea is no exception. This public relations exercise is similar to Koreans' habit at the micro level of checking their appearance on publicly located mirrors. They want to ensure they look their best, their skin is glowing, and every hair is in place.

After the games, I wondered if Koreans who were touched by recent tragedies, or any Koreans in general, identified with the country's glossy image presented to the world during the opening ceremony. Results of an informal and non-scientific survey of my Korean friends indicate that although they felt proud of hosting the games, some did not identify with the opening ceremony.

The Perfect Storm

Unsurprisingly, the country's stellar economic and technological trajectory has been accompanied by growing pains, challenges, and tragic catastrophes. Other developed and developing countries that have matured from an agrarian stage through the Industrial Revolution and eventually to the Information Age have also encountered similar growing pains. For Korea, one such challenge was the Asian Financial Crisis (ca. 1997-2001). The nation rallied to overcome a critical economic situation by accepting harsh austerity measures, liberalizing its trade, and restructuring its corporate governance. Today, although the Korean economy ranks 13th globally, according to the IMF and The World Bank, the country faces some tough macroeconomic challenges. These obstacles may signal the ripe conditions for a perfect storm. The nation's challenges include the following:

- a long-standing low fertility rate;
- limited immigration, which fails to offset the economic impact of a low fertility rate;
- an increasingly aging population that requires additional spending on social services;
- a widening of the gap between the haves and have-nots;
- real estate prices have increased significantly, fueled by pervasively low interest rates, which may promote speculative investments, particularly in metropolitan areas like Seoul and Busan, and make other investments less attractive;
- a high self-employment rate, which makes up a high percentage of the economically active population;
- a proliferation and a high bankruptcy rate of small mom-and-pop businesses;
- record high youth unemployment;
- a high rate of "intentional harm" as the primary cause of death among youth aged nine to 24;
- the highest suicide rate in the developed world.[1]

Since we have discussed some of these challenges at length in previous chapters, we will focus only on those that require further discussion to connect the dots.

Several capitalist economies, including Japan and the United States, are experiencing similar conditions, including a persistently low fertility rate, an increasingly aging population, a widening gap between the haves and have-nots, and high real estate prices. However, some prevailing conditions, including a high rate of self-employed, do not exist in the U.S. and other developed countries. Another advantage in countries like the U.S. is that historically, immigration has offset the economic impact of a low fertility rate. The fertility rate, as measured by total births per woman in the U.S., was less than 2.0 from 1973 through 1988 and from 2010 through 2017.[2]

Countries like Japan face similar conditions caused by comparable circumstances, including a low fertility rate, a growing aging population, skyrocketing real estate prices, and limited immigration, which fails to offset the economic impact of a persistently low fertility rate. However, Japan appears to be proactively coping with labor shortages by increasing the number of foreign workers. Specifically, as of the end of October 2023, foreign workers exceeded two million for the first time.[3] According to *Kyodo News*, "The foreign worker population has logged consecutive annual highs since 2013, but last year's [2023] increase dwarfed the 5.5 percent rise in the previous year [2022]."[4]

Korea's unique cultural attributes may exacerbate the perfect storm outlook. Several reasons lead us to believe that Korea's potential perfect storm forecast may be more pronounced than that of other capitalist countries. Some differences appear to be culturally driven, such as immigration policies. Korea makes immigration difficult, one reason why the nation has remained homogenous. We are not suggesting that liberalizing immigration is the answer for Korea, for it may exacerbate the high unemployment rate.

The proliferation and high cost of private education are unique conditions in Korea. This situation often causes parents to have limited retirement savings. Their investments are usually concentrated on home ownership. This tendency is due to speculative investment and persistently low-interest rates. Consequently, if real estate prices decrease or interest rates increase significantly, the impact on parents' net worth and disposable income will be much more severe.

As discussed in Chapter Ten, insufficient jobs, the emphasis on cost efficiency in businesses, the imbalance between supply and demand, and high competition in the job market enable employers to push Koreans in their mid-40s to mid-50s into "retirement." This, in turn, causes a proliferation of small businesses with a high probability of bankruptcy due to a lack of training in small business management and entrepreneurship. Given Korea's relatively small economy compared to other capitalist countries and the high percentage of self-employed, a high bankruptcy rate in this segment of the economy has a sizable impact.

The following two factors are directly related to high youth unemployment. First, the democratization of higher education has caused an enormous degree inflation challenge at the undergraduate and graduate levels by producing an overabundance of overeducated and overqualified individuals for the available jobs. This reality has intensified job competition. Second, the economic imbalance caused by the concentration of wealth and resources in the conglomerates or *chaebols* has also contributed to high youth unemployment. Since *chaebols* are robust job creators, they are job eliminators when the economy contracts.

The pervasively low-interest rates present other potential macroeconomic problems besides the public's tendency to engage in risky investments. One such option is real estate. Rampant speculative real estate investments often make homeownership challenging for a sizable portion of the population. They can end badly by creating an economic bubble and hurting investors and the overall economy. Typically, ultra-low interest rates also may contribute to capital flight. However, any changes in interest rates need to be approached cautiously. Government leaders must consider the potential negative impact on the already high bankruptcy rate of small mom-and-pop businesses with outstanding loans. They must also weigh the possible adverse effects on existing mortgages generated by a speculative real estate frenzy and parents' debt, given their willingness to sacrifice everything to afford their children the best private education possible, including assuming loans.

These conditions prompt us to maintain that Korea has a more concentrated form of capitalism. Consequently, a more challenging perfect storm may loom on the horizon than in other developed nations under similar circumstances. The economic adversities appear more daunting, given the unique cultural factors. Should the perfect storm materialize, it would behoove government, business leaders, and the public to resort to one of Korea's cultural traits—unity—to face the challenges together. However, they must recognize that these issues will require long-term rather than short-term solutions, which the government has proposed and the general population tolerated.

The emphasis on efficiency that permeates the culture and is reinforced by private education may prompt some people to blame the present situation on the administration in power. This reaction resembles the general public's attitude after a national disaster. They seek to identify a scapegoat, pinpoint the key culprits and the individuals in charge, and punish them to get back to business as usual as soon as possible.

Some people become impatient with the administration in power when positive results are not forthcoming, especially when they propose what is viewed as short-term, Band-Aid solutions to systemic challenges. Short-term solutions gloss over the fact that many of the nation's challenges developed before the administration in power took office or are rooted in the culture. Societal attitudes and behavioral patterns that reflect the competitive nature of the culture, the emphasis on efficiency, and quick financial gains fueled a good portion of these challenges.

- The transformation of Korea's public face to the world began in 1988 when Seoul hosted the Summer Olympics. To this day, the country continues to polish its image.
- Since *chaebols* are powerful job creators, they are also job eliminators when the economy contracts.
- Rampant speculative real estate investments often make homeownership difficult to afford for a sizable portion of the population. They can end badly by creating an economic bubble and hurting investors and the overall economy.
- Some people become impatient with the administration in power when positive results are not forthcoming, especially when they propose what is viewed as short-term, Band-Aid solutions to systemic challenges.
- Short-term solutions gloss over the fact that many of the nation's challenges developed before the administration in power took office.

Afterword

Happiness Indicators

At first glance, Korea appears to be the epitome of perfection, given the status it has achieved worldwide in a relatively short time. It is considered a model economy and has become a technological and cultural powerhouse and a trendsetter in areas such as entertainment and cosmetics. However, underneath the public façade lies a culturally imposed, overwhelming affliction. Several metrics indicate a streak of unhappiness underneath the public smiles of beautiful, chiseled faces and carefully choreographed dances.

While Korea has become more prosperous based on GDP and GNI per capita, and Koreans have focused on materialism, efficiency, and short-term financial gains, the country's ranking in the *World Happiness Report* has dropped significantly. It fell from 41st in 2012 to 57th in 2017.[1 and 2] Then, in 2018, it rose slightly to 54th out of 156 countries reporting.[3] Finally, it reached a ranking of 59th in the 2022 edition.[4] This iteration of the report contains survey results collected during a portion of the COVID-19 pandemic since it includes data from 2019 through 2021.[5] However, the decline in the Happiness Report began before the pandemic. Therefore, it is safe to assume that the pandemic was not the leading cause of the drop.

Given these rankings, we conclude that, as far as Korea is concerned, the fluctuation in the last three iterations of the report is not significant. However, the decline from 2012 to 2017 is. Notably, Korea's ranking has remained consistently in a lower range for six years compared to its high mark in 2012.

According to the report: "The overall rankings of country happiness are based on the pooled results from Gallup World Poll surveys […] and show both change and stability."[6] The survey results are organized by country. Therefore, the comparison of Korea's ranking from 2012 to 2017, 2018, and 2022 indicates how Koreans view their happiness level based on the corresponding survey results. In other words, based on the drop in the rankings, the survey results suggest that Koreans felt less happy from 2017 through 2021 than in 2012.

The 2017 report identifies the six variables that support well-being. They are as follows:

GDP per capita, healthy years of life expectancy, social support (as measured by having someone to count on in times of trouble), trust (as measured by a perceived absence of corruption in government and business), perceived freedom to make life decisions, and generosity (as measured by recent donations). The top ten countries rank highly on all six of these factors.[7]

Because Korea has made significant strides in areas such as technology, entertainment, education, health care, and cosmetics, yet Koreans' happiness level has decreased, two variables deserve attention: First is trust, as measured by a perceived absence of corruption in government and business. Second is GNI per capita, formerly known as GDP per capita.

The trust metric should provide food for thought and reflection for politicians, business leaders, and the public, particularly given the country's recent history at the top level of government. It is up to the entire Korean nation to determine whether the country has the fortitude to eradicate this cancer or continue to live with it.

Several incidents taking place during the period of decline in Korea's ranking between 2012 and 2017, discussed in this book, may account for the plummeting in the happiness metric. Some of these incidents include the *Sewol* ferry disaster, a litany of man-made and industrial accidents, the corruption issues associated with Seoul Metro, and the impeachment of President Park Geun-hye on charges of abuse of power, bribery, and coercion.

Focusing on GNI per capita, Korea is doing well based on the latest government statistics. However, what is the quality of the growth achieved? The *World Happiness Report 2017,* cited above, underscores the importance of emphasizing both happiness and GNI per capita. The report quotes the UN Development Program leader as speaking against what she referred to as "the tyranny of GDP,"

…arguing that what matters is the quality of growth [:] 'Paying more attention to happiness should be part of our efforts to achieve both human and sustainable development.'[8]

The *World Happiness Report* ranking is highly significant. It should be taken seriously because human beings, by nature, strive to be happy. Furthermore, the happiness metric can determine human progress. The Korean people's actions and culture, by nature, reflect their pursuit of happiness. For instance, parents want their children to be happy; therefore, they do everything possible to ensure their offspring receive the best education possible. They know that doing so will increase their children's chances of success in a competitive environment. If successful, their offspring will afford their own children a high-quality education. They, too, will be happy, and the cycle will repeat. However, people express less happiness when the old formula becomes less dependable despite parents' and children's efforts and sacrifices.

As discussed in Chapter Two, the contradictions prevalent in Korean culture include conformity versus differentiation and traditional norms versus modern values in all their multi-faceted forms. These encompass the pressure to conform to established norms versus the desire to differentiate from the crowd and the pressure to accept and live by traditional norms while surrounded by the urgency to actualize and adopt new values. These contradictions can cause individuals to feel like they are being pulled in different directions. As a result, they can feel a sense of helplessness, hopelessness, worthlessness, loneliness, deep unhappiness, and frustration at the inability to be themselves.

The contradictions and pressures in Korean culture discussed in this book make it difficult for all Koreans to achieve true happiness. By "all," I mean people on opposite sides of the ledger: the rich and the poor, the glamorous and famous, including movie stars and K-pop artists, and average citizens, the middle-aged husbands being forced out of the labor force and *chaebol* family members, students attending exclusive private or international academies and average students enrolled in Korean schools. On the surface, it would appear that those born with gold or even silver spoons can easily cope with cultural challenges. However, that is not the case. They are all under pressure to succeed and to be the best they can be. Their ethnicity, cultural and historical background, and pressure from society, their families, and even from within represent commonalities. However, their differences are abysmal. Given these contrasts, the question is, do people have compassion for those on the other side of the street?

An article appearing in the *Korea Times* describes the existing contradictions and the resulting polarization in Korean culture in the following manner:

> On normal days, … the disparity between the rich and the poor, between the rural and the urban is stark and real. It causes discomfort and brings to light the many contradictions the country is home to. On one side of the street we see gaudy pleasure palaces and Luis Vuitton stores caked in gold and offering plastic surgery in the basement; on the other side, old people clutch their meatless

kimbap and collect cardboard in the hope of earning a few thousand won. It is like sitting in a multi-screen cinema and seeing a comedy and a tragedy play at the same time.

Surrounded by Korea's new demonstrable affluence and wealth, many have become blind to the poverty that exists on the other side of the road. And that, more than the hunger and the cold, is the real tragedy of the story: not the suffering itself but rather the willful indifference to the suffering that takes place. The rising tide will raise all boats, they say. Yet there are some places in the concrete jungle that the tide does not reach, starved of the water of wealth experienced by others.[9]

Taking the argument a step further, I would stipulate that the suffering and indifference are actually taking place on both sides of the street.

Sustainable Development Solutions Network has published the *World Happiness Report* annually since 2012. According to the 2017 iteration of the document,

[it was published] …in support of the UN High Level Meeting on happiness and well-being. Since then, we have come a long way. Happiness is increasingly considered the proper measure of social progress and the goal of public policy.[10]

Therefore, we ask, is happiness one of Korea's public policy goals?

Korea's significant descent in the *World Happiness Report* ranking appears to triangulate with the country's high suicide rate. Based on 2019 World Health Organization data, Korea's suicide mortality rate per 100,000 is 28.6, the highest in the developed world.[11] The nation's rate was above the OECD average from 2000 to 2019. The average suicide rate for OECD countries in the same period fluctuated consistently between 12 and 13.2, while Korea's was as low as 14.5 and as high as 34.5. It was above 34 in three consecutive years from 2009 to 2011.[12]

In 2021, Korea's suicide rate of 26 per 100,000 people was not much better. The nation still led OECD countries in this unenviable statistic. "Suicide was the main cause of death for those aged 10 to 39, with 44% of teenage deaths and 56.8% of deaths of those in their 20s attributed to it. Mental illness was identified as the leading cause of suicide."[13] The latter is explained by the country's stigma associated with mental health, which is seen as a sign of "personal weakness or failure."[14 and 15] It is common for families to discourage individuals with mental illness from seeking treatment.

Not surprisingly, suicide cases in the entertainment industry receive the most media attention. However, entertainers do not have a monopoly on this devastating crisis. People of all ages and from all walks of life fall victim to this calamity. Academic pressure, bullying, economic hardship, poverty, shame over seeking help for depression, feelings of isolation, gender inequality, lack of social protection for seniors, discrimination for not conforming or being different, and violence are often cited as causes of suicide.

Korea's substantial drop in the *World Happiness Report* rankings coincides with another potential happiness indicator discussed in this book, also seen as a sign of distress. This potential happiness indicator is the use of the term *Hell Joseon* by weary, disenchanted, and disenfranchised young people to reflect their frustration with the existing socioeconomic inequality.

This unhappiness about the situation among young people is a call for change. Some may argue that this condition only applies to a small subset of the Korean population. However, in a free society, societal change often originates not with the masses behind a cause but with a cadre of citizens who voice their discontent with an injustice caused by a socioeconomic condition. Their voices then sensitize others who are impacted or may sympathize with the cause. Finally, the voices grow louder, and the larger society heeds the calls for change.

The nation's highly competitive economic environment negatively impacts another segment of the population: individuals in their mid-40s to mid-50s who are part of the workforce but are compelled to retire early. They are particularly financially vulnerable if they are parents who had to dip into their retirement savings to afford costly private education and university tuition for their children. At that age, they are still productive citizens with family obligations; however, society squeezes them out of the workforce. Therefore, if they wish to remain productive, self-sufficient citizens, they have no choice but to take an economic risk by joining the self-employed ranks. They usually undertake this new role with little to no training in business management. Even though this segment of the population does not use the term *Hell Joseon*, the stress level of their situation is understandable.

The indicators we have discussed, including the drop in the *World Happiness Report* ranking, the high suicide rate, the high rate of intentional harm, identified as the primary cause of death among youth 9 to 24 years of age, the nation's high suicide rate, and the young people's dissatisfaction with Korea's socioeconomic conditions as expressed through the *Hell Joseon* epitaph, should raise a red flag among policymakers and the public at large.[16]

These factors are far from trivial, particularly for a country with the fifth largest economy in Asia and 13th in the world.[17] Is this the price people must pay to achieve economic success? Is this the price people must pay for adopting a capitalist economy? Or is this the price people must pay when a radical transformation takes place relatively quickly? Do the ends justify the means? At what point does the balance tip to being humane and genuinely caring for one another as fellow human beings versus being efficient for achieving economic prosperity that falls short of attaining true happiness?

Suppose Koreans wish to be among the happier countries in the world. In that case, they might consider examining policies and programs that have been successful in other countries, such as initiatives aimed at promoting greater work-life balance, reducing income inequality, admitting that mental health exists instead of denying it, learning to recognize the symptoms, and improving mental health services to grapple with the suicide crisis. Most, if not all, of these issues have cultural overtones; thus, they are monumental obstacles to overcome, particularly the mental health question, since it is considered taboo. They may also wish to examine the behavior patterns, such as disregard for safety regulations, that tend to repeat and are entrenched in the culture instrumental in lifting the nation out of the rubble after the war, recognizing that the country is in a much different stage of development.

Given Korea's stellar trajectory since the end of the Korean War, it would not be surprising to find that people from other countries, such as China and Vietnam, may look to Korea as an economic and technological success model. One cannot underestimate the power of movies, television, and social media. As we have seen, Korea exports its modern, high-tech culture through glossy images, finely sculpted faces, and extravagant glamour in soap operas, movies, K-pop, and worldwide sports events. Before embarking on a similar path, it would behoove developing countries that wish to emulate Korea to consider the price Korean adults and children have had to pay for the nation's economic and technological accomplishments.

In the 1950s, 1960s, and 1970s, while Korea was recovering from the ravages of the Korean War, Japan was playing a leading role economically and technologically among Asian countries. Now, it is Korea's turn. The nation that replaces Korea in this enviable position would benefit significantly from studying Korea's successes and the areas where it has fallen short of the mark. Equally important would be examining the cultural and capitalist-driven behavioral trends that propelled the country's success, such as emphasizing efficiency and short-term financial gains at all costs, even public safety.

- Although South Korea has become more prosperous based on GDP and GNI per capita while emphasizing materialism, efficiency, and short-term financial gains, the country's ranking in the *World Happiness Report* has dropped significantly.
- Based on 2019 World Health Organization data, Korea's suicide mortality rate per 100,000 is 28.6, the highest in the developed world.[11]
- Before embarking on a similar path, it would behoove other developing countries that wish to emulate Korea to consider the price Koreans have had to pay for the nation's outstanding economic and technological accomplishments on the international stage.
- Other developing countries that see Korea as a role model would benefit greatly from studying the successes and areas where Korea has fallen short of the mark.

Notes

Introduction

1. Dangremond, Sam. "Here's Everything You Need to Know About Soju, the National Drink of Korea: Never Heard of It? The Low-Alcohol Spirit Is the Best-Selling Liquor in the World." *Town and Country Magazine*, 8 February 2018, *townandcountrymag.com*. Last accessed 19 February 2024.
2. Wolinski, Cat. "The Differences Between Soju, Shochu, and Sake, Explained." *Vinepair*, *vinepair.com*. Accessed 27 June 2019.

Chapter One

1. According to the *World Atlas*: "The phrase ['the Miracle on the Han River'] was introduced by South Korea's Prime Minister, Chang Myon, as part of his New Year address in 1961 in which he requested his fellow South Koreans to withstand the discomfort that came with change and be optimistic of economic growth. The phrase was derived from a similar phrase, 'Miracle on the Rhine,' coined in reference to the dramatic economic resurgence of West Germany soon after the Second World War." Kiprop, Joseph. "What Was the Miracle on the Han River?" *World Atlas*, 6 February 2018, *worldatlas.com*. Last accessed 2 February 2023.
2. World Bank. "GDP (Current US$)." *World Development Indicators*. The World Bank, *data.worldbank.org*. Last accessed 30 August 2023.
3. Ibid.
4. Ibid.
5. World Bank. "GNI per Capita, Atlas Method (Current US$)." Graph. *World Development Indicators*. The World Bank, *data.worldbank.org*. Last accessed 2 September 2023.
6. "The Korean Economy – the Miracle on the Hangang River." *Economy*. Korea.net, *korea.net*. Last accessed 3 September 2023.
7. Ibid.
8. "Mixed Economy." *Business Dictionary*, *businessdictionary.com*. Accessed 7 February 2019.
9. Workman, Daniel. "Electronic Circuit Component Exports by Country." *World's Top Exports*, *worldstopexports.com*. Accessed 3 May 2022.
10. "17 Semiconductor Companies Forecast to Have > $10 Billion in Sales This Year." *IC Insights*, December 20, 2021, *icinsights.com*. Accessed 1 May 2022.
11. "Internet Connection Speed by Country." *Fastmetrics*, *fastmetrics.com*. Accessed 25 June 2019.
12. Cheng, Roger. "The 5-G Wireless Revolution, Explained." CNET, 27 October 2019, *cnet.com*.
13. "Seoul City to Operate Autonomous Night Bus." *The Korea Herald*, 3 December 2023, *koreaherald.com*. Accessed 4 December 2023.
14. Ibid.

15. Ibid.

16. Salmon, Andrew. "A Sporting Host: How South Korea has Continued to Build on the Legacy of the Seoul Olympics." *South China Morning Post*, 5 July 2015, *scmp.com*. Last accessed 24 May 2023.

17. Kim, Sohee. "The 4.7 Billion K-pop Industry Chases Its 'Michael Jackson Moment.'" *Bloomberg*, 22 August 2017, *bloomberg.com*. Accessed 13 February 2019.

18. "BTS Are the 1st Act Since The Beatles to Have 6 No. 1 Songs on the Billboard Hot 100 in Just Over 1 Year." *ShowBiz CheatSheet*, 4 October 2021, *cheatsheet.com*. Accessed 29 April 2022.

Chapter Two

1. Tizzard, David A. "Understanding Korean Modernization." The *Korea Times*, 23 September 2023, *koreatimes.co.kr*. Accessed 24 October 2023.

2. Huus, Kari. "The Cost of the Olympics from the 1940s to Today." *MSN* 15 August 2018, *msn.com*.

3. Struck, Doug. "Hosts Left to Foot the World Cup Bill." The *Washington Post*, 29 June 2002, *washingtonpost.com*. Last accessed 1 August 2023.

4. Ibid.

5. "Flag of South Korea." Image. *Wikipedia, en.wikipedia.org*. Accessed 14 November 2019.

6. "Three Most Prestigious Universities in South Korea." *Your University Guide, youruniversityguide.wordpress.com*. Accessed 1 July 2019.

7. "Best Global Universities in South Korea." *U.S. News & World Report, usnews.com*. Accessed 4 February 2022.

8. A university student's retrospective look at his decision to select Singapore over Australia for an internship in hotel management, and the consultation process that helped him arrive at his decision. Anonymous. Personal interview by John Gonzalez. Text interview, 12-13 July 2019.

9. Holmes, Frank. "How Gold Rode to the Rescue of South Korea." *Forbes*, 27 September 2016, *forbes.com*. Accessed 17 March 2018.

10. "Ppalli Ppalli Culture – Korean's Disposition to Like Fast-Paced Lifestyle." *Korea Daily*, 26 February 2016, *koreadailyus.com*. Accessed 31 August 2018.

11. World Bank. "GDP Growth (Annual %) – Korea, Rep." *World Development Indicators*. The World Bank, *data.worldbank.org*. Last accessed 3 September 2023.

12. "Irregular Workers." Trans. Young Lee, *Wikipedia.com, ko.wikipedia.org*. Accessed 23 October 2019.

13. "Homepage." *Fair Test: The National Center for Fair and Open Testing, fairtest.org*. Accessed 13 November 2019.

14. "[News]: 1700+ Bachelor-Degree-Granting Colleges and Universities Do Not Require ACT/SAT Test Scores from Fall 2022 Applicants; Will Upcoming U.S. News Guide Accurately Reflect the 'New Normal' of Test-Optional Admissions?" *Fair Test: The National Center for Fair and Open Testing*, 9 September 2021, *fairtest.org*. Accessed 13 November 2019.

15. Hoover, Eric. "An Ultra-Selective University Just Dropped the ACT/SAT. So What?" The *Chronicle of Higher Education*, 14 June 2018, *chronicle.com*. Accessed 4 July 2019.

16. The *Washington Post* reports James G. Nondorf's title as "Dean of Admissions and Finan-cial Aid," whereas The *Chronicle of Higher Education* titles Nondorf as "Vice President for Enrollment," Anderson, Nick. "A Shake-Up in Elite Admissions: U-Chicago Drops SAT/ACT Testing Requirement." The *Washington Post*, 14 June 2018, *washingtonpost.com*. Accessed 4 July 2019.

17. Ibid.

18. Hoover, Eric. "An Ultra-Selective University Just Dropped the ACT/SAT. So What?"

19. "Destinations by Region." *VisitKorea,* Official Korea Tourism Organization, *english.visit-korea.or.kr*. Accessed 9 July 2019.

20. Ibid.

21. "Top Things to Do and See: Seoul." *CNN, cnn.com*. Accessed 9 July 2019.

22. "McDonalds in South Korea." *Modern Seoul*, 16 February 2013, *modernseoul.org*. Last accessed 1 August 2023.

23. Park, Sangyoub. "What's Behind South Korea's Shake Shack Fever?" *NPR*, 6 September 2016, *npr.org*. Accessed 13 March 2018.

24. Anonymous. Personal interview by John Gonzalez, in-person, 19 June 2018.

25. Jung, Hemin. "Koreans' Love for Luxury Handbags Has Surpassed the French... Now, the 4th Biggest Market in the World." Trans. Young Lee, *News 1*, 1 October 2018, *naver.me/GdvyOwGg*. Accessed 7 July 2019.

26. Ibid.

27. "The World Factbook." *Central Intelligence Agency, cia.gov*. Accessed 8 July 2018.

28. "Discovery is No. 1 as Bench Season Ends." The *Korea JoongAng Daily*, 26 February 2018, *koreajoongangdaily.com*. Accessed 10 July 2019.

29. Ibid.

30. "Discovery Expedition's 'Leicester' Bench Coat." Image. "Discovery is No. 1 as Bench Season Ends." The *Korea JoongAng Daily*, 26 February 2018, *koreajoongangdaily.com*. Accessed 10 July 2019.

31. Lee, Sun-young. "[Weekender] One Coat that Conquered Street Fashion in South Korea." The *Korea Herald*, 1 December 2017, *koreaherald.com*. Accessed 8 January 2018.

Chapter Three

1. "JEONJU, South Korea Population." *Population Stat, populationstat.com*. Accessed 7 August 2019.

2. "About KTX." *Life in Korea, lifeinkorea.com*. Accessed 7 August 2019.

3. "KTX Overview." *Korail, info.korail.com*. Accessed 7 August 2019.

4. Jeon, Sung-Won. "Food Delivery Gets Its Apps." *Koreana, koreana.or.kr*. Accessed 11 July 2019.

5. Jeon, So-Young. "Food Delivery Paradise." *Korean Culture and Information Service, kocis.go.kr*. Accessed 11 July 2019.

6. "Incheon Port: The Door to Economic Vitality." *Port of Incheon, icpa.or.kr*. Accessed 7 August 2019.

7. Do Rosario, Louise. "Seoul's Invisible Chinese Rise Up." The *Straits Times*, 22 October 2000, *straitstimes.com*. Last accessed 31 July 2023.

8. Jeon, So-Young. "Food Delivery Paradise."

9. Jeon, Sung-Won. "Food Delivery Gets Its Apps."

10. Jeon, So-Young. "Food Delivery Paradise."

11. Ibid.

12. Jeon, Sung-Won. "Food Delivery Gets Its Apps."

13. Ibid.

14. "Currently, 30 to 40 delivery apps are engaged in fierce competition. The combined number of downloads of the top three delivery apps—Baedal Minjok, Yogiyo, and Baedaltong—has reportedly exceeded 40 million. To stay ahead of the pack, the Baedal Minjok app allows customers to use its 'all-in-one' location-based services, skipping the process of entering user information." Ibid.

15. Chung, Younshik, Tai-Jin Song, Byoung-Jo Yoon. "Injury severity in delivery-motorcycle to vehicle crashes in the Seoul metropolitan area." *Accident Analysis and Prevention*, no. 62, 2014, p. 79-86.

16. Ibid.

17. Ibid.

18. "#1442 Naver." *Forbes, forbes.com.* Accessed 8 July 2019.

19. Ibid.

20. Ibid.

21. *New Choice Health, newchoicehealth.com.* Accessed 7 July 2019.

22. KBS. *Naver, naver.me.* Accessed 7 July 2019.

23. See Chapter Seven.

24. Anonymous, personal interview by John Gonzalez, email, 10 June 2019.

Chapter Four

1. World Bank. "Population, Total – Korea, Rep." *World Development Indicators.* The World Bank, *data.worldbank.org.* Last accessed 3 September 2023.

2. "International Educational Attainment." *NCES National Center for Education Statistics,* last updated May 2020, *nces.ed.gov.*

3. Ibid.

4. Ibid.

5. Ibid.

6. Ibid.

7. Kim, Young-Nam. "Enrollment in Vocational Schools Surges." The *Korea JoongAng Daily,* 23 January 2017, *koreajoongangdaily.joins.com.*

8. Statista. "Share of High School Students Enrolling in University in South Korea from 2013 to 2022." *Education and Science.* Statista, January 2023, *statista.com/statistics/628656/south-korea-share-of-high-school-students-enrolling-in-university/.* Accessed 14 September 2023.

9. "Parents Spend More and More on Private Tuition." The *Chosun Ilbo,* 27 March 2017, *english.chosun.com.* Last accessed 10 May 2023.

10. Ibid.

11. Fenton, Siobhan. "President Obama Praises South Korea for Paying Teachers as Much as Doctors." The *Independent,* 18 July 2015, *independent.co.uk.* Last accessed 10 May 2023.

12. "Statistical Database." *Korean Statistical Information Service, kosis.kr.* Accessed 20 July 2019.

13. "Monthly Spending on Private Education Up 33%." The *Korea Herald*, 17 March 2018, *koreaherald.com*.

14. "Gangnam District." *Wikipedia, en.wikipedia.org*. Last accessed 10 May 2023.

15. "International Education Attainment." *NCES National Center for Education Statistics*, *nces.ed.gov*. Accessed 16 August 2019.

16. "Monthly Spending." The *Korea Herald*.

17. Yim, Hyun-Su. "Viewers Gush Over 'Sky Castle.'" The *Korea Herald*, *koreaherald.com*. Accessed 16 August 2019.

18. Ibid.

19. "Hit Drama Reveals Sky High Pressure of South Korean School System." The *Jakarta Post*, *thejakartapost.com*. Accessed 30 June 2019.

20. Ibid.

21. Park, Jin-Hai. "Sky Castle captures elite moms' education craze." The *Korea Times*, *korea-times.kr*. Accessed 29 June 2019.

22. "Monthly Spending." The *Korea Herald*.

23. Ibid.

24. Chakrabarti, Reeta. "South Korea's schools: Long days, high results." *BBC*, 2 December 2013, *bbc.com*. Last accessed 10 May 2023.

25. Ibid.

26. "Total." *Statistics Korea, kostat.go.kr*. Accessed 16 August 2019, and "Suicide No. 1 cause of death for S. Korean teens, youths." The *Korea Herald*, 1 May 2019, *koreaherald.com*. Accessed 16 August 2019.

27. Farrugia, Christine. "Globally Mobile Youth: Trends in International Secondary Students in the United States, 2013-2016." 2017. Institute of International Education, Center for Academic Mobility, Research, and Impact, August 2017, *iie.org*. Accessed 16 August 2019.

28. "List of Countries by Population." *Statistics Times*, 29 July 2019, *statisticstimes.com*. Last accessed 8 May 2023.

29. Based on estimates by the United Nations Department of Economic and Social Affairs, the population for the other countries in this category is as follows; China: over 1.415 billion, Vietnam: over 96.491 million, Mexico: over 130.759 million, and Japan: over 127.185 million. United Nations, Department of Economic and Social Affairs, Population Division (2022). *World Population Prospects 2022*: Press Release. Last accessed 10 May 2023.

30. Reed, Bronwen. "'Wild Geese Families': Stress, loneliness for South Korean families heading overseas to gain edge in 'brutal' education system." *Australian Broadcasting Corporation*, 15 June 2015, *abc.net.au*. Last accessed 11 May 2023.

31. "Suicide No. 1 cause of death," The *Korea Herald*.

32. Anonymous. Personal interview by John Gonzalez. Text interview, 17 July-5 November 2023.

33. The Korean Research Institute for Vocational Education and Training conducted the research. Jun, Jin-Young. "Master's and Ph.D. Market demand is only 250,000." Trans. Young Lee, *Munhwa Ilbo*, 2 May 2018, *munhwa.com*.

34. Ibid.

35. "Did you go to college to do this? 1 in 3 unemployed." Trans. Young Lee, *Naver*, 23 June 2018, *naver.com*.

36. Ibid.
37. Ibid.
38. Ibid.
39. Ibid.
40. Ibid.

Chapter Five

1. Fendos, Justin. "Why Korean Students Lack Creativity." The *Korea Herald*, 15 October 2017, *koreaherald.com*. Last accessed 15 May 2023.
2. Ibid.
3. "Youth." *Statistics Korea, kostat.go.kr*. Accessed 22 August 2019.
4. "Current Cigarette Smoking." *Korean Statistical Information Service, kosis.kr*. Accessed 20 November 2019.
5. "Daily Smokers (indicator)." *OECD, data.oecd.org*. Accessed 28 July 2019.
6. "At the moment [November 26, 2017], there are 17,500 public areas where smoking is prohibited, which include some 3,400 areas close to education facilities such as kindergartens and daycare centers. About 6,800 bus stops, 1,700 subway exits, [and] 1,700 parks and squares are also designated as non-smoking areas. In addition, 57 streets in areas with heavy foot traffic, including Insa-dong and part of Gangnamdaero, are now non-smoking zones, and violators face fines of up to 100,000 won ($92). There are also another 23,900 indoor locations–buildings of public offices, restaurants, hospitals, and some apartments–designated as smoke-free zones." Kim, Da-Sol. "Seoul Delays Plan to Ban Public Smoking." The *Korea Herald*, 26 November 2017, *koreaherald.com*. Last accessed 15 May 2023.
7. Ibid.
8. Ibid.
9. "2017 Statistics on the Youth." *Statistics Korea, kostat.go.kr*. Accessed 22 August 2019.
10. Ibid.

Chapter Six

1. Duncan, Arne. "Parent Voices for World-Class Education: Remarks of U.S. Secretary of Education Arne Duncan to the National Assessment Governing Board Education Summit for Parent Leaders." *U.S. Department of Education*, 13 January 2014, *ed.gov*. Accessed 10 May 2018.
2. Ibid.
3. Ibid.
4. Obama, Barack. "Remarks of President Barack Obama in State of the Union Address." The *White House Office of the Press Secretary*, 25 January 2011, *obamawhitehouse.archives. gov*. Accessed 9 May 2018.
5. Obama, Barack. "Remarks by the President on Education in Arlington, Virginia." The *White House Office of the Press Secretary*, 14 March 2011, *obamawhitehouse.archives.gov*. Accessed 21 May 2018.

6. Obama, Barack. "Remarks by the President on the Launch of ConnectHome Initiative." The *White House Office of the Press Secretary*, 15 July 2015. *obamawhitehouse.archives.gov*. Accessed 5 June 2018.

7. "Best Paying Jobs." *U.S. News and World Report*, 10 January 2018, *money.usnews.com*. Accessed 30 August 2019.

8. Given the 2017 OECD data, starting Korean teacher salaries at the elementary and secondary levels are much lower than their American counterparts. At the 15-year experience mark, the salary gap between the two remains vast, with American teacher salaries remaining higher than those in Korea. However, Korean teachers' wages at the top of the scale in the two education segments are higher than those of American instructors. Therefore, it appears that in preparation for President Obama's speech, the analysis for the comparison between teacher salaries in the two countries was made at the top of the pay scales without consideration of wages at the starting point or the 15-year mark. These statistics support President Obama's argument that Korean teachers' wages are higher than their American counterparts. However, for accuracy and full disclosure, the comparison should be made at various points in the wage scales. One such option is to compare salaries for the first year, after 15 years of experience, and at the top of the scale. This analysis would draw a complete picture of the teacher salary comparison argument. However, a comprehensive assessment would require a thorough discussion of other factors, such as cost of living, fringe benefits, teacher retention, and professional longevity. Absent these considerations, the teacher salary comparison is inconclusive at best and misleading at worst.

9. Strauss, Valerie. "Arne Duncan: Why Can't We Be More Like South Korea?" The *Washington Post*, 18 January 2014, *washingtonpost.com*. Accessed 31 July 2019.

10. Ibid.

11. Ibid.

12. Ibid.

13. Ibid.

14. Ibid.

15. Ibid.

16. Obama, Barack. "Remarks by the President to the Hispanic Chamber of Commerce." The *White House Office of the Press Secretary*, 10 March 2009, *obamawhitehouse.archives.gov*. Accessed 9 May 2018.

17. "Obama Lauds Korea's Education of Children." The *Korea Times*, 11 March 2009, *koreatimes.co.kr*. Accessed 9 November 2019.

18. "Korean Kids Unhappiest in OECD." The *Chosun Ilbo*, 6 May 2010, *english.chosun.com*. Last accessed 19 May 2023.

19. Ibid.

20. Ibid.

21. "Korean Kids Most Stressed in the World." The *Chosun Ilbo*, 12 March 2015, *english.chosun.com*. Last accessed 19 May 2023.

22. Ibid.

23. "Korean Kids Spend Barely Half an Hour a Day Outdoors." The *Chosun Ilbo*, 11 May 2016, *english.chosun.com*. Last accessed 19 May 2023.

24. "Korean Teenagers Study Hard but Feel Unhappy." The *Chosun Ilbo*, 25 April 2017, *english.chosun.com*. Last accessed 19 May 2023.

25. "Self-Harm on the Rise Among Korean Teens." The *Chosun Ilbo*, 27 July 2019, *english.chosun.com*. Accessed 1 August 2019.

26. Singer, Alan. "Obama, Korea, and American Schools." *HuffPost*, 18 March 2010, *huffpost.com*. Last accessed 19 May 2023.

27. Ibid.

28. Ibid.

Chapter Seven

1. "Hours Worked." *OECD Data*, *data.oecd.org*. Accessed 5 September 2019.

2. World Bank. "Urban Population (% of Total Population)." *World Development Indicators*. The World Bank, *data.worldbank.org*. Last accessed 2 September 2023.

3. Ibid.

4. World Bank. "Urban Population Growth (Annual %)." *World Development Indicators*. The World Bank, *data.worldbank.org*. Last accessed 2 September 2023.

5. Nikola. "The Last Citizen Apartment of Seoul." *KO-JECTS*, 23 November 2015, *kojects.com*. Last accessed 28 May 2023.

6. See the charts above on urban population and urban population growth.

7. Jeon, Sang-Soo. "Man-Made Disasters in Korea: Case Histories and Improvement Plans." *International Journal of Scientific and Research Publications,* vol. 4, no. 7, July 2014, pp. 1-6. https://www.ijsrp.org/research-paper-0714/ijsrp-p3102.pdf. Last accessed 28 May 2023.

8. This figure does not include injuries, of which there were many more.

9. Sawe, Benjamin Elisha. "The Sampoong Department Store Disaster of 1995." *WorldAtlas*, 25 April 2017, *worldatlas.com*. Last accessed 28 May 2023.

10. Nikola. "The Last Citizen Apartment of Seoul."

11. Kong, Kanga. "South Korea's History of Building Collapses." The *Wall Street Journal*, 18 February 2014, *blogs.wsj.com*. Last accessed 28 May 2023.

12. Nikola. "The Last Citizen Apartment of Seoul."

13. Jeon, Sang-Soo. "Man-Made Disasters in Korea: Case Histories and Improvement Plans."

14. Nikola. "The Last Citizen Apartment of Seoul."

15. Kong, Kanaga. "South Korea's History of Building Collapses."

16. Ibid.

17. Nikola. "The Last Citizen Apartment of Seoul."

18. The various reports consulted show a minor discrepancy in the accident's exact date. Most news sources report that it occurred on October 10, 1993, while one claims it happened on October 12. "Disasters: Sampoong Collapse Worst Disaster in Korea's History." *Yonhap News Agency*, 15 July 1995, *en.yna.co.kr*. Accessed 20, April 2019. "Sinking of MV Seohae." *Wikipedia*, *en.wikipedia.org*. Accessed 10, June 2023. Jeon, Sang-Soo. "Man-Made Disasters in Korea: Case Histories and Improvement Plans," and "List of Maritime Disasters in the 20th Century." *Revolvy*, *revolvy.com*. Accessed 5 September 2019.

19. Jeon, Sang-Soo. "Man-Made Disasters in Korea: Case Histories and Improvement Plans," and "Sinking of MV Seohae." *Wikipedia*, *en.wikipedia.org*. Accessed 10, June 2023.

20. Jeon, Sang-Soo. "Man-Made Disasters in Korea: Case Histories and Improvement Plans," and "Disasters: Sampoong Collapse Worst Disaster in Korea's History." *Yonhap News*, 15 July 1995, *en.yna.co.kr*. Accessed 20 April 2019.

21. Sawe, Benjamin Elisha. "The Sampoong Department Store Disaster of 1995."
22. "Failure Case Studies: Sampoong Superstore." ASCE Technical Council on Forensic Engineering (TCFE), The University of North Carolina at Charlotte, *eng-resources.uncc. edu*. Last accessed 6 November 2019.
23. Sawe, Benjamin Elisha. "The Sampoong Department Store Disaster of 1995."
24. "Sampoong Department Store Collapse." The *Distributed Wikipedia Mirror Project*, *en.wikipedia.org*. Last accessed 31 March 2019.
25. Lankov, Andrei. "The Dawn of Modern Korea: Collapse of Sampoong Department Store." The *Korea Times*, 14 October 2004, *times.hankooki.com*. Accessed 31 March 2019.
26. Sawe, Benjamin Elisha. "The Sampoong Department Store Disaster of 1995."
27. Ibid.
28. "Failure Case Studies: Sampoong Superstore." ASCE Technical Council on Forensic Engineering (TCFE), The University of North Carolina at Charlotte.
29. Lankov, Andrei. "The Dawn of Modern Korea: Collapse of Sampoong Department Store."
30. Jeong, Andrew. "Itaewon Halloween Tragedy Conjures Ghosts of 1995 Seoul Store Collapse." The *Washington Post*, 4 November 2022, *washingtonpost.com*. Accessed 26 June 2023.
31. "Failure Case Studies: Sampoong Superstore." ASCE Technical Council on Forensic Engineering (TCFE), The University of North Carolina at Charlotte.
32. Ibid.
33. Jeon, Su-yong. "Prosecution Investigation Report on Sewol Ferry Accident." Trans. Young Lee, The *Chosun Ilbo*, 7 October 2014, *chosun.com*. Accessed 8 September 2019.
34. Liljas, Per. "Investigations into the South Korea Ferry Disaster Reveal a Litany of Errors." *Time*, 24 April 2014, *time.com*. Accessed 10 September 2015.
35. "[Editorial]: Preventing Disasters." The *Korea Herald*, 20 April 2014, *koreaherald.com*. Accessed 31 March 2019.
36. Groll, Elias. "Why do So Many People Die in Ferry Accidents?" *Foreign Policy*, 16 April 2014, *foreignpolicy.com*. Accessed 21 April 2019.
37. "Fire at Apartment Blocks Kills 4, Leaves 124 Injured." The *Korea JoongAng Daily*, 11 January 2015, *koreajoongangdaily.joins.com*. Accessed 11 February 2019.
38. Lee, Seul. "Police Closes Investigation of Uijeongbu Fire… Committing Illegal Acts and Cutting Corners Started Fire." *Newshankuk*, 26 March 2015, *eng.newshankuk.com*. Accessed 26 January 2018.
39. "4 Dead, 100 Injured in Apartment Fire in Ujeongbu." The *Korea Times*, 11 January 2015, *koreatimes.us*. Accessed 26 January 2018.
40. "Four People Were Killed and 100 Others Injured in a Fire that Swept through a 10-Story Apartment Building in Uijeongbu, North of Seoul on Saturday (Yonhap)." Image. "4 Dead, 100 Injured in Apartment Fire in Ujeongbu." The *Korea Times*, 11 January 2015, *koreatimes.us*. Accessed 26 January 2018.
41. Gyeonggi Fire Service. Image. "Police Closes Investigation of Uijeongbu Fire… Committing Illegal Acts and Cutting Corners Started Fire." *Newshankuk*, 26 March 2015, *eng.newshankuk.com*. Accessed 26 January 2018.
42. Lee, Hyun-Jeong. "Police Launch Probe into Uijeongbu Fire." The *Korea Herald*, 11 January 2015, *koreaherald.com*. Accessed 11 February 2019.

43. "Dryvit Method Suspected as Cause of Instant Spread in Uijeongbu Fire." The *Dong-A Ilbo*, 13 January 2015, *donga.com*. Accessed 26 January 2018.

44. Huber, Jeanne. "Why Does the Inside of this Door Keep Getting Damaged by Rain?" The *Washington Post*, 21 January 2019, *washingtonpost.com*. Accessed 5 September 2019.

45. Haag, Benjamin A. "Exterior Insulation Finish Systems: Hazard Considerations for the Fire Service." *University of Cincinnati*, 10 February 2016, *ceas.uc.edu*.

46. Ibid.

47. "Dryvit method." The *Dong-A Ilbo*.

48. "Fire at Apartment Blocks." The *Korea JoongAng Daily*.

49. Ibid.

50. Emphasis my own. "Dryvit Method," The *Dong-A Ilbo*.

51. Emphasis my own. Ibid.

52. Ibid.

53. Bak Se-hwan. "[Newsmaker] South Korean Gyms Face Scrutiny after Jecheon Deadly Fire." The *Korea Herald*, 25 December 2017, *koreaherald.com*. Accessed 11 February 2019.

54. "Police Closes Investigation of Uijeongbu Fire." *Newshankuk*.

55. Bak, Se-hwan. "[Newsmaker] South Korean Gyms."

56. You, Soo-Sun. "Electrical Spark Started Fire in Jecheon." The *Korea Times*, 23 December 2017, *koreatimes.ko.kr*. Accessed 27 December 2017.

57. Ibid.

58. Ibid.

59. Ibid.

60. Ryu, Hyo-jin. "Firefighters and Forensic Investigators Examine an Eight-Story Building, which was Destroyed by a Massive Fire…" Image. You, Soo-sun. "Electrical Spark Started Fire in Jecheon." The *Korea Times*, 23 December 2017, *koreatimes.ko.kr*. Accessed 27 December 2017.

61. "(LEAD) State Crime Lab Confirms Jecheon Fire Started from Ceiling." *Yonhap News Agency*, 23 December 2017, *en.yna.ko.kr*. Accessed 3 February 2019.

62. Ibid.

63. Lee, Jae-Min. "Liberal Parking not Condoned Practice." The *Korea Herald*, 9 January 2018, *koreaherald.com*. Accessed 4 February 2019.

64. "Understanding Negligence and Liability." *Ameriprise Auto & Home Insurance, ikkeiise. com*. Accessed 5 September 2019.

65. Kim, Jin-Kyu. Image. "Double Parking is Common in Parking Lots in Jinju, South Korea." *NEWSIS*, 20 May 2009, *newsnavercom*. Accessed 11 September 2019.

66. Lee, Jae-Ho. Image. "Unenforced Illegal Parking Laws in Gwangju Residential Area are Inconveniencing Residents." *Asia News Agency*, 20 February 2013, *anewsa.com*. Accessed 11 September 2019.

67. Park, Jin-Young. "Fire Inspection of Bath Houses in Seoul: One Out of Three Fail Inspection." Trans. Young Lee, *KBS*, 1 February 2018, *naver.me*.

68. "Death Toll from Hospital Fire in Southern Korea Rises to 46." *Yonhap News Agency*, 6 February 2018, *m-en.yna.co.kr*. Accessed 2 February 2019.

69. Lee, Kyung-min. "Miryang Hospital Faces Probe over Safety Breaches." The *Korea Times*, 29 January 2018, *koreatimes.ko.kr*. Last accessed 29 May 2023.

70. "Hospital Apologizes for Deadly Blaze but Claims Compliance with Fire Prevention Rules." *Yonhap News*, 26 January 2018, *en.yna.co.kr*. Accessed 2 February 2019.

71. Choe, Sang-hun. "South Korea Hospital Fire Kills at Least 37 People." *The New York Times*, 25 January 2018, *newyorktimes.com*. Accessed 3 April 2019.

72. "12 Indicted for Hospital Fire in Southern S. Korea that Killed Dozens." *The Korea Herald*, 15 March 2018, *koreaherald.com*. Accessed 2 February 2019.

73. Kim, Hoo-ran. "Safety Checks on 'High-Risk' Facilities Begin Next Week." *The Korea Herald*, 2 February 2018, *koreaherald.com*. Accessed 3 February 2019.

74. "Framework Act on Fire-Fighting Services, Article 25." *Korea Law Translation Center*, *elaw.klri.re.kr*. Accessed 4 February 2019.

75. Migiro, Geoffrey. "Countries with the Most High Speed Rail." *World Atlas*, 19 April 2018, *worldatlas.com*. Accessed 31 October 2022.

76. Ibid.

77. "Mission and Vision," *Korail, info.korail.com*. Accessed 23 October 2019.

78. Lee, Suh-Yoon. "Korail Under Fire After Yet Another Accident." *The Korea Times*, 9 December 2018, *koreatimes.co.kr*. Accessed 23 October 2019.

79. Ibid.

80. Ibid.

81. Ibid.

82. "Incessant Safety Failures: Buildings, Trains, Hot Water Pipes, What Else?" *The Korea Times*, 14 December 2018, *koreatimes.co.kr*. Accessed 22 March 2022.

83. Ibid.

84. Kim, Hoo-ran. "Culture Closely Tied to Korea's Vulnerability to Disasters." *The Korea Herald*, 13 May 2014, *koreaherald.com*. Accessed 31 March 2019.

85. Hwang, Kyung Moon. "Lesson from Disasters," *The Korea Times*, 30 April 2014, *koreatimes.co.kr*. Accessed 11 April 2019.

86. "Recurring Disasters." *The Korea Times*, 29 May 2014, *koreatimes.co.kr*. Accessed 8 March 2019.

87. Ibid.

88. Park, Yoon-bae. "Old Habits Die Hard." *The Korea Times*, 4 June 2014, *koreatimes.co.kr*. Last accessed 10 September 2023.

89. Ibid.

90. Ibid.

91. "(3rd LD) Loft Collapse Inside Gwangju Night Club Kills 2 Injures Athletes at FINA Championships." *Yonhap News Agency*, 27 July 2019, *en.yna.co.kr*. Accessed 27 July 2019.

92. Ibid.

93. Ibid.

94. Ibid.

95. Kwon, Oh-Eun. "The Collapsed Structure at Gwangju Nightclub Was Built by an Acquaintance of the Owner Who Does not Have a License." Trans. Young Lee, *The Chosun Ilbo*, 30 July 2019, *naver.me*. Accessed 30 July 2019.

96. Ko, Do-Yea, "25 out of 35 Two-Story Night Clubs Added Structure Without Permit." Trans. Young Lee, *The Dong-A Ilbo*, 30 July 2019, *naver.me*. Accessed 30 July 2019.

97. Ibid.

98. Lee, Michelle, Hee Ye, Meg Kelly, Atthar Mirza, Grace Moon, Min Joo Kim, and Stefanie Le. "Crucial Lapses Led to Tragically Delayed Rescue in a Seoul Alley." The *Washington Post*, 16 November 2022, *washingtonpost.com*. Accessed 28 June 2023.

99. Lee, Michelle, Hee Ye and Min Joo Kim. "South Korea Admits Police Crowd Control was 'Inadequate' before Crush." The *Washington Post*, 1 November 2022, *washingtonpost.com*. Accessed 28 June 2023.

100. Rashid, Raphael. "Crowds Exit Itaewon Station in the South Korean Capital on 29 October 2022." Image. "A Visual Guide to How the Seoul Halloween Crowd Crush Unfolded." The *Guardian*, 31 October 2023, *theguardian.com*. Accessed 6 July 2023.

101. "South Korea: How the Halloween Tragedy Unfolded." *BBC News*, 2 November 2022, *bbc.com*. Accessed 4 July 2023.

102. Lee, Michelle. "Crucial Lapses Led to Tragically Delayed Rescue in a Seoul Alley."

103. Kobara, Junnosuke. "The Site of the Halloween Crowd Crush in Seoul's Itaewon District is No Longer Blocked off from the Public." Image. "Itaewon Tragedy: One Month on, Search for Blame Continues." *Nikkei Asia*, 30 November 2022, *asia.nikkei.com*. Accessed 28 June 2023.

104. "Interview: Seoul's Deadly Halloween Crowd Crush Was Avoidable." The *Korea Times*, 17 November 2022, *koreatimes.co.kr*. Accessed 28 June 2023.

105. "Police Wrap up Monthslong Probe into Itaewon Crush; 23 Officials Referred to Prosecution." The *Korea Times*, 13 January 2023, *koreatimes.co.kr*. Accessed 28 June 2023.

106. "Satellite 2022 Naver/Spot/ National-Geographic Information Institute." Image. Lee, Michelle, Hee Ye, Meg Kelly, Atthar Mirza, Grace Moon, Min Joo Kim, and Stefanie Le. "Crucial Lapses Led to Tragically Delayed Rescue in a Seoul Alley." The *Washington Post*, 16 November 2022, *washingtonpost.com*. Accessed 28 June 2023.

107. *Yonhap/Reuters*. "A Street in Itaewon Fills with People before the Deadly Crowd Crush." Image. "A Visual Guide to How the Seoul Halloween Crowd Crush Unfolded." The *Guardian*, 31 October 2023, *theguardian.com*. Accessed 6 July 2023.

108. Lee, Michelle. "Crucial Lapses Led to Tragically Delayed Rescue in a Seoul Alley."

109. Kobara, Junnosuke. "Itaewon Tragedy: One Month on, Search for Blame Continues." *Nikkei Asia*, 30 November 2022, *asia.nikkei.com*. Accessed 28 June 2023.

110. "Police Wrap up Monthslong Probe into Itaewon Crush; 23 Officials Referred to Prosecution." The *Korea Times*.

111. Ibid.

Chapter Eight

1. "Industrial Accidents," The *Collins English Dictionary*, *collinsdictionary.com*. Accessed 9 September 2019.

2. Emphasis added. Dupree, Deb. "Definition of Industrial Accident." Career Trend, 27 December 2018, *careertrend.com*.

3. Cho, Han-Dae and Esther Chung, "Subway Workers Are Still Hustling." The *Korea JoongAng Daily*, 17 June 2016, *koreajoongangdaily.joins.com*. Accessed 7 April 2019.

4. Emphasis added.

5. Lee, Kyung-min. "Subway Accident Shows Safety Ignored." The *Korea Times*, 1 June 2016, *koreatimes.co.kr*. Accessed 7 April 2019.

6. "Metro Worker Crushed by Train." The *Korea JoongAng Daily*, 30 May 2016, *koreajoon-gangdaily.joins.com*. Accessed 2 May 2019.

7. Ibid.

8. Ibid.

9. Ibid.

10. Leejojoba. "Young Korean Man Loses His Life in Subway Accident; Was Doing Repair Work Alone Despite Regulations," *Soompi*, 1 September 2015, *soompi.com*. Accessed 4 May 2019.

11. Ibid.

12. Ibid.

13. Kim, Rahn. "Worker Dies While Repairing Screen Door at Subway Station." The *Korea Times*, 30 August 2015, *koreatimes.co.kr*. Accessed 5 May 2019.

14. Ibid.

15. Ibid.

16. Ibid.

17. Leejojoba. "Young Korean Man Loses His Life in Subway Accident; Was Doing Repair Work Alone Despite Regulations."

18. Lee, Kyung-min. "Subway Accident Shows Safety Ignored."

19. Ibid.

20. Ibid.

21. Cho, Han-Dae and Esther Chung. "Subway Workers Are Still Hustling."

22. Kim, Da-Sol. "Subway Maintenance Worker Dies during Repairs." The *Korea Herald*, 4 September 2016, *koreaherald.com*. Accessed 9 April 2019.

23. Cho, Han-Dae and Esther Chung. "Subway Workers Are Still Hustling."

24. Lee, Kyung-min. "Subway Accident Shows Safety Ignored."

25. Ibid.

26. Ibid.

27. Lee, Kyung-min. "One Year after Guui Station Accident, Not Much Has Changed." The *Korea Times*, 28 May 2017, *koreatimes.co.kr*. Accessed 5 May 2019.

28. Ibid.

29. Ibid.

30. Ibid.

31. Yang, young-yu. "Looking into the Mirror." The *Korea JoongAng Daily*, 24 October 2018, *koreajoongangdaily.joins.com*. Accessed 9 April 2019.

32. Lee, Kyung-min. "One Year after Guui Station Accident."

33. Ibid.

34. Ibid.

35. Lee, Kyung-min. "Subway Accident Shows Safety Ignored."

36. Cho, Han-Dae and Esther Chung. "Subway Workers Are Still Hustling."

37. Ibid.

38. Ibid.

39. Choe, Sang-hun. "Park Geun-hye, Ex-South Korea Leader, Gets 25 Years in Prison." The *New York Times*, 24 August 2018, *newyorktimes.com*. Accessed 18 August 2019.

40. Lee, Joyce. "South Korean Court Raises ex-President Park's Jail Term to 25 Years." *Reuters*, 23 August 2018, *reuters.com*. Last accessed 3 August 2023.

41. Kim, Da-Sol. "Subway Maintenance Worker Dies during Repairs."

42. Ock, Hyun-ju. "Explosion at a Subway Construction Site Kills 4 Workers, Injures 10." The *Korea Herald*, 1 June 2016, *koreaherald.com*. Accessed 12 January 2018.

43. Kim, Se-jeong. "Subcontracting Causes Accidents through Negligence." The *Korea Times*, 2 June 2016, *koreatimes.co.kr*. Accessed 5 May 2019.

44. This claim derives from the information published in The *Korea Times*, which is factually correct to the best of our knowledge.

45. Ock, Hyun-ju. "Explosion at a Subway Construction Site Kills 4 Workers, Injures 10."

46. Ibid.

47. Kim, Se-jeong. "Subcontracting Causes Accidents through Negligence."

48. Ibid.

49. Ibid.

50. Krishnamoorthy, Nandini. "South Korea: 4 Dead, 10 Injured in Explosion near Seoul," *International Business Times*, 1 June 2016, *ibtimes.co.uk*. Accessed 2 May 2019.

51. Shin, Jae-woong. "Technician Fell to His Death during Air Conditioning Installation, Working without Safety Devices Because of Pressure Due to Tight Schedule." Trans. Young Lee, *Naver*, 25 June 2016, *n.news.naver.com*. Accessed 25 June 2016.

52. Ibid.

53. Gang, Hee-Yeon. "Collapse during Installation... Repeated Tragedy Every High Demand Season for Air Conditioning." Trans. Young Lee, *Naver*, 13 July 2017, *n.news.naver.com*. Accessed 15 August 2019.

54. Ibid.

55. Yi, San. "South Korea: Death of a Young Worker Galvanizes a New Movement." *Labor Notes*, 2 January 2019, *labornotes.org*. Last accessed 4 August 2023.

56. Kang, Seung-woo. "Subcontractor Operations Criticized after Young Man's Death." The *Korea Times*, 13 December 2018, *koreatimes.co.kr*. Last accessed 4 August 2023.

57. Ibid.

58. Yi, San. "South Korea: Death of a Young Worker Galvanizes a New Movement."

59. Jung, Hae-myoung. "Subcontractors' Death Not Counted in Gov't Evaluation." The *Korea Times*, 17 December 2018, *koreatimes.co.kr*. Last accessed 4 August 2023.

60. Yi, San. "South Korea: Death of a Young Worker Galvanizes a New Movement."

61. Kang, Seung-woo. "Subcontractor Operations Criticized after Young Man's Death."

62. Jung, Hae-myoung. "Subcontractors' Death Not Counted in Gov't Evaluation."

63. Jo, He-rim. "Original Contractors Should Be Responsible for Subcontractor Accidents." The *Korea Herald*, 16 December 2018, *koreaherald.com*. Accessed 25 December 2018.

64. Jeong, Eun-joo. "How S. Korea Has a Low Industrial Accident Rate, Alongside the Highest Death Rate." *Hankyoreh*, 27 June 2016, *english.hani.co.kr*. Last accessed 4 August 2023.

65. Jung, Hae-myoung. "Subcontractors' Death Not Counted in Gov't Evaluation."

66. Emphasis added. Yi, San. "South Korea: Death of a Young Worker Galvanizes a New Movement."

67. Jeong, Eun-joo. "How S. Korea Has a Low Industrial Accident Rate, Alongside the Highest Death Rate."

68. Ibid.

69. Harris, Bryan, Jung-a Song, and Buseong Kang. "S. Korea Industry's Deadly Conditions Built on Culture of Cover-Up: Job Sites Officially among World's Safest but Death Rates

Tell Different Story." *Financial Times*, 5 December 2017, *ft.com*. Last accessed 7 January 2024.

70. Ibid.
71. Ibid.
72. Ibid.
73. Ibid.
74. "Outsourcing." *NIBusinessInfo.Co.uk*, nibusinessinfo.co.uk. Accessed 9 September 2019.
75. Kim, Da-Sol. "Subway Maintenance Worker Dies during Repairs."
76. "The Ultimate List of Outsourcing Statistics." *Microsourcing, microsourcing.com*. Accessed 28 February 2019.
77. Allnutt, Charles. "The Ultimate List of Outsourcing Statistics." *Microsourcing*, 28 February 2020, *microsourcing.com*. Accessed 14 March 2022.
78. Our definition of millennials is as follows: Anyone born between 1981 and 1996 (ages 28 to 43 in 2024) is considered a millennial. Dimock, Michael. "Defining Generations: Where Millennials End and Generation Z Begins." *Pew Research*, 17 January 2019, *pewresearch.org*. Last accessed 5 August 2023.
79. Choi, Young-ae, Chief of the National Human Rights Commission, was quoted in an article published in The *Korea Herald* on December 16, 2018, calling "for an amendment to the Occupational Safety and Health Act (OSHA) to ban 'outsourcing dangerous' work at infrastructure sites and to mandate that prime contractors take responsibility for accidents that occur at work sites." He was reported as saying, "To cut down labor costs, society is outsourcing even the responsibility to prevent accidents and disasters to subcontractors – 'outsourcing the danger.'" Jo, He-rim. "Original Contractors Should Be Responsible for Subcontractor Accidents." The *Korea Herald*, 16 December 2018, *koreaherald.com*. Accessed 25 December 2018.
80. Ock, Hyun-ju. "Explosion at a Subway Construction Site Kills 4 Workers, Injures 10."
81. Kim, Se-jeong. "Subcontracting Causes Accidents through Negligence."
82. Ock, Hyun-ju. "Explosion at a Subway Construction Site Kills 4 Workers, Injures 10."
83. Jo, He-rim. "Original Contractors Should Be Responsible for Subcontractor Accidents."
84. Yi, San. "South Korea: Death of a Young Worker Galvanizes a New Movement."
85. Nam, Ji-Won and Hyeong-guk Jo. "Lawmakers Reach an Agreement on the 'Kim Yong-gyun Bill' at the Last Minute." The *Kyunghyang Shinmun*, 28 December 2018, *english.khan.co.kr*. Accessed 5 January 2019.
86. Ibid.
87. Yi, San. "South Korea: Death of a Young Worker Galvanizes a New Movement."
88. Nam, Ji-Won and Hyeong-guk Jo. "Lawmakers Reach an Agreement on the 'Kim Yong-gyun Bill' at the Last Minute."

Chapter Nine

1. Park, Yoon-bae. "Old Habits Die Hard." The *Korea Times*, 4 June 2014, *koreatimes.co.kr*. Last accessed 26 May 2023.
2. "Hongik Ingan." *Wikipedia, wikipedia.com*. Accessed 1 September 2019,
3. Compton, Robert W. *Transforming East Asian Domestic and International Politics: The Impact of Economy and Globalization*, Ashgate Publishing, 2012, p. 109.

4. Lee, Jung-Soo. "Safety before Money – People Have to Change in Order for the Country/ Government to Change." Trans. Young Lee, The *Seoul Times*, 16 April 2018, *theseoultimes. com*. Accessed 1 May 2018.

5. "Belatedly, everyone now realizes just how dangerous a threat this problem [random or liberal parking] poses. We have learned that in the deadly blaze in Jecheon City in December [2017], 20-plus cars were lined up along the alleys and passages, only to block the access of fire trucks and delay rescue operations. As what happened there may repeat itself elsewhere in major cities in the country, the public now perceives it as an important social safety issue. In response, relevant laws have been recently amended to provide firefighters on the field with more discretion and authority in emergency situations: Illegally parked cars can be pushed out of the way, towed, or even destroyed, when necessary, without […] concern over associated liability and compensation problems. An appropriate amendment, indeed. There are other regulatory changes that need to be [made]. Penalties should be made effective and more strictly enforced. [The] requirement for proof of parking space should be imposed on constructors of at least certain sizes of buildings and facilities. Perhaps, restaurants that do not have their own parking spaces should be required to show how they will handle their customers' cars before they run valet parking booths. Right now, [restaurant] owners make money because of increased customers, valet parking operators also make money if they park as many cars as possible, and customers benefit as well because they can forget about their cars after [they arrive] at a restaurant. The price for these gains and benefits is being paid by all of us. Most importantly, the public attitude should change. Random […] or liberal parking, whatever you may call [it], is not an inevitable or condoned practice in Seoul. It has now become a serious social safety issue." Lee, Jae-Min. "Liberal Parking not Condoned Practice." The *Korea Herald*, 9 January 2018, *koreaherald. com*. Accessed 23 October 2019.

6. The Gangnam District Office ordered an emergency safety inspection of the structure and "determined that the building's safety was at level E, the lowest in its safety measuring index." "Incessant Safety Failures: Buildings, Trains, Hot Water Pipes, What Else?" The *Korea Times*, 14 December 2018, *koreatimes.co.kr*. Last accessed 13 January 2024.

7. "Korean Government Policy Briefing for 4th Industrial Revolution and Innovative Growth." Trans. Young Lee, *Naver*, 24 January 2018, *n.news.naver.com*. Accessed 26 October 2019.

Chapter Ten

1. MacDonald, Joan Vos. "Makgeolli in Seoul: Why This Speciality Liquor is Only at Its Best in the Korean Capital." The *Independent*, 30 August 2017, *independent.co.uk*. Accessed 26 August 2023.

2. Ibid.

3. Callaghan, Adam H. "Should You Be Drinking Makgeolli? – How One Seattle Brewer Hopes to Make Korean Liquor Big in America." *Eater*, 20 February 2017, *eater.com*. Last accessed 23 August 2023.

4. "Tteok." *Trifood*, *trifood.com*. Accessed 2 November 2019.

5. Ko, Dong-hwan. "Paris Baguette to Open 150th Store in North America." The *Korea Times*, 13 September 2023, *koreatimes.co.kr*. Last accessed 6 November 2023.

6. Yen, Michelle. "First McDonalds Locations in Asia." *Getchee*, 20 February 2014, *blog. getchee.com*. Last accessed 24 July 2023.

7. "Number of McDonald's Restaurants in the Asia-Pacific Region and Middle East in 2022, by Country or Territory." *Statista*, February 2023, *statista.com*. Accessed 13 January 2024.

8. Yi, Whan-woo. "30 People Purchased 8,000 Homes: Data." The *Korea Times*, 21 September 2023, *koreatimes.co.kr*. Accessed 22 September 2023.

9. Ibid.

10. Ibid.

11. Kim, Jiyeon. "Growing Hate toward Elders: 'Good Reasons to Hate Elders' vs. 'Still Need to Respect Elders.'" Trans. Young Lee, the *Segye Ilbo | Naver*, http://naver.me/G1v6Svag, 18 September 2018. Accessed 21 August 2019.

12. Ibid.

13. *Boys Over Flowers*. Dir. Jeon Ke-Sang, *Netflix, Netflix.com*. Accessed 23 August 2019.

14. *Secret Garden* (2010). *MyDramaList, mydramalist.com*. Accessed 10 October 2019.

15. *The Heirs. MyDramaList, mydrmalist.com*. Accessed 10 October 2019.

16. D'Addario, Daniel. "Squid Game Review: Netflix's Global Hit Wants to Condemn Violence While Reveling in It." *Variety*, 8 October 2021, *variety.com*. Accessed 23 January 2023.

17. Ibid.

18. "Cosmetics." *Export.gov, export.gov*. Accessed 10 October 2019.

19. Ibid.

20. Thilbodeaux, Wanda. "Is There a Law Against Asking for a Photo with a Job Application?" *BizFluent, bizfluent.com*. Last accessed 2 November 2019.

21. "Hospitals." *Visit Medical Korea, english.visitmedicalkorea.com*. Accessed 21 August 2019.

22. Park, Sung-Jin. "Small Business Owners Work 11 Hours a Day and Take 3 Days off Per Month." Trans. Young Lee, *Yonhap News, http://naver.me/5oOh6Ami*. Accessed 21 August 2019.

23. Ibid.

24. "Self-Employment Rate." *OECD Data, data.oecd.org*. Last accessed 2 November 2019.

25. Heo, In-Hoe. "6.7 Million Small Business Owners Angry about High Rent and Minimum Wage Regulation." Trans. Young Lee, *JoongAng Magazine* no. 11, 17 October 2018, *http://me2.do/5zjzfV1P*. Accessed 21 August 2019.

26. Chang, Ha-Joon. *23 Things They Don't Tell You about Capitalism*. New York: Bloomsbury Press, 2010, p. 159.

27. Ibid.

28. "The Young and Sick: 'Opo' to 'Chilpo,' The 'Give-Up' Generation." *Korea BANG, koreabang.com*. Accessed 22 August 2018.

29. Ibid.

30. "Cost of Living." *Numbeo, numbeo.com*. Last accessed 29 August 2023.

31. Ibid.

32. "The Young and Sick." *Korea BANG*.

33. Ibid.

34. Ibid.

35. World Bank. "GDP Growth (Annual %)." *World Development Indicators*. The World Bank, *data.worldbank.org*. Accessed 23 August 2023.

36. World Bank. "GDP Growth and GNI Per Capita (Atlas Method, Current US$)" *World Development Indicators*. The World Bank, *data.worldbank.org*. Last accessed 16 August 2023.

37. "South Korea Proposes Extra Budget, Bigger Subsidies to Address Youth Unemployment." *Reuters*, 14 March 2018, *reuters.com*. Last accessed 10 October 2019.

38. World Bank. "Unemployment, Youth Total (% of Total Labor Force Ages 15-24 Modeled ILO Estimate)." *World Development Indicators*. The World Bank, *data.worldbank.org*. Accessed 23 August 2023.

39. Ibid.

40. "The Government's Wage Subsidy for Jobs in Small and Medium-Sized Enterprises – Could it Convince Young Job Seekers?" Trans. Young Lee, the *Segye Times*, 21 March 2018, *segye.com*. Accessed 8 April 2018.

41. Ibid.

42. Anonymous, personal interview by John Gonzalez, text message, 8 September 2019.

43. World Bank. "Fertility Rate, Total (Births Per Woman)." *World Development Indicators*. The World Bank, *data.worldbank.org*. Last accessed 16 August 2023.

44. Ibid.

45. Yon, Hwangbo. "Parents Spending Roughly a Quarter of Their Income on Raising Their Kids." *Hankyoreh*, 1 January 2017, *english.hani.co.kr*. Accessed 3 June 2018.

46. Ibid.

47. Ibid.

48. Ibid.

49. *Statistics Korea, kostat.go.kr*. Accessed 10 October 2019.

50. Ibid.

51. "Household Projections for Korea, 2015-2045." *Statistics Korea, kostat.go.kr*. Accessed 10 October 2019.

52. Ibid.

53. *Statistics Korea, kostat.go.kr*.

54. Steger, Isabella. "South Korea is Aging Faster than Any Other Developed Country." *Quartz*, 31 August 2017, *qz.com*. Accessed 10 April 2018.

55. Ibid.

56. Kim, Sam. "Korea to Triple Baby Payments After It Smashes Own Record for World's Lowest Fertility Rate." *Bloomberg*, 30 August 2022, *bloomberg.com*. Accessed 15 August 2023.

57. Ibid.

58. Ibid.

59. Kim, Tae-Yun and Esther Chung. "Rural Schools Struggle to Stay Open in the Face of Dwindling, Aging Populations." The *Korea JoongAng Daily*, 25 January 2023, *koreajoongangdaily.join.com*. Accessed 28 June 2023.

60. Ibid.

61. Ibid.

62. Lee, Yeon-woo. "Remorse, Pride Intersect as Seoul's High School Set for Closure: Experts Call for Shift in Education Policy as School Sizes Become Smaller Due to Population Decline." The *Korea Times*, 2 September 2022, *koreatimes.co.kr*. Accessed 28 June 2023.

63. Ibid.

64. Kim, Tae-Yun and Esther Chung. "Rural Schools Struggle to Stay Open in the Face of Dwindling, Aging Populations."

65. "1 in 6 Elementary Schools in Seoul to Have under 40 Students per Grade: Study." The *Korea Herald*, 15 February 2024, *koreaherald.com*. Accessed 16 February 2024.

66. Ibid.

67. Kim, Tae-Yun and Esther Chung. "Rural Schools Struggle to Stay Open in the Face of Dwindling, Aging Populations."

68. Kim, Hyo-Hye. "60 4-Year Universities May Not Receive Any Students in 2020." Trans. Young Lee, *Maeil Economy*, 18 June 2018, *http://naver.me/G356KEC4*. Accessed 22 August 2019.

69. Ibid.

70. Ibid.

71. Jun, Ji-hye. "Korea Aims to Attract 300,000 Foreign Students by 2027." The *Korea Times*, 16 August 2023, *koreatimes.co.kr*. Accessed 21 August 2023.

72. "South Korea Unveils 5-Year Plan to Attract 300,000 Foreign Students." The *Straits Times*, 16 August 2023, *straitstimes.com*. Accessed 21 August 2023.

73. Ibid.

74. Ibid.

75. Ibid.

76. Jun, Ji-hye. "Korea Aims to Attract 300,000 Foreign Students by 2027."

77. "More S. Koreans Go Back to Rural Life in 2015." *Yonhap News Agency*, 30 June 2016, *en.yna.co.kr*. Accessed 15 July 2018.

78. Ibid.

Chapter Eleven

1. World Health Organization 2023. *data.who.int*, Suicide Mortality Rate (per 100,000 population) [Indicator]. *https://data.who.int/indicators/i/16BBF41*. Accessed 27 October 2023.

2. World Bank. "Fertility Rate, Total (Births Per Woman)." *World Development Indicators*. The World Bank, *data.worldbank.org*. Last accessed 16 August 2023.

3. "Japan's Foreign Worker Population Tops 2 Million for First Time." *Kyodo News*, 26 January 2024, *english.kyodonews.net*. Last accessed 8 February 2024.

4. Ibid.

Afterword

1. Helliwell, John F., Richard Layard, and Jeffrey Sachs, eds. 2013. *World Happiness Report 2013*. New York: UN Sustainable Development Solutions Network. Last accessed 13 February 2024.

2. Helliwell, J. F., R. Layard, and J. Sachs, *World Happiness Report 2017*. New York: Sustainable Development Solutions Network, 2017. Accessed 19 August 2018.

3. Helliwell, J. F., R. Layard, and J. Sachs, *World Happiness Report 2018*. New York: Sustainable Development Solutions Network, 2018. Accessed 16 March 2018.

4. Helliwell, J. F., R. Layard, J. D. Sachs, J.-E. De Neve, L. B. Aknin, and S. Wang (Eds.). *World Happiness Report 2022*. New York: Sustainable Development Solutions Network, 2022. Accessed 26 April 2023.

5. Ibid.

6. Helliwell, J. F., R. Layard, and J. Sachs, *World Happiness Report 2018*. New York: Sustainable Development Solutions Network, 2018. Accessed 16 March 2018.

7. Helliwell, J. F., R. Layard, and J. Sachs, *World Happiness Report 2017*. New York: Sustainable Development Solutions Network, 2017. Accessed 19 August 2018.

8. Ibid.

9. Tizzard, David A. "The Korean Pendulum of Disparity." The *Korea Times*, 2 September 2023, *m.koreatimes.co.kr*. Accessed 8 October 2023.

10. Ibid.

11. "Globally, the availability and quality of data on suicide and suicide attempts is poor. Only some 80 Member States have good-quality vital registration data that can be used directly to estimate suicide rates. This problem of poor-quality mortality data is not unique to suicide, but given the sensitivity of suicide – and the illegality of suicidal behaviour in some countries – it is likely that under-reporting and misclassification are greater problems for suicide than for most other causes of death." World Health Organization 2023 *data. who.int*, Suicide Mortality Rate (per 100,000 population) [Indicator]. *https://data.who.int/ indicators/i/16BBF41*. Accessed 27 October 2023.

12. The suicide mortality rate is the number of suicide deaths in a year divided by the population and multiplied by 100,000. Ibid.

13. Rashid, Raphael. "South Korea May Look Perfect, but Behind the Façade Lies a Devastating Suicide Crisis." The *Guardian*, 29 April 2023, *theguardian.com*. Accessed 6 September 2023.

14. Ibid.

15. Kim, Sam. "Korea's Suicide Rate Rises, Remains Highest in Developed World." *Bloomberg*, 26 September 2022, *loomberg.com*. Accessed 6 September 2023.

16. "Suicide No. 1 Cause of Death for S. Korean Teens, Youths." The *Korea Herald*, 1 May 2019, *koreaherald.com*. Accessed 16 August 2019.

17. World Bank. "GDP (Current US$)." *World Development Indicators*. The World Bank, *data.worldbank.org*. Last accessed 30 August 2023.

Acknowledgments

Looking back at my trajectory as an educator, I am grateful to the role models and mentors who saw a diamond in the rough in me and took me under their wings. Their support and guidance, both in and out of academia, enabled me to access the highest echelons and enriched my educational experiences. Education opened the doors for me to make a difference in other people's lives. I am grateful to my parents for all their sacrifices to support my quest and to my brother Jorge for his moral support and inspiration.

John Gonzalez

Most Koreans with whom I shared my idea about the book, including most of my family members, advised me not to write it because they believed that I, as a Korean, should not write anything negative about my country. I owe special thanks to my uncle, Ja Heung Koo, who understood my good intentions and encouraged me to write the book.

Young Lee

About the Authors

John Gonzalez was born in a small town of 12,000 people in the highlands of Mexico. While growing up, Gonzalez dreamed of becoming an educator. He traveled thousands of miles from his hometown to make his childhood dream come true. At age 13, his family immigrated to the United States, hoping he would forge a solid future for himself. Gonzalez always remembered why his parents decided to leave their home country and the sacrifices they made while uprooting the family. He learned English and French and earned several degrees, including a doctorate in educational leadership from UCLA. After receiving his doctorate, Gonzalez was appointed American Council on Education Fellow. He has worked in academic positions from middle to graduate school in the U.S. Subsequently, he lived in South Korea for five years, where he worked at an American school as a Spanish teacher and academic counselor. After completing his assignment, he was offered the position of school principal. While living in Korea, he immersed himself in the culture. He chose to write this book as a way to express his gratitude to the Korean people. Gonzalez enjoys traveling, spiritual retreats, and meeting people from all walks of life. In his spare time, he volunteers to teach yoga and meditation in the community.

Young Lee was born and raised in Seoul, South Korea. At age 20, he immigrated to the U.S., where he attended college and received a baccalaureate and a master's degree in applied mathematics. Most of his professional experience is in financial analysis in U.S. companies. Twenty-five years after leaving his native Korea, Lee returned and taught as a visiting professor at a university for three years. During this visit, he experienced an unexpected culture shock related to the question: How could South Koreans achieve such remarkable financial success so quickly? This question inspired him to write this book using the analytical and problem-solving skills he learned from his educational and professional experience. Lee enjoys camping in the mountains, meditating in his home in California, and traveling the world to learn about different cultures, beliefs, and lifestyles.

Printed in Great Britain
by Amazon

50811280R00155